THE
SACKETT
COMPANION

Bantam Books by Louis L'Amour
Ask your bookseller for the books you have missed

NOVELS

BENDIGO SHAFTER
BORDEN CHANTRY
BRIONNE
THE BROKEN GUN
THE BURNING HILLS
THE CALIFORNIOS
CALLAGHEN
CATLOW
CHANCY
THE CHEROKEE TRAIL
COMSTOCK LODE
CONAGHER
CROSSFIRE TRAIL
DARK CANYON
DOWN THE LONG HILLS
THE EMPTY LAND
FAIR BLOWS THE WIND
FALLON
THE FERGUSON RIFLE
THE FIRST FAST DRAW
FLINT
GUNS OF THE TIMBERLANDS
HANGING WOMAN CREEK
THE HAUNTED MESA
HELLER WITH A GUN
THE HIGH GRADERS
HIGH LONESOME
HONDO
HOW THE WEST WAS WON
THE IRON MARSHAL
THE KEY-LOCK MAN
KID RODELO
KILKENNY
KILLOE
KILRONE
KIOWA TRAIL
LAST OF THE BREED
LAST STAND AT PAPAGO WELLS
THE LONESOME GODS
THE MAN CALLED NOON
THE MAN FROM SKIBBEREEN
THE MAN FROM THE BROKEN HILLS
MATAGORDA
MILO TALON
THE MOUNTAIN VALLEY WAR
NORTH TO THE RAILS
OVER ON THE DRY SIDE
PASSIN' THROUGH
THE PROVING TRAIL
THE QUICK AND THE DEAD
RADIGAN
REILLY'S LUCK
THE RIDER OF LOST CREEK
RIVERS WEST
THE SHADOW RIDERS
SHALAKO
SHOWDOWN AT YELLOW BUTTE

SILVER CANYON
SITKA
SON OF A WANTED MAN
TAGGART
THE TALL STRANGER
TO TAME A LAND
TUCKER
UNDER THE SWEETWATER RIM
UTAH BLAINE
THE WALKING DRUM
WESTWARD THE TIDE
WHERE THE LONG GRASS BLOWS

SHORT STORY COLLECTIONS

BOWDRIE
BOWDRIE'S LAW
BUCKSKIN RUN
DUTCHMAN'S FLAT
THE HILLS OF HOMICIDE
LAW OF THE DESERT BORN
LONIGAN
NIGHT OVER THE SOLOMONS
THE RIDER OF THE RUBY HILLS
RIDING FOR THE BRAND
THE STRONG SHALL LIVE
THE TRAIL TO CRAZY MAN
WAR PARTY
WEST FROM SINGAPORE
YONDERING

SACKETT TITLES

SACKETT'S LAND
TO THE FAR BLUE MOUNTAINS
THE WARRIOR'S PATH
JUBAL SACKETT
RIDE THE RIVER
THE DAYBREAKERS
SACKETT
LANDO
MOJAVE CROSSING
MUSTANG MAN
THE LONELY MEN
GALLOWAY
TREASURE MOUNTAIN
LONELY ON THE MOUNTAIN
RIDE THE DARK TRAIL
THE SACKETT BRAND
THE SKY-LINERS

NONFICTION

FRONTIER
THE SACKETT COMPANION:
  A Personal Guide to the
  Sackett Novels
A TRAIL OF MEMORIES:
  The Quotations of Louis L'Amour,
  compiled by Angelique L'Amour

THE SACKETT COMPANION

◆

A PERSONAL GUIDE TO THE SACKETT NOVELS

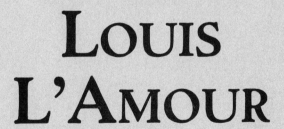

LOUIS L'AMOUR

BANTAM BOOKS

TORONTO · NEW YORK · LONDON · SYDNEY · AUCKLAND

THE SACKETT COMPANION

A Bantam Book / November 1988

Produced by Ink Projects
Book design by Lynne Arany
Maps by William B. and Alan McKnight:
Sackett's Land, To The Far Blue Mountains, Lando, Mustang Man,
The Lonely Men, Treasure Mountain, and The Sackett Brand.
All other maps by Alan McKnight.

Library of Congress Cataloging-in-Publication Data

L'Amour, Louis, 1908–1988
 The Sackett companion.

 Includes index.
 1. L'Amour, Louis, 1908–1988—Handbooks, manuals, etc. 2. L'Amour,
Louis, 1908–1988—Characters—Sackett family. 3. Western stories—
Handbooks, manuals, etc. 4. Sackett family (Fictitious characters)—
Handbooks, manuals, etc. I. Title.
PS3523.A446Z459   1988   813'.52   88-47530
ISBN 0-553-05305-1

Published simultaneously in the United States and Canada

PRINTED IN THE UNITED STATES OF AMERICA

DH   0 9 8 7 6 5 4 3 2 1

To the many readers who
asked for this book

CONTENTS

EDITORS' NOTE:

Louis L'Amour died on June 10, 1988. He completed the manuscript for THE SACKETT COMPANION some months before his death, and throughout it he refers to future stories and characters whose tales were still to be told. Rather than delete these references, we felt his many readers would be interested in knowing what he hoped to write.

INTRODUCTION

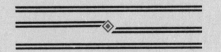

A question I am often asked is: How long does it take to write a book?

It seems to me a ridiculous question. If the questioner stopped to think, he or she would understand that it takes as long as is necessary. Is the book to be two hundred pages or two thousand? Is much research required or very little? No book can be written without some research, for no matter how much one believes he knows, it will always prove to be less than enough.

I rarely do research on a book I am writing. That research has, except for the unexpected detail, been done long before. By the time I begin to write, I am saturated with the background of my story. Yet one never knows enough. There is always more to be learned.

Another question I am asked at least once a month or during the question-and-answer period at a lecture: What book can I read to learn about the West?

What part of the West? During what period? What phase of western settlement?

I have read, scanned, or browsed through literally thousands of books, documents, diaries, and reports and am only beginning to understand what happened; how, why, when, and where it happened; to say nothing of all the problems and influences that contributed to what the West was at various stages in history.

No story of the frontier can be written without knowledge of the physical environment, of the terrain, vegetation, animal, and insect life. Each state differs from every other, and within each state there are many widely diverse environments. Montana is unlike Texas, and both differ in many respects from Arizona, New Mexico, Nevada, or Colorado.

The Plains states present other problems, as do those rimming the Pacific. Oddly enough, some readers have never realized that California was as much a cowboy state as any other, and her vaqueros were among the greatest riders and ropers this country ever saw. It was second in cattle population only to Texas.

Oregon, Washington, and Idaho had their big ranches, their stagecoach hold-ups, and gunfighters, so the West was and is a very large area, indeed.

To really know the western frontier requires a lifetime of study. And there will always be those unexpected pockets of history that have developed in relative isolation so far as the reading public is concerned.

The western American frontier went through many phases of development. The Spanish who settled in the Southwest and the French in the North and Northwest were the first. Then the so-called Long Hunters (because they were out a long, long time!) ventured west of the Appalachians. Daniel Boone, who is considered by many to be the original western pioneer, was, in fact, preceded by many others. Gabriel Arthur was living with the same Indians Boone was to meet, but one hundred years earlier, and he was but one of many.

Our histories are based largely upon official or semi-official reports that appeared at a time when only a small number of people could read and write. Few of the hunters and explorers even thought of writing what had happened to them or where they had been. In our western histories, and indeed, in the history of the world, we are basing all our conjectures on only a small number of accounts. Moreover, most of these come from a relatively few countries; reports from elsewhere in the world are rarely considered.

At a rough guess, I would estimate that ninety percent of the fiction written about the West has concerned the Plains states or those few others that were in the cattle business or provided a trail westward that moved from Missouri to California. For some reason the man on horseback has always intrigued, whether he be knight in armor, a Bedouin of the desert, or an American cowboy. He has always been a figure of romance.

Is it because he is mobile? Because he can ride away into the sunset? Or that he comes from out of nowhere, a mysterious, romantic figure who appears without warning and is seemingly free of everyday trials and troubles?

4

Contemporary man has tried to substitute the car for the cow pony, but it simply doesn't work. True, in a car he is mobile, and once behind the wheel he can feel the excitement of command, but nevertheless the car is bound to the road, inhibited by traffic, and frustrated by regulations essential to his safety but which he often feels rob him of the true freedom he wants.

====

To write well of the West there is so much one should know. Horses, cattle, weapons, the way a saddle was rigged, the way a cowhand used a rope, and the lifestyles of Indians varied greatly from place to place.

The English saddle, for instance, was intended for the hunt or for brief rides, but a cowhand *lived* in his saddle from daylight until dark. It was not only where he spent a major part of his life, it was his workbench, and had to be structured as such. The ancestor of the cowboy saddle was that of the armored knight who needed a secure seat, or the Conquistador who followed Cortes, Coronado, and their kind. These men established settlements in New Mexico, with churches and schools, long before the Pilgrims landed in 1620.

As for the importance of physical environment: the land itself was always present in the thoughts, the emotions, and calculations of the pioneer. No story of the West can be written where the terrain is not a factor. The distance from here to there, the existence of waterholes, the condition of the grass, the trails (if any existed), and many other factors had to be considered. The country demanded consideration in any pioneer's plans, but it also exerted its influences on the emotions. Many simply could not stand the rolling plains that seemed to go on forever with a vast sky arching overhead. Many turned and ran for cover in city streets or small villages where they had lived. Some went insane from the ever-blowing wind and the isolation of life on a government claim.

To write well of the West one must understand not only what happened here, but what caused it to happen.

My own western experience began with stories told by my grandfather, who had fought in the Civil and Indian Wars; my father, who had grown up with a Huron Indian as his only playmate; and an uncle who came to visit at least twice when I was very young. He was an uncle by marriage, a man born with a wanderlust and no desire to own or possess. In his lifetime he covered much of the West from British Columbia to Sonora. He delivered mail, punched cows, managed a large ranch, and did just about everything a man could do in western country.

My father was a veterinarian who worked largely with farm or ranch stock, and doubled as a deputy sheriff for a number of years, off and on. As a veterinarian, one of his jobs was the inspection of cattle shipped through on the Northern Pacific Railroad, and frequently, when I was very young I went with him to the stockyards, listening to his conversations with the cowboys who were riding east with the cattle.

Later, at the age of fifteen, when I started to make my own way in the world, I worked on ranches, in mines, on construction gangs, and in the sawmills and lumber woods. Often I worked beside men who had lived through the younger, wilder days of America's growing years.

As a child I learned to listen and remember, and later, sitting around cow camps and in mining towns, I listened more than I talked. The men and women I met were the survivors. Some survived by skill, some by chance, I learned, as my questions or comments helped revive memories. I had already acquired an interest in everything western.

Although I knew I would be a writer and a teller of tales, I had no idea of writing about the West. It was simply that the stories I heard were exciting, and it was simply that I was interested. The collectors of oral history today would give their eyeteeth for what I was hearing nearly every day, and I'd have given mine for any kind of a recording device, but I had to rely on my memory.

Sometimes today I am not sure just where I learned something, remembering the information but not the source. Miners I worked with had before my time worked the mines from Butte to Tombstone, from Cripple Creek and Tonopah to Grass Valley. Now they are gone, and the old cattlemen are gone too, taking their memories with them. Four of the old-time gunfighters I knew passed on down the trail in the 1940s, another in '53. As I've said elsewhere, "if you didn't shoot 'em they'd live forever."

If I have written good stories, much is due to those with whom I worked or saw around town, and who contributed their bits of western lore or their memories of the old days and the people who lived them.

Often their opinions varied, and often what they told me in later years was colored by hearsay, but it was what was believed at the time. All this must be weighed in the balance with newspaper accounts, diaries, or other documentation. Somewhere out of it all comes something resembling the truth.

Occasionally there will be an "old-timer" who has told the same story so many times he believes it (and others do, too), telling you "he was there!".

One such story was an anecdote about Wyatt Earp in Dodge City. The only trouble with it was that Wyatt was a gambler in Silverton, Colorado when the so-called event took place and had not been in Dodge for over a year.

Diaries were and are important. They were written at the time events happened and represented the information at least as one man saw it.

Diaries have been a rich source of material for me. Not the events recorded in such journals, but the mental attitude, the moral standards, and the feelings of people at the time. It is all right to imagine, but the imagination must have a takeoff point, it must have a basis in fact.

Newspapers—and nearly every western town had at least one—are valuable sources. Often the reporting was good, and just as often the writing was opinionated, a fact one should easily detect, for people of the time—and that included newspaper reporters—made no secret of their opinions. Many a western editor set his type with a six-shooter on the table beside him, ready to back up his opinions, if need be.

A story can begin anywhere but may be years in germination, the idea lying quietly as the subconscious slowly gathered the materials needed for the telling. Many of my stories have been in my mind for upwards of twenty years before actually being recorded, and in at least two cases, twice that long.

The people who speak so glibly about "cranking them out" have never attempted it. Writing is a matter of temperament and character, and probably no two writers ever wrote alike or approached their writing in the same way. Some are very slow and painstaking, while others write with great speed and facility. Gustave Flaubert was one of the former, William Shakespeare one of the latter.

Flaubert needed seven years to write *Madame Bovary*, while Shakespeare's entire body of work—thirty-six plays, many sonnets, and several long poems—was produced in sixteen years. Yet even that doesn't begin to tell the story. During those sixteen years Shakespeare was a working actor, an actor-manager, and busy with many details of play production. During much of that time he was appearing in two plays each week, one old play and one new play that still needed some rehearsal.

The event that led to the birth of the Sackett stories began on a hot, dusty morning in New Mexico.

I was a stranger in another town, sixteen but passing as twenty-four, hunting any kind of a job that could be done with two hands.

The town was crowded for a gathering, a county fair, perhaps, or a carnival, something that attracted many people. Exactly what it was I do not remember.

A stranger and alone, I drew comment from some rowdies. Maybe they were decent enough fellows most of the time, but just feeling their oats that day. One word led to another, and one of them, under the mistaken belief that he was a fighter, selected me for a demonstration. No doubt he wished to augment a reputation he already had, or create one he wished to have.

Always I tried to avoid trouble, but, being a stranger, have learned to expect it. If I walked away the chances were that they would follow, and I was young enough to wish not to be considered a coward.

He was husky and confident, but I had begun working out with professional boxers when I was fourteen. I was by no means a great fighter, yet I did know how to handle myself in a fight. However, I had a problem: if I broke a hand, altogether too easy when fighting bare-fisted, I would starve. When the fight began I slipped his right to the head and hit him with a right in the midsection where there was less chance of hurting a hand.

When that punch landed the way it did, he knew and I knew the fight was over, but he dared not quit in front of his friends. He tried to clinch, but I pushed him away and hit him again, in the same place. Two of his friends, seeing him in trouble, started to move in to help.

A crowd had gathered. Two cowpunchers stepped out and stopped his friends, advising them to lay off and leave us to settle it. I hit him again and when he fell, walked quickly away, pausing only to thank the two cowboys.

They were, as it happened, cousins. Two rawboned, lean-bodied young men, one of them twenty-one, the other a year or two older.

As I had been a stranger in other towns before this, I knew no one could get anywhere by whipping a local boy, and the best thing to do was to leave. I said as much to Red, one of the cowboys.

He asked me if I could ride, as they had horses and were heading south. At the moment almost any direction looked good, so I joined them.

That night before a campfire we discussed the events of the morning, and Red commented, "We never get into fights."

"You're lucky," I agreed.

"It isn't luck," his cousin suggested, "it's our family. There's thirteen boys in his family and sixteen in mine. If they tackle any one of us they'll have to whip us all."

In the rough years that followed, I often remembered that.

West of Yuma, Arizona a few years later I had occasion to look for and find a desert water hole (if you dug out two barrels of sand) called Sackett's Well. Arthur Woodward, in his excellent notes to *The Journal of Lt. Thomas Sweeny, 1846–1855* says the wells were named for Russell Sackett, a stationkeeper on a stageline. I believe this to be a mistake. The wells were named for Lt. Delos B. Sackett who discovered the water hole in time to save the expedition's mules.

That was my introduction to the Sackett name. Crudely lettered on an old piece of board were the words: SACKETT'S WELL. A few years later I stopped by again but the sign was gone, carried off by some thoughtless souvenir hunter or used to start a fire.

It was from Sackett's Well I got the name, and from the two cowboy cousins, whose family came from the Appalachians, that I got the idea. A lot of wandering, hard work, and World War II intervened before I wrote the first of the Sackett stories, which was THE DAYBREAKERS.

Much of American history has been the story of families moving westward, and after I had written THE DAYBREAKERS, I decided to tell the story of the opening of a continent as seen through the eyes of three families, the Sacketts, Chantrys, and Talons.

Historians as a rule follow the main lines of history—the wars, the politics, the rise and fall of empires—yet the true history is that of the people themselves: where they lived, their ways of making a living, their inventions, discoveries, problem-solving, business dealings, and their relations with each other.

The curious involvement of families with each other has always intrigued me. When one is constantly researching, certain family names recur again and again. Shortly after my wife and I were married, I was glancing over some of her family history and it immediately became apparent that our families must have known each other at several times in the past. If such was the case with our families, it must have happened often.

Samuel Maverick, one of the first half-dozen settlers on the site of what is now Boston, and a minor character in my book THE WARRIOR'S PATH, was an ancestor to the Maverick whose name was given to unbranded calves in Texas. Two members of my own family had occasion to meet Tench Tilghman, aide to General George Washington in the Revolutionary War, and about one hundred and fifty years later Bill Tilghman, frontier marshal at Dodge City and in Oklahoma, showed me how a six-shooter should be used.

There is, of course, no end to the number of such chance meetings, each a part of a thread woven into the tapestry of history. We are all much more closely connected than is generally assumed and a good genealogist can demonstrate that everybody is related, in one way or another, with everybody else.

In the stories of the Sacketts, Chantrys, and Talons, which will eventually become one story, there are casual meetings between the families. Occasionally they will be associated in business, feud, or war, and sometimes a character friendly with one family will appear in the history of another. Or perhaps they will have dealings with the same enemies.

Over a period of nearly four hundred years a family can have many relationships with other families, and with these intermarriages will come many family traditions and memories.

History and historical fiction have most often related the stories of kings, nobles, presidents, and generals. They have dealt, until recently, largely with wars and politics, or with exploration of the land through stories that have survived. But what of the countless other, largely unrecorded explorations and discoveries? What of the many seafaring men and explorers who could not write, so left no written accounts of their ventures? What of the many who went out and did not return? What of the many who are known but are ignored by history?

What we must always remember when reading history is that we can never have more than a small part of the story, and it is a story often told in highlights. The story of a party of French people from Illinois who traveled west before Lewis and Clark and went to live in Idaho and Washington, is almost unknown, and only a little more is known of several explorers who supplied Lewis and Clark with maps and information.

Many of the names of the first men who went west are unknown. In some of my stories I have tried to let my readers know that others were there, and something of how they reached the western mountains and what they did there.

History has to follow main lines or the story would never be told. The average historian cannot afford the time to explore the bypaths or follow trails that had no recognizable influence upon subsequent events.

My stories are history of a kind. The difference is that I write of the nameless ones, and when they have left no stories I write what must have been, what could have been, using knowledge of the country itself, how it was traveled, how many people lived by hunting and gathering, and what their relationships might have been with the Indians and others.

Yet my stories or any others, as well as history itself, must always be read with the understanding that we know only a small part of the whole picture.

There are many indications that others were here before us, yet as the scattered clues indicate no pattern that fits into known events, they are ignored.

THE DAYBREAKERS was the first of the Sackett stories to be written, and was largely the story of Orrin and Tyrel Sackett who came west after the Civil War to try to find a new home for their mother and their family. What happened to them was simply what was happening to many people; their involvement and their reactions to events was due to their personalities and character.

Growing up in the mountains of Tennessee and North Carolina, the Sacketts were accustomed to farming their few acres, hunting and gathering food from the forests around them. They were also accustomed to feuding and fighting, and had just ended a long-running feud with the Higgins family, whose menfolks were rugged as the Sacketts themselves, although the Sacketts edged them somewhat when it came to rifle shooting.

Hard work was a way of life for them and they understood nothing else, so when they hired on with the first cattle drive they ever saw they were no strangers to long hours and short rations. What else was needed they soon learned, and when trouble came they were prepared for it. They'd served their apprenticeship in a rough school.

Later, when they became involved in a land grant fight, they were equally at home.

These were things happening at the time. Nothing was dragged in for effect, nothing manufactured. It was all there waiting for them, and what they did was just what many others were doing, except that their early life had prepared them well. The Sacketts were, like most of the mountain people, simple, God-fearing folk who attended meetin' on a Sunday and went to "sings" to compete with singing of songs, and accompanying themselves on the fiddle, the dulcimer, or whatever instrument was handy. The men attended barn-raisings and turkey-shoots, the women went to quilting bees, and the like. Those who favored strong drink could find stills a-plenty making moon- shine of quality.

Boys in the mountains of those days all went to church, even if they were not religious. And many were not, so they went because that was the place to meet the girls. Most of what they knew of sinning they learned from preachers who told them about it; where else would you hear such stories, even with fire and brimstone added?

When mountain boys got right down to Hell-bent-for-Georgia sinning, they found it right disappointing, compared to what the preachers had been telling them.

What happens in my stories is what was happening in reality. My method of telling such tales is simple: I place my characters in an existing situation and let it happen to them.

No man can be judged except against the background of his own time. The standards of yesterday are not the standards of today, and the circumstances of daily life were vastly different. Before one attempts to render judgment, one should consider the world in which the man existed, and the customs of the time and the place.

The men who came west following the Civil War were accustomed to weapons. Most were veterans of that war on one side or another, and many who had not been active participants in the war had been active resisting attacks by guerrillas, outlaws, or Indians.

Such men did not hesitate to use weapons to defend their lives or property. The law, when it existed, was often many miles away. So if cattle or horses were stolen it was easier to pursue and recover, if possible, than to take the time to call the law. By the time a man had ridden to town, the cattle could be miles away and beyond the jurisdiction of local law or hope of recovery. Moreover, in many areas a man was expected to handle such problems himself, until about 1890 or later.

The pistol was the accepted way to settle disputes in the West, but not only in the West. Those were the last days of the Code Duello, when gentlemen settled their disputes by personal combat. It was considered a matter of honor to respond when challenged, not only in the West but over much of the world.

For many years it was believed that the outcome of a duel was the judgment of God, hence trial by combat was accepted as just and right. Even a king could be challenged but as it was not considered wise, for the good of the state, that he risk his life, each king had a champion, a noted fighting man, who would respond on his behalf.

A century before the gunfighting days in the American West, an English diplomat at the court of France commented that he did not know even one man about the court who had not killed his man in a duel.

At the time of Louis XIII the Chevalier d'Andrieux was reputed to have killed seventy-four men in duels, and no western gunfighter ever reached such a total, although Alexander McClung is said to have killed almost as many. McClung was a former attorney turned riverboat gambler.

Our American Navy of the period encompassing the War of 1812 and the fights with the Barbary pirates had as many gunfighters and duellists as ever came out of Texas. Stephen Decatur was one of the best known.

Andrew Jackson, before he became president of the United States, participated in a number of duels in one capacity or another, but killed only one man, Charles Dickinson.

Jackson was defending the honor of his wife, and both men were noted pistol shots. Dickinson fired first and Jackson was seen to waver. He then returned the fire and killed Dickinson. Not until Dickinson fell was it noticed that Jackson was bleeding badly. Dickinson's bullet had broken three ribs, inflicting a severe chest wound.

Where most men carried weapons, it was natural that some would prove more skillful than others. When a fight ensued, he who was most skillful, better coordinated, and coolest usually won. By the time he had won several such fights, he had the reputation of being a gunfighter, whether he wanted it or not. Among those who became known as gunfighters were doctors, lawyers, and cattlemen, as well as gamblers and cowboys (the latter but rarely), and men from all walks of life.

Temple Houston was a lawyer, Doc Holliday a dentist, John Slaughter a cattleman, and Buckskin Frank Leslie a bartender.

For every known gunfighter there were a dozen just as capable who did not become famous for one reason or another. Ninety percent of Wyatt Earp's reputation is due to his biographer, Stuart Lake. Without a doubt Wyatt's brother Virgil was as good with a gun and had a longer career as an officer of the law. Wild Bill Hickok, a known and respected man in his time, owed much of his later notoriety to a story written by George Ward Nichols who came west looking for sensationalism. Nichols credited Hickok with saying he had killed a hundred men. Those who knew Hickok doubted he ever made such a remark, and if he did he was undoubtedly referring to those killed during the war when he was, for a time, a sharpshooter.

Most of the famous gunfighters were peace officers, with—when all is considered—remarkably few shootings in line of duty. Most of them were fully aware there were men in the town or the surrounding country who were as good with a gun as they were. Men who survived Gettysburg, Shiloh, and the battles in the Wilderness not only possessed weapons but were prepared to use them if necessary. Such men as Hickok, Tilghman, and the Earps walked the streets so storekeepers, bankers, and cattle buyers could carry on their lives in peace.

A fact too little understood is that in the decade of the 1860s as well as just before and after, moral and social standards were vastly different than now. A large percentage of those who lived on the frontier attended church regularly, and a person who did not had little place in the community, and small chance of success in business.

Women did not drink in public and only a few drank in private. It simply was not done. In the East a woman might have wine at a formal dinner. Anything else was frowned upon.

Juvenile problems were, for the most part, almost nonexistent, as a boy simply could not wait to become a man and be accepted as such. He sought approbation not from his peers but from adults. Boyhood ended at thirteen or fourteen, and from that time on a boy was apt to be doing a man's work and drawing a man's wages.

What made the difference then, as now, was the boy's willingness to accept responsibility. Few allowances were made for youth. If you were working with men you were expected to do a man's share of the work. If you did not, it placed an added burden on those who worked with you. However, almost any range hand was willing to show a new boy or man the ropes, and guide him during his first weeks on the job.

An example of a boyhood in the West is that of Buffalo Bill Cody. By the time he was twelve Cody was carrying messages from one train of wagon freighters to another, riding long distances on horseback and alone, and in Indian country. He was in his first Indian fight at about that time, when one of the wagon trains was attacked while he was present. Often remembered only as a showman, Cody had done it all, from riding for the Pony Express to buffalo hunting, scouting for the Army to working as a guide.

Buffalo Bill Cody was one of those who, though never considered a gunfighter, could have coped with the best of them. Another was Major Frank North, commander of the Pawnee Scouts. In target shooting North out-shot Hickok on several occasions and was accredited as one of the best. His brother, Luke North, was nearly as good.

The western frontier was a place of hard work and hardship, and as far as the range was concerned it was a case of first come, first served, if you could hold what you claimed. Unhappily, the story of the West has often been badly told by those who simply did not know or did not care. Recently a failed film, *Heaven's Gate*, told the story of western ranchers riding roughshod over some poor Russian immigrants in what they called the Johnson County War.

The actual Johnson County War was a fight waged between the big cattlemen and nesters, and there were no Russian immigrants anywhere around. The men involved on both sides were of Anglo-Saxon and Irish origin.

The simple truth of the war was that the big cattlemen imported something more than fifty hired gunmen to come into the state of Wyoming to murder eighty or more nesters or so-called rustlers. An armed body of citizens surrounded them, and was on the verge of wiping them out but for the intervention of the United States Army, who escorted the invaders back to Cheyenne, from which place they faded into the sunset. Due to the influence of those involved, there was no prosecution of any of the invaders, despite the fact that they murdered Nate Champion and Nick Ray.

Often the motion picture maker has neither respect for nor knowledge of history, and they believe their audience is the same. The Nate Champion who was killed after a daylong siege, and who was the man the cattlemen most wanted to kill, appears in the movie as one of the killers! The Russian immigrants were a product of the producer's imagination.

The sort of men and women it took to open the West were the kind of whom stories are told. Strongly individual, willing to risk all they possessed as well as their lives, they were also prepared to fight for what they believed was theirs. Right or wrong, they had both strength and character, and about such people stories gather.

The land was crossed and recrossed by explorers, fur traders, and trappers, as well as prospectors for gold and silver who often left nothing behind but fading footprints. Those who came later tried to dig in and stay. They built homes on range land or government claims, they established towns, schools and hospitals, and later raised grain enough to feed half the world.

There were blizzards and dust storms, crops were destroyed by hail or by clouds of hungry grasshoppers, but the pioneers survived. Often the ownership of cattle or land was disputed at gunpoint. From all of this are stories born. But there is no way the fiction writer with all his imagination can surpass the truth.

The story of the West is our story, an American story, but

one for all the world, and all the world contributed. First came the French and the Spanish, then the Anglo-Saxon and Irish, and afterward the Germans, the blacks, the Scandinavians, and others.

Through the eyes of the Sacketts I invite you to see it happen in many of its phases.

The story of the opening of the West did not begin with the march of the pioneers beyond the Mississippi. It began long before in the towns and villages of England, France, and Spain. It began in the Netherlands, in Ireland, and in the Highlands of Scotland. It began with a few men and women who were willing to dare, to risk all that they might better themselves and their children. It began with a few who made a choice.

Why did some go, and some stay? What was it in those who were willing to venture all to begin a new life that made them take the risk?

What was it that made them, even after they had arrived and established good homes, good farms, or good businesses, pack up and move further westward still?

What was it that led them to round the next curve, to top the next hill?

Many of them died, but they left sons and daughters to carry on the tradition, to pioneer in new lands, wherever they might be. Some said it was the lure of free land, of gold for the taking, or to get rich with cattle or furs or silver, but it was none of these. They were the excuses offered to more reasonable and less imaginative men, men who could understand the lure of land or gold but would never know the lure of an uncrossed mountain, of a place beyond the plains.

In the chapters that follow I have written about each of the Sackett novels, adding for the reader's interest some additional information about the books, and a few notes for those who may wish to check back on what they have read.

It will be observed that I have not commented on everything or listed all the characters. This book is simply what it is named, a companion to the Sackett stories, and an effort to answer some of the questions I have received in the mail or in person from readers over the years.

Unfortunately, I can answer but a few of the many letters I receive. To reply to them all, I would have to cease writing books and only reply to letters. So this COMPANION is, in a way, a chance to respond to those many wonderful letters I have received.

Several attempts have been made by readers to put together a family tree of the Sacketts, an impossible task as I have not supplied all the names and relationships. In this COMPANION I mention many members of the Sackett family, and in the genealogy, explain some of the connections between them.

In some cases I have offered no more information about the characters than can be found in the books themselves. Often I have nothing further to say. Perhaps some of those characters will appear again and we will learn more about them then.

A companion can be fun. Now it is easy to check back to see which characters appeared in which book, and to establish the locale of the book and its time.

Do not expect every generation's story to be filled with adventure. Some of the Sacketts, as with all families, lived quiet lives and died quietly. When a man has four sons, only one may survive to become a man. Childbirth was never easy on the frontier, nor was medical attention often available. If someone became ill, he or she was treated with what simple remedies were known. The way west was marked with the graves of those who died en route, for that way was never easy.

My stories may seem to be the stories of men, but a check of my books will show that I have probably written the stories of more strong women than any other writer. I will not list them all here, but Miss Nesselrode of THE LONESOME GODS, Ruth Macken of BENDIGO SHAFTER, Echo Sackett of RIDE THE RIVER, Em Talon of RIDE THE DARK TRAIL are some, and there are so many others. I believe there are at least fifty such in my books—some major characters, others who had minor roles. I must admit that one of my favorites is Miss Jessica Trescott, of MATAGORDA. She was a lady of style, in everything she did.

Those who have read the books know something of them; only here and there I have added bits of extra information. If this COMPANION adds a bit of extra enjoyment to the reading of the Sackett stories I am amply repaid. So read, and enjoy.

SACKETT'S
LAND

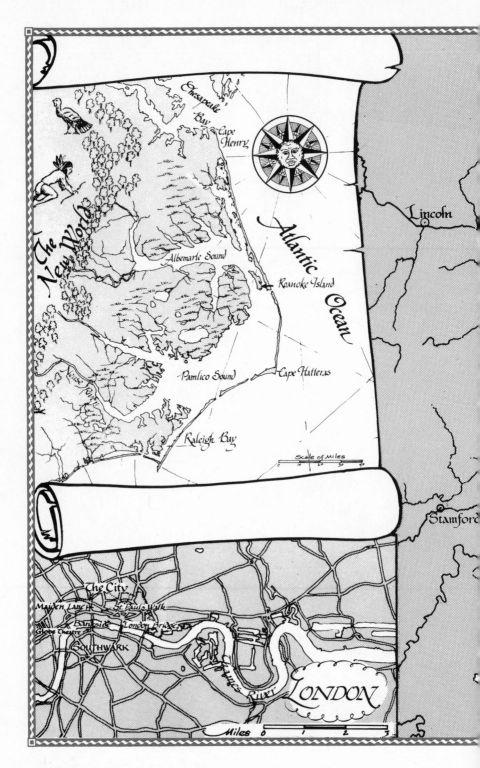

The New World

Chesapeake
Bay
Cape
Henry

Atlantic Ocean

Albemarle Sound

Roanoke Island

Pamlico Sound

Cape Hatteras

Raleigh Bay

Scale of Miles
0   10   20   30   40

Lincoln

Stamford

The City
Maiden Lane   St Paul's Walk
Bankside   London Bridge
Globe Theatre
SOUTHWARK

Thames River   LONDON

Miles 0   1   2   3

24

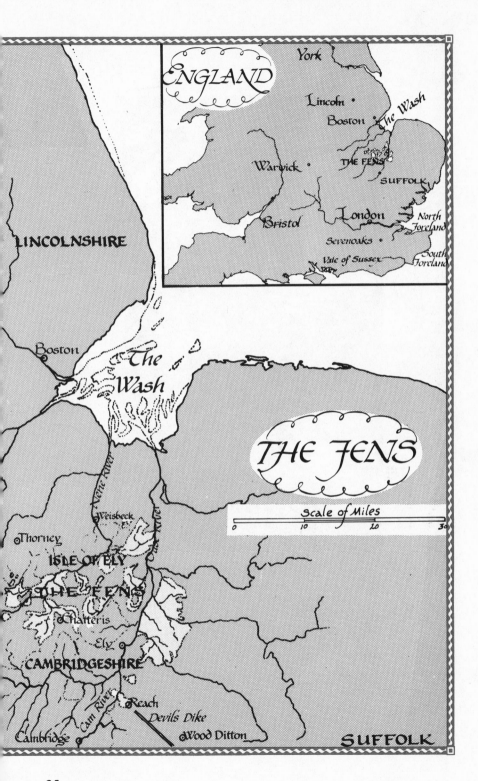

ENGLAND

York
Lincoln ·
Boston · The Wash
THE FENS
SUFFOLK
Warwick ·
London
North Foreland
Bristol
Sevenoaks ·
Vale of Sussex
South Foreland

LINCOLNSHIRE

Boston

The Wash

THE FENS

Scale of Miles

0   10   20   30

Weisbeck
Thorney
ISLE OF ELY
THE FENS
Chatteris
Ely
CAMBRIDGESHIRE

Reach
Devils Dike
Cambridge
Wood Ditton

SUFFOLK

SACKETT'S LAND

First publication: Saturday Review Press hardcover, May 1974;
    Bantam Books paperback, May 1975
Narrator: Barnabas Sackett
Time Period: c. 1600

This is the story of Barnabas, the son of Ivo, and of his migration to a strange land beyond the sea, of his discovery of a purse of gold coins in the mud of Devil's Dyke that began it all, and the mischief it brought him.

It is also the story of Abigail, the daughter of Captain Brian Tempany, and how she met and married Barnabas of the Fens.

And it begins the story of those who accompanied them into the far land, and those who joined them later, and of all that came to be as they began the westward trek.

And here are related various and sundry tales of the people who were concerned with them, and what became of them in the years that followed, at least so far as we have been told. And here are given some of the trails to the future, and some of the memories too, so that you who read may know all that can be told of those who followed the path to Shooting Creek, and beyond.

IVO: Of Ivo we will speak, who left the fens to follow the Earl of Blencope to foreign wars; a yeoman born, of stout arm and heart, he achieved modest fame at the battles of Lepanto and Zutphen, as well as in skirmishes hither and yon between those battles, and in traveling.

Later he saved the life of his fallen lord, standing over him to smite hard his enemies with sword and axe, then carrying him from the bloody field when the fighting was ended.

In the ancient days of Ivo there was yet a chance for a bold young man if he handled his blade well. Land was held by the King or the great nobles of the realm; all others were yeomen or peasants, yet a good fighting man might win wealth and preferment. In later years, many a great family was to forget that its high position in life was won by a husky nobody whose valor and strength were rewarded with a gift of lands, and a title to accompany them.

It is often forgotten that all lands, everywhere, were won by the sword. The followers of William the Conqueror, whose flimsy claim to the throne of England was backed by his Norman relatives and allies, descendants of Vikings who were seized off the land known thereafter as Normandy.

For generations these Northmen, or Normans, as they came to be called, had sailed out from their fjords to raid and conquer, sailing at first only to loot and destroy. Then they became enamored of the warm southern lands and remained there.

There were some who settled on lands in what we now call France, others in Scotland or England. They founded the city of Dublin in Ireland, and went still further south to establish a kingdom in Sicily.

But Ivo of the Fens was not of these, being a Celt of ancient line. He wedded Megan, a maid of Talybont in Wales, who was to become the mother of Barnabas. Ivo had won her fair, rescuing her from pirates in the western isles. And she, the fairest maid in all the isles, was of the blood of Nial.

For some pages now we shall speak of places and people, some not too familiar, some with whom the reader may have met at least in passing upon this lane or that.

LONDON BRIDGE: For many years it was the only bridge over the Thames, until Westminster Bridge was added in 1750. London Bridge rested on nineteen stone arches, and there was a wooden drawbridge that allowed ships to pass upstream. London Bridge was considered a street and lined with shops and residences, which in time became decrepit and rat-infested.

The current as well as the tide caused whirlpools and rapids around the arches, and "running the bridge" became a sport, albeit a dangerous one where many a strong lad lost his life.

At either end of the bridge was a gate over which were displayed the heads of malefactors, especially those of traitors or those perceived to be such. At one time a huge monster was destroyed near the bridge, but little is known of its actual size or nature.

Nor is there information as to when the first London Bridge was built. Details of the construction of the Bridge in 1176 have been found, yet there seems to have been a bridge in the time of King Ethelred, and it's likely the Romans had themselves bridged the Thames as early as A.D. 100 or shortly after.

LEPANTO: One of the decisive battles of history, and the last in which oar-propelled vessels were engaged. Don John of Austria, then but twenty-four years of age (not unusual for a ruler in those years), defeated Ali Pasha. Don John had at his command some three hundred ships provided by Venice, the Papal States, and Spain against the two hundred seventy-three Turkish vessels. This battle marked the end of Moslem power in Europe. The date was 1571, and Ivo Sackett was but a young man.

ZUTPHEN: A fortified city in the Netherlands, on the right bank of the Ysel. This battle took place in September of 1586, sadly remembered in England as the battle in which Sir Philip Sidney, the poet-soldier, was killed. Formerly the seat of the Counts of Zutphen, whose line became extinct in the twelfth century. Some six thousand British soldiers were involved.

In the fifteen years between these battles Ivo divided his time between living in the Fens and fighting in other wars, elsewhere.

It was the custom in those years to hold prisoners for ransom if they happened to be important men or had friends who might provide ransom. One such capture might make his captor wealthy, but the riches of captured cities were often divided among the rank and file as well if they followed a successful leader. Any young man with a sword might return from the wars with wealth enough to buy an estate.

SAKIM: Called a Moor, a term given to designate an African-born Arab; a name he sometimes accepted rather than offer an explanation few would understand. His actual home was farther away, in Jurjan, on the shores of the Caspian Sea. A fighting man when necessary, and one of those who taught the Sacketts to wield a blade, he was in his own land known for his wisdom. An occasional official, he was also a philosopher, physician, astronomer, and judge.

Taken by pirates after his trip to Mecca, he escaped from one ship only to be taken by another. He joined Barnabas in escaping from Nick Bardle's ship, and went with him to Shooting Creek. Called back to his native land by the death of his father, he discovered his travels had only begun. He was to think often of his old friend Barnabas, of Shooting Creek, and of Barnabas' children, who were like his own.

His story is also told in TO THE FAR BLUE MOUNTAINS. Such a man might appear anywhere, so who knows?

JEREMY RING: A wandering soldier of fortune following his luck wherever it chanced to take him. A landless man without home or fortune, selling his sword to the highest bidder, he asked only that the cause be just. A man with a fierce pride, a strong sense of loyalty, and a skilled swordsman and fighting man, he knew much of war, of men, and of the dark streets of evil. A chance acquaintance who became Barnabas' best friend, Jeremy Ring went with him to America and found a home there, with true love and happiness as well.

In that far land to which he had gone with Barnabas he founded a family and built an estate beyond his wildest expectations, if not beyond his dreams. His story continues in TO THE FAR BLUE MOUNTAINS, and elsewhere, as well.

THE LONGBOW: A weapon that revolutionized war in its time, enabling England to dominate every war in which it engaged for over one hundred years. The origin of the longbow is unknown but generally attributed to Wales, where it appeared in the hands of Welsh yeomen in the twelfth century. Although later bows were made of yew when that wood was available, it is said the earliest bows were of elm, and were usually the height of the man who was to use the bow. Some longbows were even taller, measuring as much as seven feet. What was called the warbow was usually six feet with a pull of one hundred pounds, and it needed a strong man to handle it. Good yew was rare in England, and even more scarce in Wales, so the first bows were also of ash or hazelwood. The appearance of the longbow on the field of battle spelled the death knell to the armored knight, although they were slow to accept the idea.

The armored knights were an undisciplined lot, unaccustomed to any but individual battle, and either unwilling or unable to work in concert. The archer well knew where his arrows were most effective, and his marksmanship was excellent. Every battle had its tales of some phenomenal shooting by archers with the longbow. In the earliest days each man made his own bows and arrows, but later these were provided for him, and had some uniformity.

By the time of Ivo, most English soldiers had seen the longbow in action, and many favored them over the crossbow as quicker to loose a second arrow, and easier to replace if lost or broken in battle. The effective range was considered to be 200 to 240 yards, although there were many stories of effective shooting at greater distances by archers of skill.

CORVINO: Former acrobat, injured in a fall, who lives by his wits in London, a man who once belonged to a troupe of acrobats and jugglers, and who wishes to belong again, who seeks someone worthy of his loyalty.

JUBLAIN: A former soldier from Mayenne, in France; a difficult man, cross-grained and cynical, but a fine swordsman. Returned to England with John Tilly, in TO THE FAR BLUE MOUNTAINS, but a bad penny always turns up, so. . . .

RUFISCO: A Neapolitan shipmate of Barnabas who deserted the *Jolly Jack* with Barnabas and Sakim. Dies in a boat after being shot with Indian arrows.

THE HULK: The wreck of a ship, half-buried in sand, where Barnabas took shelter. It also appears in TO THE FAR BLUE

MOUNTAINS, and in a future book, as yet unwritten. If you wish to know its origin you might read FAIR BLOWS THE WIND, a story of Tatton Chantry. A ship with a cargo of silver bars and perhaps other treasure, left to the mercy of wind, wave, and whatever chance might bring, but buried at last on a small, sandy islet in a Carolina river.

JOHN LELAND: An historical character, author of *Itinerary in England and Wales*. Supposedly born in London in 1506, but it could have been a year or so earlier, and died in 1552. Perhaps the most dedicated antiquary in English history, he devoted much of his adult life to wandering the English countryside noting old castles and ruins, searching out the histories of towns and scholars, recording whatever he discovered. What we have, however, are only notes taken en route, for Leland did not live to write the work he planned.

No doubt much was lost, for if I were to judge him by my own practice, I know his notes might serve only to fix certain places or ideas in mind that he planned to develop later from memories. The notes were merely keys to unlock memories he had filed away for future reference.

Leland had demonstrated considerable scholarship, and his education was excellent. Offended by what he considered slighting remarks about England and her kings, he had followed his studies by on-the-spot research. The map he planned was never drawn, yet his books remain a fascinating area for research on the England of his time, and offer significant clues to a sometimes unrecorded past.

PETER TALLIS: A man of varied talents, providing from a booth in St. Paul's Walk legal papers of various kinds, and purveying information for all those who could pay. A man of considerable education but no wealth; an interesting rascal, but a good friend to those to whom he took a fancy. Whatever you wanted, he either had or could acquire for you, always for the proper payment. A man not above ignoring business for good conversation, a sifter of truth from gossip; a man aware of who was plotting against whom, and why. If he did not know what you wanted, he could find out; if he did not know today he would tomorrow. Occasionally he loaned money, always for exorbitant interest. A friend to Barnabas, he appears again in TO THE FAR BLUE MOUNTAINS, and no doubt will be heard from elsewhere, again and again.

RICHARD HAKLUYT: An historical figure, birthdate uncertain, but probably 1552, died 1616. Compiled *Principal Navigations, Voyages and Discoveries of the English Nation*, a remarkable collection of accounts of exploration and travel, in many volumes, and a most valuable reference for the time. The Hakluyt Society continues to gather and publish accounts from various parts of the globe. I read from this many times, in many places, before I finally could add the set to my library.

It must be remembered that the accounts of exploration provided in the usual histories are those considered important by the compiler. During the years following the first voyage of Columbus there were several hundred ships of several nationalities off the coasts of America, exploring or trading with Indians. But only a few names remain known to us. The records of the French towns of Dieppe, St. Malo, and La Rochelle, for example, have suffered from time as well as wars and sieges. Seamen and fishermen from these and many other ports went often to the West, both before and after Columbus, as did those of Bristol, in England.

BARTHOLOMEW GOSNOLD: Died in 1607. Commanded an expedition that reached southern Maine, and south as far as Narragansett Bay in 1602; second in command of the expedition that carried settlers to Jamestown. Gosnold was a gentleman of Suffolk, a man not only of seagoing experience (he had been a privateer as early as 1599) but with family connections. Very early he had the idea of planting a colony in Virginia. It was he who enlisted Captain John Smith, among others. His death came at a time when he was sorely needed by the colony he helped to plant, leaving them poorly equipped for what was to come.

CHRISTOPHER NEWPORT: Of Limehouse, in London. He had sailed with Sir Francis Drake. His first voyage and his first command were in 1590, and he spent the following fifteen years at sea, or largely so. He had lost a hand on his first voyage, but his skills as a navigator were not affected. The first settlers for Virginia's Jamestown colony arrived on a ship he commanded.

RICHARD FIELD: Of Stratford-on-Avon, he came to London just as William Shakespeare did. Established a shop in Blackfriars, becoming one of England's best known printers. He lived from 1561 to 1624 and published the first works of Shakespeare to appear in print: *Venus and Adonis* in 1593 and *The Rape of Lucrece* in 1594. His father was a tanner; Shakespeare's was a glover.

THE BELLE SAVAGE: On Ludgate Hill. The site is now a garden and the building itself was removed in 1873. It first appeared in 1452 as Savage's Inn, and its courtyard was used as a theatre for the presentation of plays. Pocohontas stopped there for a time when living in England, and according to rumor the Devil himself made an appearance there once during a play. This must not be considered extraordinary, as the Devil was making quite a few appearances in London at the time, as well as later. The Inn could stable up to one hundred horses and house about the same number of guests.

Many explanations have been offered for the name of the Inn, including a claim that it had been named for Pocohontas. It is more than likely it was simply named for the first owner. Much could be written on its history and its place in historical events. Travel in those days offered many trials and tribulations, not the least of which were the creatures inhabiting the beds in most inns. Parson Woodforde commented that he had been "savagely bitten" while stopping the night at La Belle Savage.

COVENEY HASLING: A gentleman of Stamford, a collector of antiquities, and a man of modest means but varied interests.

The Society of Antiquaries of London was not formed until 1707 when a group of interested men began meeting in the Bear Tavern in the Strand, and later on Fleet Street. However, there was a Society of Antiquaries in the country at large at a much earlier date.

TABARD: The inn from which Chaucer's pilgrims began their trek as recorded in *The Canterbury Tales*, and a popular resort for many years. It lay near the end of London Bridge, and was a large, rambling structure. Plays were frequently performed there as the architecture of such inns offered balconies overlooking the courtyard, and provided a natural setting for theatre. The Tabard burned in 1676 but was rebuilt and stayed in business in one way or another for over a hundred years after that date. Later it was demolished.

JULIUS CAESAR: Barnabas Sackett was fortunate enough to attend the first performance of this play written by William Shakespeare. That performance took place on September 21, 1599, at the Globe Theatre in London.

WILLIAM SHAKESPEARE: Born in Stratford-on-Avon; an actor of character roles (he often played kings) who also wrote plays. A thoroughgoing professional writer who knew what he was doing at all times. He was prolific, writing thirty-six plays, many sonnets, and several narrative poems, all in less than twenty years. He did this while he was regularly performing one old play and rehearsing a new one. We do not know how many roles he was prepared to offer at any given moment but Edward Alleyn, an actor performing in the same era, was prepared to go on stage in any one of seventy roles. It can be assumed that Shakespeare was equally prepared.

A canny businessman, he soon became an actor-sharer, owning a small piece of the company and sharing in its profits and losses. That he saved his money cannot be doubted, for from the first he bought real estate in Stratford and maintained his family there. Later he became an actor-manager.

When he left the theatre, he retired to live the life of a country gentleman in the surroundings he loved. It has been suggested with some probability of truth that in earlier years, before choosing London and the theatre, he had been a school teacher. There are frequent references in his plays to various school texts and the conduct of school boys, so this seems a strong possibility.

There has been a tendency to enshroud him in mystery for one reason or another. As a matter of fact, we know more about his life than that of almost any commoner of the time, and there is no mystery. The only reason for imagining that anyone else but Shakespeare wrote his plays is that he did not attend a university, which seems to have offended some small-minded scholars from time to time. The school he did attend in Stratford was one of the best in England, and several of the nobility sent their sons to school there for that reason.

The sources of his plays, many of which he merely rewrote from other sources and improved, are obvious and well-known. At one time or another, more than fifty people or organizations have been credited with writing his plays. There is no logical reason to suppose they were written by anyone but Shakespeare himself.

Sir Francis Bacon, to whom some misguided people have attributed the plays, simply did not have the time. He never completed the work he had laid out for himself and which was dear to his heart. Moreover, there are errors in Shakespeare's plays that Bacon would never have made.

Unfortunately we miss many points in Shakespeare's plays because we are not familiar with personalities and discussions current in his time. Personalities known to everyone in England are often portrayed in an oblique manner recognizable to his audience. Topical allusions are common throughout his plays, all of which would have amused his audience.

The Tempest was based upon a well-known shipwreck in Bermuda, much discussed at the time. And not many years before the first performance of *Hamlet*, Eustachio had discovered the Eustachian tube, which was used in the murder of the King, Hamlet's father.

Aside from his use of language (and an actor was constantly rehearsing the finest writing of the period) his greatest asset was something that could not be obtained from books: his knowledge of people, character, and psychology. That he was a keen observer of his fellow man is obvious, and none of his rivals came close to him in that respect.

One must also remember that the age in which he lived was not one given to introspection. His age was a time of outward movement, of exploration. This was the period of Sir Francis Drake, Hawkins, Frobisher, and others who were capturing ships and raiding ports along the Spanish Main.

Shakespeare's plays are open to many interpretations but surely those based on Freudian or other modern psychological theories are furthest from what the author himself had in mind. The Elizabethan period was a time of action, not for looking inward. Ben Jonson, an equally famous playwright in his day, once killed an enemy soldier in single combat between the assembled armies, and later killed at least one man in a duel. Another playwright, Christopher Marlowe, was involved in several violent actions and was finally murdered in what has been described as a brawl in a tavern. It is more likely, I believe, considering Marlowe's career as a spy, that it was an assassination.

All in all, it was a time when direct action was the order of the day, and Shakespeare knew his audience and what they wished to see. The man of the Elizabethan period would have been equally at ease at the siege of Troy or in the American West. Drake or Achilles would have been perfectly at home at the Alamo, and Jim Bowie in the Trojan war. Achilles and Bowie could have walked a deck with Drake. The times were similar, as were the men.

WILL KEMPE: Also, Kemp. An actor in the same company as Shakespeare; a portrayer of low comedy, vastly popular in his time. He also appeared in several plays by Ben Jonson.

RICHARD BURBAGE: The matinee idol of his day; played leads in many of Shakespeare's plays as well as others. His father, James Burbage, was the owner of a theatre, inherited by his sons, Cuthbert and Richard. The latter lived 1567 to 1619.

DEVIL'S DYKE: Built by the Iceni, a Celtic people whose leaders included Queen Boudicca. The Dyke was about six miles long, covering a gap between the fens and the heights, from Reach to Wood Ditton.

THE WASH: A shallow bay, some 22 miles by 15, opening upon the North Sea, on the east coast of Lincolnshire and Norfolk. It includes the estuaries of several small rivers; the Nene, the Ouse, the Witham, and the Welland. It was here that King John lost the royal treasure—the sceptre and the crown of England, as well as many unset rubies, diamonds, and emeralds. The crown of Matilda, the sword of Tristan, nearly two hundred gold and silver cups, rings, jeweled belts, pendants, clasps, and sacks of gold coins were also lost. King John felt safer when keeping the royal treasure close to him. Aside from the long train of wagons, he also had the army with him.

King John knew nothing of the Wash or its vagaries, nothing of what could happen when the incoming tide met the outflowing currents of the rivers. His plan was to spend the night at a Cistercian abbey at Swineshead, and when they reached the place where the river flowed across the sand into the Wash he saw no danger in those slight waters. Eager to get on, tired and wanting rest, as did those he commanded, he had no idea that when the tide met the river currents the Wash became a maelstrom, a mad whirling of fresh and salt water against which nothing could stand.

King John rode through the shallow waters and his army followed. Behind came the heavily loaded wagons, just in time to catch the first of the tide. In a moment the wagon train was engulfed. There were cries for help, madly struggling horses fighting to be free of their harness, and fleeing men. Then the waves swept over the train and King John's royal treasure was swept away to be buried in the mud and sand of the Wash.

The King rode on to spend the night at the abbey, and ate a hearty meal. The combination of the meal, the stress, and perhaps a bit of poison was fatal for the King. But not while at the Cistercian abbey, for he rode away, no longer trusting them, if he ever had. Riding on did not help, however, for he died soon after.

The memory of that vast treasure lost in the Wash did not die. So far as is known, only one small piece was ever found, a bit of gold broken from a cup.

That the treasure was not forgotten Barnabas was soon to discover.

POTAKA: An Eno Indian, encountered in Carolina by Barnabas. Decimated by intertribal warfare as well as smallpox, the last of the Eno joined forces with the Catawba. They were of Siouan ancestry.

KING ARTHUR: Barnabas mistakenly believed that he lived before the Romans. His existence is disputed, some believing the stories of Arthur and his Round Table were figments of someone's imagination. There is considerable evidence, however, that some such Celtic chieftain did live and organized resistance against the invaders of England after the Romans had left.

Recently further evidence has been discovered on the Isle of Man. Much of the story of King Arthur did not, however, take place in England, but across the channel in Brittany. Now a part of France, Brittany was for many years a part of England, and several of the places referred to in the stories of King Arthur and his Knights can be found in Brittany. If he existed, and I, for one, believe he did, then it was in that period of turmoil that followed the retreat of the Roman legions from England. The Roman presence had long held the barbarian hordes at bay, but once the soldiers were gone the English shores were exposed. In those hectic times a strong leader was necessary.

WHITE HART: An inn known in Southwark (a borough of London near the docks), mentioned by Charles Dickens. Open as early as 1406, it was partly destroyed by fire in 1669 (after it was known by Barnabas and his friends), later rebuilt, and then finally torn down in 1889.

ST. PAUL'S WALK: The news that Jesus had driven the moneylenders from the temple apparently did not reach St. Paul's Cathedral in London. What really happened, of course, was that after Henry VIII broke with the Catholic Church there was a time when St. Paul's could not be maintained as it formerly had. The nave of the cathedral, known as St. Paul's Walk, became a shortcut from Paternoster's Row to Carter Lane. That "street" became a place of popular resort. Various people set up booths and all manner of business was conducted there, moneylending being the least of these. It was also a veritable "Peacock Alley" where the very latest in fashion might be seen and where ladies of the evening, or any other time of day, might be found. Lawyers received their clients, horsefairs were conducted, murderers were hired. It was a gossip center and a place for strollers, newsgatherers, and hawkers of every description.

The first state lottery was held at the west door. Scenes from many plays of the time were set in St. Paul's, particularly in the plays and masques written by Ben Jonson, obviously a frequenter of the place. His duel with Gabriel Spencer, however, took place at Hoxton's Fields, some distance away. Ben Jonson, poet and playwright as well as occasional actor, former bricklayer's apprentice and a notable fighting man, killed Spencer in that duel. He himself was wounded.

DOLL BARTHRAM: An historical character who was hanged as a witch on July 12th, 1599. Accused by Joan Jordan, a servant of Simon Fox, of sending her three toads and then a spirit that came knocking at eleven o'clock at night. Witnesses: a chief constable, a vicar, and Anthony Aldham, a gentleman.

LUKE HUTTON: Hanged. A noted highwayman, formerly a scholar at Cambridge, and rumored to be the son of the Archbishop of York. Condemned on nine-score and seventeen indictments. Obviously an active young man, Hutton wrote a book while in prison called *The Black Dog of Newgate*.

NICK BARDLE: Master of a merchant vessel, half a pirate, ready to take any advantage or engage in any nefarious activity that promised a profit. He shanghaied Barnabas aboard his ship, the *Jolly Jack*, intending to lose him over the side somewhere en route to the Indies. But Barnabas proved one of his best seamen and Bardle delayed until too late.

Hence Barnabas became the first of his name in America, the first to look westward from the sea toward the blue distant mountains, and to wonder what lay there, and what lies beyond. Little did he know that ten generations of his name would look westward with wonder in their eyes and in their minds, and then, perhaps, still other generations would look outward to the stars.

TO THE
FAR BLUE
MOUNTAINS

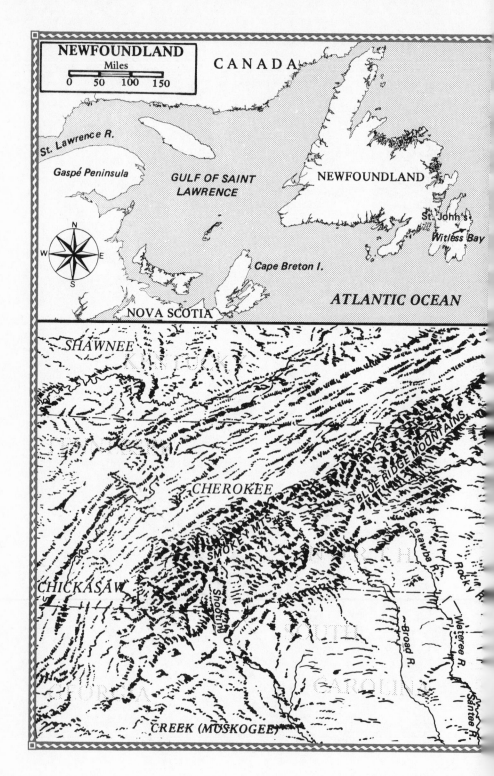

NEWFOUNDLAND
Miles
0   50   100   150

CANADA

St. Lawrence R.

Gaspé Peninsula

GULF OF SAINT
LAWRENCE

NEWFOUNDLAND

St. John's

Witless Bay

N
W   E
S

Cape Breton I.

ATLANTIC OCEAN

NOVA SCOTIA

SHAWNEE

BLUE RIDGE MOUNTAINS

CHEROKEE

SMOKY MTS.

Catawba R.

Rocky R.

CHICKASAW

Shooting

Broad R.

Wateree R.

Santee R.

CREEK (MUSKOGEE)

44

ENGLAND

Miles

25   50   100

THE NEW WORLD
"RALEIGH'S LAND"

Miles

0   25   50   75

TO THE FAR BLUE MOUNTAINS

First publication: E.P. Dutton hardcover, October 1976;
Bantam Books paperback, June 1977
Narrator: Barnabas Sackett
Time Period: c. 1600–1620

I n which Barnabas Sackett returns briefly to the land of his birth, and relates what he found there, including an order for his arrest. Because of the gold coins he found and sold to Coveney Hasling, he is suspected of having found the royal treasure of King John in the Wash.

Barnabas encountered some old friends and some enemies, found his bride Abigail again, and took a ship for America. This is the story of how Abigail went with him to the far lands and became mother to his sons and daughter, and how his first born was birthed to the sounds of battle with a man standing over Abigail with a sword as she gave birth to Kin-Ring, the first son.

And how they found, at last, a home at Shooting Creek in the shadow of Chunky Gal Mountain, and what happened there and thereafter.

BLACK TOM WATKINS: A sailor and a soldier, but a smuggler as well, with his name on a list to be hanged at Tyburn, when he was caught. A man of the fens he was, and one who stopped by the cottage in times past. Now he would escape the country with Barnabas, knowing little of where they went, nor little caring whether it was to life or death. Like all men, he knew he owed life a death; only he wished to die cleanly with a sword in hand, perhaps, and a friend to stand beside.

THE PROSPECT OF WHITBY: A pub, originally built in 1520, and perhaps the oldest public house in the London area. It was where Barnabas expected to meet Peter Tallis. Originally it had been known as the Devil's Tavern, and was in the beginning a hang-out for smugglers, river pirates, and thieves of every vintage. Not far away is Execution Dock where pirates were hanged, including Captain Kidd, less a pirate than many. Charles Dickens, Whistler, Pepys, and Turner all visited here, as well as John Taylor, the Water Poet.

There is a river terrace from which the traffic on the Thames may be watched. Although it was still called the

Devil's Tavern in the time of Barnabas, I have chosen to call it by its present name for the sake of those readers who might someday wish to visit the place. Its name was changed to Prospect of Whitby in 1777 because of a vessel named the *Prospect* that used to tie up there.

THE GRAPES: A waterfront tavern where Barnabas left the borrowed boat. An inn well known to Charles Dickens who also used it in a story. Few inns along the river front were better known. It was established in the sixteenth century.

MAG: A sailor's wife who kept a sleeping place for sailors and others; a respectable woman whose place was clean, and whose cooking rivaled the best. Her Jack was a gunner aboard a Queen's ship. A friend to Jeremy Ring.

PIMMERTON BURKE: A vagabond, and a landless man, a wild and reckless young man given to fisticuffs in taverns and fairs. He went over the seas with Barnabas and found a home there, and modest wealth as well, until he met a lady who proved to be somewhat less than a lady. She took his gold and his emerald and went off to England, no doubt to meet a man who was less than a gentleman. Pimmerton then opened an inn, and no doubt met another lady.

NICK BARDLE: A sea captain who first appears in SACKETT'S LAND, he is an enemy to Barnabas and all his kin. His ship is the *Jolly Jack*. This sea-going rascal could turn up anywhere.

ROBERT MALMAYNE: A courtier and a man of power, involved in intrigues of various kinds, all of which either increase his power or his wealth. A skilled swordsman and a plotter, he believes Barnabas has found the treasure of King John and means to have it for himself. A treacherous man, believed to be loyal to the Queen but actually loyal to none but himself.

CONRAD POLTZ: A shrewd, dangerous man, a spy and an informer. A henchman of Robert Malmayne, skilled at obtaining information, with secret friends in most of the taverns and places of resort as well as along the waterfronts and in the homes of the mighty.

ODIHAM: A pleasant village on a prehistoric trade route with architecture of many styles, from many centuries. If you are in the vicinity, pay it a visit and you will enjoy the day. Nobody there will remember Barnabas Sackett, for many years have passed, but Barnabas remembered the village and with pleasure.

ROCKBOURNE: Another pleasant village, and a bit south was the site of a Roman villa. Also worth a side trip.

CRICKLADE: Near the source of the Thames, where Barnabas met Darby, a man known to Peter Tallis, who knew many men who could be useful in a quiet way. He provided horses to enable Barnabas to continue on his way with some speed. A town located on the old Roman road.

DARBY: A canny man who found ways of being useful to friends of Peter Tallis, and no doubt to others as well.

NIAL: A spaeman, a foreteller of the future, born with the gift of second sight. His mother was the daughter of Ar the Silent, master of a great land in Norway. The legend of Nial was known in Wales but as far as Iceland, too, and not forgotten elsewhere. It was said that all of his blood had the Gift, to a greater or lesser extent.

EDMUND PRICE: A poet and a man of talent and taste. He was of Merionethshire in Wales, but well known at Cambridge and Oxford.

GUDLIEF GUDLAUGSON: Who sailed from the west of Ireland in 1029 with a northeast wind and was driven far to the southwest. There upon a lonely coast he found Bjorn Ashbraudson who had left Ireland thirty years before.

ANGLESEY: Separated from Wales by Menai Strait, an island of legend and mystery.

GLANDORE: A deep inlet sheltered from the sea. The Castle of the O'Donovans was there, on the south coast of Ireland. A lovely place where we spent some happy days while I picked up bits of legend and lore. Not far off the coast is where the *Lusitania* was sunk by a German submarine in World War I.

TO SPIKE A GUN: Often written of in old historical novels but rarely explained. Cannon were fired by holding a match to a touch-hole in the top of the gun. To render a cannon useless, or at least for the time being, a spike was driven into the touch-hole so the flame could not reach the powder charge.

PETER FITCH: A shipwright who married a Catawba woman. A man who loved working with wood and understood its properties, and which woods were better to use for selected projects. A strong man, a good man.

JOHN QUILL: A man from the sea who had been a farmer and wished to be so again.

NATHANIEL CAUSIE: He came over with Captain John Smith to the Virginia colony. One of the first to be attacked when the massacre began, he killed one of his attackers with an axe (he was chopping wood at the time) and managed to fight off the others until he could escape to carry word to the colonists.

THE KILLIGREWS: A trading and shipping family who were a power in their own area. One of them went on to London and became an actor there in Shakespeare's time.

SIR FRANCIS WYATT: He took over administration of the Virginia Colony in 1621. An able and considerate man, he was unfortunately in command when disaster struck, a disaster that had been brewing for some time. Oppecancanough had assured the governor that peace between the Indians and the colonists would be forever, that all was well. A few hours later, on the morning of March 22, 1622, the Indians attacked without warning and massacred nearly one-third of the colonists. There were a few cases where individual Indians friendly to certain colonists did warn them of what was to come. Some did not believe the warnings; others put themselves in a position of readiness in well-guarded compounds and so survived. Generally it was a major disaster.

JOHN TILLY: A ship's master and ordained minister; it was he who married Abigail and Barnabas, and at a later time, Lila and Jeremy Ring. A strong, capable, quiet man, he had been promoted from seaman to captain by Barnabas, who recognized his ability. He also appears in THE WARRIOR'S PATH.

THE LOST COLONY: Planted by Sir Walter Raleigh, it endured from 1584 to 1587, then vanished. There has been much speculation about the lost colonists, and of Grenville's men, who were also left in Virginia. Such speculation is interesting but, it seems to me, needless. It would seem obvious that when ships did not return with the promised and necessary supplies, as well as additional colonists, that those people who came with Raleigh simply went to live with friendly Indians and adopted their way of life.

John Lawson, the naturalist, who arrived in Virginia-Carolina in 1700, tells of meeting many Hatteras Indians. "These tell us," he writes, "that several of their ancestors were white, and could talk in a book (read) as we do; the Truth of which is confirmed by gray eyes being found frequently amongst these Indians, and no others. They value themselves extremely for their Affinity to the English and are ready to do them all friendly offices. It is probable this settlement miscarried for want of supplies from England; or through treachery of the natives, for we may reasonably suppose that the English were forced to cohabit with them, for Relief and Conversation; and that in the process of Time they conformed themselves to the Manners of their Indian relations."

—from *A New Voyage to Carolina*, by John Lawson.

Lawson spent much time among the Indians and was the first to make a comprehensive list of plants and animals in the

Carolinas. He also discussed the Indian method of scalping, and was later killed and scalped himself.

CHOWAN RIVER: On the spot where in my story Captain Tempany's vessel was run aground, charred timbers were actually discovered. Their origin we do not know, but they seem to have been a ship's timbers or those of a fort, hewn by metal axes.

HORSES: Much nonsense has been written about the horse in America. Actually, the prehistoric horse, which was about three feet high, originated in America, moved to Asia and Europe by way of the so-called land bridge that joined the continents where the Bering Strait is now, and then for some unknown reason this early horse, the size of a dog, died out.

Some writers would have us believe that all horses in the Americas descended from the sixteen brought by Cortes, but nearly every Spanish expedition brought horses, and as they did not geld their stock there was no limit to the number available for breeding.

In the expedition headed by Ayllon eighty-nine horses were landed near Cape Fear; some time later Arellano, son of the governor of Yucatan, landed some two hundred forty horses. Some of the horses brought by De Soto were abandoned when his followers boarded rafts to escape down the Mississippi.

Horses were brought into the country by other would-be settlers from Nova Scotia to Florida and Texas. Some were abandoned, some stolen by Indians, and years later vast herds of wild horses were seen. One trapper-trader in Kansas reported a herd that needed several hours to pass his position.

CATAWBA: A tribe of Indians in the Carolinas who from the first were friendly to the white man and, except for one brief difficulty, soon resolved, they remained a valuable friend and ally.

ALBEMARLE AND PAMLICO SOUNDS: Protected from the Atlantic storms by barrier islands, the two sounds receive the waters of several rivers and streams. Because of the protection from the sea, ships frequently anchored there, and it has been said that the first permanent settlement in the Carolinas was between the mouths of the Chowan and Roanoke Rivers. John Pory was in the area in 1619–22 and is credited with being the first settler. The truth is we simply do not know. As mentioned before, there were many ships of several nations cruising along the Atlantic shores, many with ideas of starting settlements or trading posts. Some of those ships were fishing, some trading, some hunting Indian slaves. Aside from the already-mentioned Gosnold and Newport, there were Weymouth, Barlow, Gordillo, Quexos, Verrazano and William Hilton, to name just a few.

Hilton found several shipwrecked English sailors being held by the Indians and he bargained for their release. Nearly every part of the country had stories of white men who had been there before, and undoubtedly castaways were living among the Indians. Juan Ortiz was one such.

WA-GA-SU: A Catawba who became a friend to Barnabas and his friends. A frequent visitor at Barnabas' various camps, and at Shooting Creek.

JONATHAN DELVE: A former member of Barnabas' crew who turned pirate and became an enemy. At Jamestown, Yance and Kin-Ring slipped aboard his ship and spiked his guns.

KIN-RING: Barnabas' first son, born in the heart of an Indian battle, while his mother was defended by his father's friend, Jeremy Ring. Kin-Ring first appears in TO THE FAR BLUE MOUNTAINS, and later in THE WARRIOR'S PATH. In the latter story he finds a wife and returns with her to Shooting Creek. A skilled swordsman as well as a hunter and man of the wilderness, but he, like his brothers, had been educated in the schools Barnabas set up, with Sakim as their principal teacher.

YANCE: The sire of the Clinch Mountain Sacketts, he went north to the Puritan settlements, and there found a wife in Temperance Penney and escorted her back to Shooting Creek. Yance spent some time in the stocks before being freed by

Temperance, a feisty lass with a mind of her own, and who knew a good man when she saw one.

A woodsman, rough, impetuous and strong, loving the wilderness, always ready for fight or frolic, he is suited to the land in which he is to live. He appears in TO THE FAR BLUE MOUNTAINS, and in THE WARRIOR'S PATH, as well as many another place before the good earth claimed him.

As it was with his father, the Indians loved him even when they fought him, and the name he left became a legend among them as his father's had before him.

JUBAL: He had the gift of second sight like his father, and after many wanderings he went away alone to the far lands beyond the great river and the only word of him after was that borne on the wind. A whisper here, a whisper there. He, too, married well, an Indian daughter of the Natchez. They built their home in Colorado, almost in the shadow of the Sangre de Cristos. His story is told in TO THE FAR BLUE MOUNTAINS as well as in JUBAL SACKETT, but he will appear again, here and there.

BRIAN: Son of Barnabas; he grew up in the mountains of what is now Tennessee, North Carolina, South Carolina, and Georgia, but his yearning was always for more education and a life in the cities. He returned to England with his mother and sister, to read for the Law at the Inns of Court. He appears in TO THE FAR BLUE MOUNTAINS but his story belongs in other lands, for the most part. He is a true Sackett, however, and did not forget his native country nor his people. Before leaving Shooting Creek he had talked much with Temperance, Yance's wife, and with Diana and her father. Moreover he had looked about him and seen what manner of people these American colonies were breeding. He foresaw the break with England and planned accordingly, not only for himself but for his relatives in America.

NOELLE: Barnabas' only daughter, who at the age of ten returned to England with her mother to become a lady there, and to have many adventures before finding the man she loved; she also found an old acquaintance in a far land who was helpful when help was needed.

Noelle became a beautiful and gracious lady with much of her father in her as well as her mother, but quite a bit of Yance, too, if pushed too far.

SHOOTING CREEK: Where the Sacketts finally located. If one is driving from Chattanooga east to Franklin in Carolina, Shooting Creek will lie deep in its green valley on your left. Since the highway was re-routed, it no longer passes through the valley and it is easily missed. There is one small narrow sign to indicate where it lies.

CHUNKY GAL MOUNTAIN: It sounds like a name invented by a writer but it is not. Chunky Gal Mountain is at the head of Shooting Creek Valley and one passes over a shoulder of it going into the Valley. It is said to have been named for an Indian girl who lived there.

CLINCH MOUNTAINS: A long narrow range of mountains largely in Tennessee that bred a hardy lot of people, and was where Yance Sackett settled. It has also produced some excellent country-western singers and dancers, among whom are the Carter family, of which June Carter Cash, Mrs. Johnny Cash, is a member.

KANE O'HARA: Who married Margarita, a Spanish girl he lured from the settlements to the south. The O'Haras prospered and many years later a small inheritance was left to Echo Sackett. (RIDE THE RIVER).

TIM GLASCO: Killed at his forge, by Indians.

JOHN PIKE: A Newfoundland man, formerly a fisherman and hunter of whales. Barnabas promoted him to sailing-master and eventually left him with a ship. He did well, and was to sail and trade on many far distant shores.

MATT SLATER: A farmer who loved the earth. Killed by the Seneca in 1602.

JAGO: A sailor, a castaway.

BARRY MAGILL: A cooper and a weaver. A deft, handy man, apprenticed to a weaver, he later went on to making barrels, but could turn his hand to anything.

SIR WALTER RALEIGH: Courtier, poet, historian, soldier in France as well as Ireland; chemist, explorer, and planter of the first known colony in English America. Born in 1552, he was beheaded in 1618. A tall, handsome man of noted courage, he took a trunk filled with books on every sea voyage, and read much while at sea. He was a favorite of Queen Elizabeth, but his fortunes declined after her death. He was a prisoner in the Tower for many years, then beheaded, reportedly at the insistence of the King of Spain.

KINSALE: About 16 miles from Cork, and on the southern coast of Ireland. In 1601 the Spanish fleet with nearly four thousand soldiers aboard seized the town, and the British forces under Lord Mountjoy were attacked from the rear by the Irish. Later, in a planned, combined attack, the Spanish failed to move as planned and the Irish were defeated.

Kinsale was an important naval base during the seventeenth and eighteenth centuries, and the area has great charm. There are several ruined castles nearby. Built around Compass Hill on the banks of the Bandon, the site is a beautiful one.

It was here that Barnabas fulfilled the prophecy of his mother and killed her enemy in the flames of a burning town. If you travel to southern Ireland you will find Kinsale, Glandore, and Skibbereen, of which I have also written. You will enjoy them even more than Barnabas did.

HORSE SHOE BANK: There's a narrow passage between it and Wicklow Head, or so there was at the time of my story. Nearby is Wolf Rock, a danger to be avoided. Wicklow Head is a bold headland, easily recognized, but there is no danger if one holds a course well to the north of the Horse Shoe.

When writing such a story as SACKETT'S LAND or TO THE FAR BLUE MOUNTAINS, one must saturate oneself in all that can be learned of the times. It is futile to attempt to understand their period by our own; customs were different, as was even the language itself.

For example, the study of mathematics and especially geometry was the fad of the day. Commenting on this, John Aubrey says, "Soldiers, sailors, courtiers, and clerics all devoted themselves to this intoxicating study."

Trevelyan has commented, ". . . apart from poetry and the stage there was hardly any literature that was not serious." The novel, as we know it, scarcely existed. Inns and taverns were not only places to eat, drink, and be entertained but were meeting places for intellectual groups, a practice that was continued on this side of the water. The problems that brought on our American Revolution and the development and writing of the Constitution were discussed and argued in taverns from Georgia to Maine.

There were skeptics about, but they were few; the idea prevailed that if something was written it was true, yet the atmosphere was changing. Trevelyan also suggests that had there been newspapers and novels, there might never have been a Protestant revolution, for as these did not exist men took to reading the Bible and no longer looked to a priest or a clergyman to interpret its meaning.

Books were published under far different circumstances than today, and usually were underwritten by some wealthy or titled man. Such books often opened with a glowing tribute to the patron, whoever he happened to be. Books were rarely dedicated by the author, but more often by the printer or publisher. This fact has given rise to much needless speculation on the part of those unaware of the different practices of the time.

Travelers in different eras did not always look at the same things. I have read several accounts of travel through the Alps that mention neither the mountains nor snow. These travelers were completely uninterested in what we call scenery. Their interest lay in the taverns, in people met along the way, and in other travelers.

When I travel over an area about which I wish to write, I see it not only as it is but as it must have been at various times over the centuries. Europe, for example, had few roads as we think of them. The Roman roads had long been abandoned or did not take travelers where they wished to go. Most travel was on horseback or foot, and in the time of Queen Elizabeth carriages and stages were just coming into use. The paths followed by travelers were often mere muddy lanes or well-worn paths between fields.

London, at the time of SACKETT'S LAND and TO THE FAR BLUE MOUNTAINS or FAIR BLOWS THE WIND, was a city of about 250,000 people. The first stagecoaches were beginning to appear, but they offered rough travel at best. Nobody traveled for pleasure, and most people would have been amazed at the idea. The great lords and others traveled only when duty or some other necessity demanded, and the only others to go far afield were soldiers or sailors. The average man traveled no further than the nearest market town.

The roads, such as they were, were maintained by villagers or their children, who dropped stones in the mudholes or ruts, and made a halfhearted attempt to keep the roads in some sort of existence. One prince, traveling by coach, commented that it required six hours to cover the last nine miles of his journey.

Later, a number of inns kept horses on hand for the stages and travel became faster and much improved. Breakfast at such a place might be a cold pigeon pie, grilled kidneys, beef, ham, or eggs washed down with buttered coffee or ale. Or rum, if one was close to a seaport.

In those more leisurely days few had occasion to hurry. A despatch rider or courier rode a horse, as did many other travelers, as the stages rarely moved much faster than a man could walk. When they were not a sea of mud, the roads were apt to be a maze of frozen ruts over which the coaches (no springs!) bounced and jarred.

Rarely have I used all the material at hand in writing of a cross-country journey. To provide too much would slow the pace of the story, yet I need to know all the conditions and possibilities.

When writing of a journey I mark down the point of origin and the destination. Then, by using old books on post-chaise travel, accounts of those who traveled the route at the time or approximately so, I fill in on my outline the rivers, the bridges, the inns, the forests, swamps, and so on until I have a picture of the route almost as good as if I had traveled it at the time. (They are always routes I have personally used, and which I know in my time.) If an innkeeper is mentioned by name, I use it, and if the meals are mentioned, I use the same food or some that would easily be available at the time and place. Few of these items can be had from one source, and often I consult a dozen books and as many maps to complete what goes on one page, or even in one paragraph.

Adequate descriptions of travel are few, so one pieces the bits together as in a jigsaw puzzle. I try to write a story so that if it was read by a man of the time he would be able to say, "Yes, that is the way it was!"

Much later than my story is an extract from Stedman's journal, dated Sept. 11, 1784: "Another post-chaise for Calais through Gravelines, where we did breakfast. Today the roads were worse as possible, except where we went over quick-sands, which is exceedingly dangerous. The breakers beat into the carriage, the horses bad, and beginning to be late."

Travel was travail; one did not enjoy, one endured.

THE
WARRIOR'S
PATH

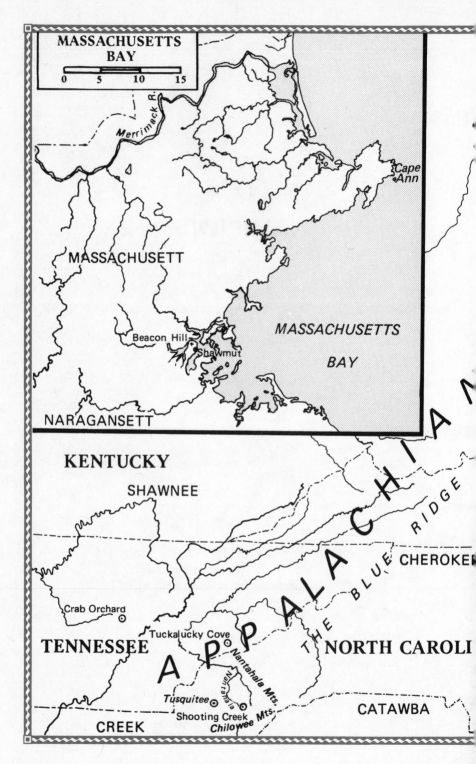

MASSACHUSETTS
BAY

0   5   10   15

Merrimack R.

Cape
Ann

MASSACHUSETT

MASSACHUSETTS
BAY

Beacon Hill
Shawmut

NARAGANSETT

KENTUCKY

SHAWNEE

APPALACHIAN

THE BLUE RIDGE

CHEROKEE

Crab Orchard

Tuckalucky Cove

TENNESSEE

NORTH CAROLI

Nantahala Mts.
Nantahla

Tusquitee
Shooting Creek
Chilowee Mts.

CATAWBA

CREEK

THE WARRIOR'S PATH
NORTH AMERICAN COAST
Scale of Miles
0   20   40   60   80   100

SENECA

PENNSYLVANIA

MOUNTAINS

Susquehanna River

NEW JERSEY

MARYLAND
Baltimore

Kent I.

DELAWARE

Nanticoke R.

Sinepuxtent
Bay

Pocomoke R.

Pocomoke
Swamp

Chesapeake Bay

Rapidan R.

Rappahannock R.

VIRGINIA

ATLANTIC OCEAN

Jamestown

OCCANEECHI

COCKPIT
COUNTRY

JAMAICA

EASTERN
JAMAICA
Scale of Miles
0   5   10   15   20

Rio Cobre

Santiago
de la Vega

Healthsire
Hills

Galleon Bay

Salt Pond

Port Royal

Great Plum Pt.

Pallisadoes

Cape
Hatteras

CARIBBEAN SEA

63

THE WARRIOR'S PATH

First publication: Bantam Books paperback, July 1980
Narrator: Kin-Ring Sackett
Time Period: c. 1620s

In which Kin-Ring and Yance respond to a call for help from Anna Penney, mother of Temperance, who is Yance's wife.

Carrie Penney, Temperance's younger sister, has disappeared in company with Diana Macklin, the beautiful daughter of Robert Macklin, who is suspected of being a witch. Supposedly the two were taken by Indians while gathering herbs in the forest. A search by local people has been abandoned, and Joseph Pittingel, a merchant, fosters the belief that they have been taken by Pequots.

Despite warnings and obstruction, Kin-Ring and Yance set out to find the missing girls, and the tracks they find are not those of Indians.

Angered by what they discover, Kin-Ring and Yance set out to find not only the missing girls but what has happened to other girls who have been lost over the past few years. Their suspicions lead them to Pittingel himself and to those employed by him. The trail leads them to Jamaica, even to Port Royal, hang-out and resort for pirates and slave traders.

TENACO: A friendly Indian who brought Anna Penney's call for help to Yance, and who was wounded by a musket ball. Did the Pequots have muskets? Who did not want a message taken?

PEQUOTS: A fierce Indian tribe, probably never numbering more than twenty-five hundred people.

The Indian population of North America has been estimated at 650,000 to 1,000,000 before the coming of the white man, which is approximately the size of the Indian population today.

Other estimates have been made, suggesting far larger populations, but these, I believe, have not considered the ability of the Indian, with his primitive methods of farming (when he farmed at all), to feed himself. It is generally agreed that a hunting and food-gathering people require one square mile per person to subsist, so the number of Pequots mentioned above

65

would require twenty-five hundred square miles of land, far more than was actually available, due to other tribes living in the vicinity, making demands upon much of the same land.

Moreover, the one constant in the Indian subsistence pattern was the near starvation period at the close of winter when food supplies began to fail and new plant growth had not begun. A long winter almost invariably led to famine.

The pursuit of agriculture varied considerably from area to area, however, and the Natchez in Louisiana harvested a wide variety of crops, living in a climate well suited to planting.

CARRIE PENNEY: A pretty young girl of ten years, learning about plants from Diana Macklin. Supposedly kidnapped by Indians along with Diana. She was the younger sister of Yance's wife, Temperance.

DIANA MACKLIN: Daughter of Robert Macklin; a quiet, self-contained girl of considerable intellect. She sewed well, spun well, and performed all domestic activities with assurance and finesse, but she also read much, and had ideas. These last were considered a very doubtful quality by many of the men of the colony. Several of the young men offered themselves as suitors but Diana manifested no interest. These suitors included Joseph Pittingel, an older man known to be well-off, one of the leaders in the community.

She knew much of herbs and their medicinal values and often went into the woods to collect herbs. Because of this and because she was not afraid of the night she was suspected of witchcraft. Pittingel, it seems, was the first to hint at such a thing. Anna Penney scoffed at this but her husband was uneasy. He was a respecter of authority and unwilling to voice opinions contrary to those of the men in power. Anna Penney, for one, recalled that no such suspicions were voiced by Pittingel until after his suit had been refused. Tom Penney liked Diana but was uneasy in the presence of a girl not afraid to speak her mind.

TOM PENNEY: A hard-working man trained as a stonemason, but skilled with tools and any kind of construction. He also has done quite well as a farmer.

Here it might be added that few of the Puritans had previous experience as farmers. A large number had been craftsmen or artisans of some kind and only a few had experience with planting, cultivating, or harvesting crops.

Another factor not always considered when reviewing the hard times the early colonists had was that they had little or no experience as hunters. In England the game belonged to the King or to the great lords, and their gamekeepers kept careful lookout for poachers.

The would-be colonists landed in a country with much game but no experience at hunting or dressing captured game. This they had to learn from the Indians, who were astonished by the white man's ignorance of something so basic.

ANNA PENNEY: Wife to Tom, mother to Temperance and Carrie, and friend to Diana, but like her husband inclined to be subservient to authority. It was only her great love for her lost child that led her to send a friendly Indian in search of Yance Sackett, who was a woodsman. Within herself she was doubtful of Pittingel's wisdom, although not suspicious of his motives. In any event, nothing more was being done and her feelings demanded the search be pursued.

JOSEPH PITTINGEL: A wealthy merchant and owner of ships; a trader with interests in the West Indies. A highly respected man and one of the officials of the community, which was unaware that he was also a slave trader, and a ruthless man to whom money and position were all-important. Contemptuous of his fellow settlers, whom he considered lesser men, he hated all who opposed or contradicted him. Success had hardened his resolves and made him even more sure of himself.

ROBERT MACKLIN: Father of Diana; a good man, a sincere man, but not one to throw his weight about unless necessary. A strong man in his own way and quite well-off, he knew nothing of Indians or their ways, nor did he know the forest. Although he distrusted Pittingel he had nothing upon which to base his distrust. A studious man, happiest when with his books, he came to the new country with some knowledge of farming as well as a small, steady income from the old country. Yet he had his own fears and worries, and had come to America to escape the scandal surrounding his wife, Diana's mother.

MAX BAUER: A slave trader; a ruthless, brutal man of great ability in his own way. Although second to Pittingel he was a stronger man in every way. A skilled tracker and hunter, a good seaman, he was all Pittingel was, only more so, but without the money. A man to be feared.

HENRY: A slave of Ashanti background. His people have always been warriors and slave traders in Africa, raiding other tribes and selling them as slaves to the Arab, Portuguese, and other traders who operated off the African coast. Enslaved himself, he had been quietly submissive, making himself useful while biding his time. He helped the girls to escape and escaped with them. His hope was, by helping them, to find a place for himself among their people. This was, at least, the story he gave himself. He was actually a kindly man, respectful of them, and aware of the life awaiting them for which they were in no way equipped to survive. A cool, self-contained man of considerable ability, and a great man in his own land where his father was a king among the Ashanti, a warrior people.

VERN, FEEBRO, AND LASHAN: Henchmen of Bauer, and hence, to some extent, of Pittingel.

JUBLAIN: Former soldier, adventurer, a friend and associate of the Sacketts. Gone to Moslem lands to seek his fortune.

PETER TALLIS: Also in SACKETT'S LAND, and TO THE FAR BLUE MOUNTAINS. Had a booth in St. Paul's Walk, a man of many parts and varied interests. Originally a man skilled in cutting not quite legal corners, he had become the agent for the Sacketts and the produce they sent for sale in England or the Low Countries. He handled such business for others as well, led into the field by the Sacketts.

DAMARISCOVE: In the Maine Islands, but rarely mentioned among the early settlements in America. Vessels had been coming to this island for generations. The first authentic date so far is 1603, four years before the Jamestown settlement and seventeen years before the Pilgrims landed. The *Mayflower*, as a fishing vessel, had visited Damariscove before its famous voyage with the Pilgrims. No longer inhabited, it was a port of call for many ships along the Atlantic coast prior to British settlement on the mainland.

SHAWMUT: Where Boston now stands. First settled by Samuel Maverick and the Reverend Blaxton. There were several springs on the site. Winthrop moved most of his colony there after the original site proved unhealthy.

SAMUEL MAVERICK: He had come over the Atlantic with Gorges, who established a colony in Maine. Maverick retained property in Maine but settled at Shawmut and built a strongly fortified trading station there. An able, interested man, he owned several trading vessels and later wrote a book called *A Brief Description of New England And Several Towns Therein.*

He was an ancestor to the Maverick for whom the unbranded Texas cattle were named, and of Maury Maverick, a Congressman from Texas in the New Deal Era.

THE REVEREND WILLIAM BLACKSTONE, OR BLAXTON: Born in Salisbury, England in 1595. Graduated from Cambridge. Came to America in 1623. As he had religious differences with the colonists he eventually left Boston for Rhode Island. He has been credited with planting the first orchards in Massachusetts. Reputed to be a reserved and studious man content to be left alone to pursue his own interests, both intellectual and agricultural.

69

PORT ROYAL, JAMAICA: Variously called the City of Gold and the Babylon of the West, Port Royal was a buccaneers' port. There was much legitimate trade, of course, but it was predominantly a port for pirates, privateers, slave traders, and those who dealt with them. Bronzed seamen with gold rings in their ears swaggered along the quays and lingered in the waterfront dives, of which there were a-plenty. The loot from many a sunken or captured ship was brought to Port Royal and it was there the riffraff of the seas spent their bloodstained gold. Brawls and dagger thrusts were an everyday matter and a man was supposed to take care of himself. Most of them were well-fitted to do so.

Dining, drinking, and wenching, the buccaneers spent fortunes because there was no need to save. The seas were a rich hunting ground for the men of the Black Flag. This continued until one sweltering morning in June, 1692, when an earthquake struck. Three rapid shocks, close together, and in three minutes or less Port Royal was destroyed as efficiently as Sodom and Gomorrah. The city slid off to the bottom of the sea, taking most of its population along with it. One moment the wild, roistering town was booming at its best and in the next there was nothing but a turmoil in the water, floating wreckage, and here and there a body the earth did not swallow.

It was to this port, still in its heyday, that Kin-Ring came on his quest for the slave traders.

THE MAROONS: Escaped slaves who took refuge in the Cockpit country of Jamaica. There were Maroons elsewhere but those in Jamaica were the best known and won themselves a position unequaled by any others.

From the Cockpit country they fiercely resisted all efforts to recapture them and finally won independent status. It is likely that many of them were of Ashanti blood. One detachment that was captured was shipped off to Nova Scotia and later to Sierra Leone, where they fell back into their old way of life. Most of those remaining in Jamaica are now Seventh-Day Adventists.

Their capital is at Accompong, and but few trails lead into the Cockpit country, so-called because of a series of pits or inverted cones in the rock. The pits are from one hundred to five hundred feet in depth, in diameter from ten to one hundred yards, many of them overgrown with brush and trees. From this hide-out of more than two hundred square miles they fought the Spanish, from whom they escaped, and later the British, until a treaty was negotiated that left the Maroons in a very favorable position.

AUGUSTUS JAYNE: A tailor in Port Royal, but he was much else besides. A man known to Peter Tallis, with whom he had dealings. A man with an ear to the ground and aware of all that was happening around him, as well as elsewhere.

RAFE BOGARDUS: A fine swordsman and a professional killer in a town where every man had done his share of killing and was prepared to do more. Kin defeated but did not kill him, so no doubt he will appear again in his own good time.

CLAIBORNE: An historical character who had a trading station on Kent Island in Chesapeake Bay.

ADELE LEGARE: A feisty young lady of unusual intelligence who matured very quickly when necessity demanded; who adapted herself to the situations in which she found herself and became a person of quality and decision. Kidnapped and sold as a slave, she did not despair, nor did she forget those responsible. From the crowd at the slave auction she selected a quiet young man and lured him into buying her, then persuaded him that she'd make a better wife than a slave. She not only became his wife, and one of whom he could be proud, but she assisted him in his business affairs. Most important, she did not forget the men who had kidnapped her.

LEGARE: The planter who became Adele's husband; a plantation owner and dabbler in government affairs who found in Adele the woman he needed, and who needed him. Kin suggested his brother Brian as London agent for Legare.

DEAL WEBSTER: A trader on Kent Island.

CAPE ANN: A granite peninsula into the Atlantic now largely occupied by Gloucester and Rockport. A place familiar to seafaring men from the first days of sail along the Atlantic coast.

GALLEON BAY: Located on the northeastern side of Goat Island, a shallow but excellent shelter for small craft; not far from Port Royal and Kingston, Jamaica.

Jamaica was for many years the most important of the West Indian Islands to the colonists, and one of the many causes leading to the Revolutionary War was the restriction put upon direct trade to and from that island. England insisted that all trade with the West Indies be routed through English ports. Traders found it much easier to sail directly from the West Indies to North American ports and so avoid two crossings of the stormy Atlantic.

Rum, the most popular drink in early America, came from the West Indies and most of it from Jamaica. The trade with the American colonies was extremely profitable, while the two crossings of the Atlantic that England demanded removed a large portion of the profit.

THE WARRIOR'S PATH: An old war trail that led from the vicinity of Chattanooga to Boston, with many branches and offshoots. A trail long used by warring Indians on their raids, north and south, but particularly the Seneca war parties attacking the Catawba and the Cherokee. It had been in use for several hundred years before the coming of the white man.

JUBAL
SACKETT

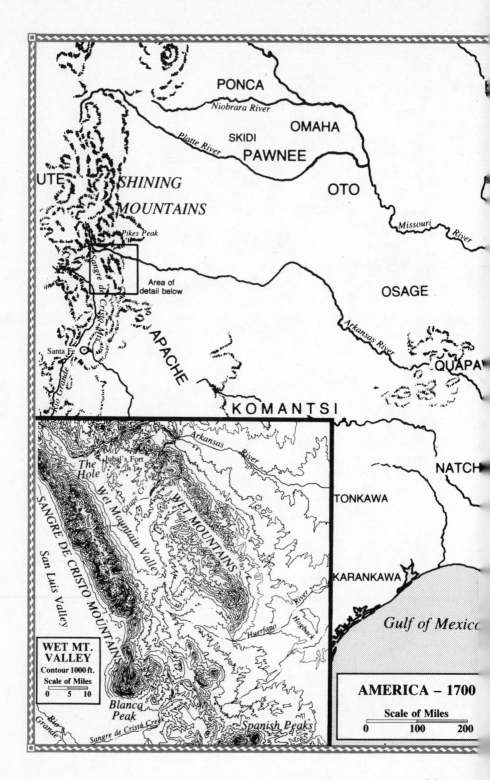

PONCA

Niobrara River

OMAHA

SKIDI

Platte River

PAWNEE

OTO

UTE

SHINING

MOUNTAINS

Pikes Peak

Missouri River

Area of
detail below

OSAGE

APACHE

Arkansas River

Santa Fe

Rio Grande

QUAPA

KOMANTSI

Arkansas River

Jubal's Fort

The
Hole

NATCH

Wet Mountain Valley

WET MOUNTAINS

TONKAWA

SANGRE DE CRISTO MOUNTAINS

San Luis Valley

Huerfano

Hogback

KARANKAWA

River

**WET MT.
VALLEY**

Contour 1000 ft.

Scale of Miles

0   5   10

Gulf of Mexico

*Blanca
Peak*

*Rio
Grande*

Sangre de Cristo Creek

Spanish Peaks

AMERICA – 1700

Scale of Miles

0   100   200

74

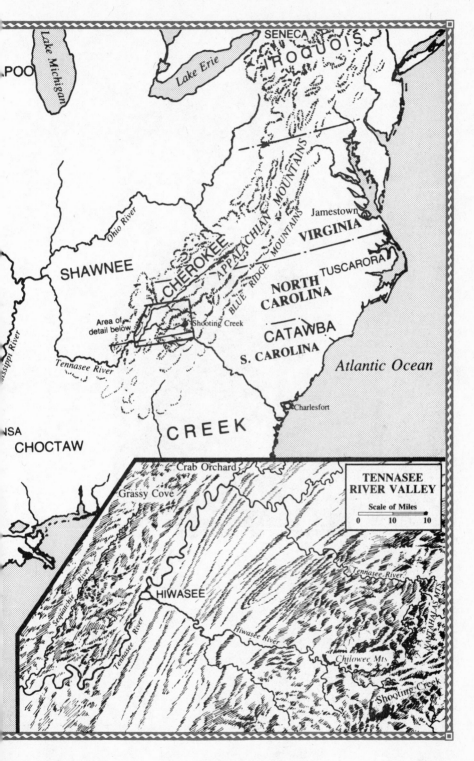

CREEK

CHOCTAW

NSA

POO

SHAWNEE

CHEROKEE

APPALACHIAN MOUNTAINS

BLUE RIDGE MOUNTAINS

VIRGINIA

Jamestown

NORTH CAROLINA

TUSCARORA

CATAWBA

S. CAROLINA

Atlantic Ocean

Charlesfort

SENECA

IROQUOIS

Lake Michigan

Lake Erie

Ohio River

Area of detail below

Shooting Creek

Tennasee River

Mississippi River

TENNASEE RIVER VALLEY

Scale of Miles

0   10   10

Crab Orchard

Grassy Cove

HIWASEE

Seqiachie River

Tennasee River

Hiwasee River

Tennasee River

Chilowee Mts.

NANTAHALA MTS.

Shooting Creek

JUBAL SACKETT

First publication: Bantam Books Hardcover, June 1985;
Bantam Books paperback, June 1986
Narrator: Jubal Sackett
Time Period: c. 1620s

In which Jubal Sackett seeks out a way to the Shining Mountains, beyond the Great River, and beyond the wide grass plains, a place where someday other Sacketts may need to go, seeking a further refuge from the King and their enemies.

He parted from his father, each knowing they would not meet again, yet each knowing they must follow the path of destiny. And Jubal had always known his way led to the unknown lands far to the West.

And in which he finds a companion, also a seeker of unknown lands, and then a girl of the Natchez, a beautiful Indian girl but with ways and customs different than any Indian he had known.

Down the Mississippi he went, and up the Arkansas, following that river until it emerged from the Rocky Mountains, and then westward into the mountains until he found the place where he wished to put down roots and remain.

Itchakomi had been sent to the West by the Ni'kwana, seeking, she supposed, a new home for the Natchez. Yet had their wise man intended more than that? Had he seen in Jubal Sackett the man for her?

How did a woman attract a man? Who could she speak to of love? She was a Sun, perhaps even destined to be the Great Sun, or to hold the leadership until he came of age or another was chosen, and a Sun did not share thoughts with women of lower caste.

JUBAL SACKETT: A son of Barnabas, gifted as was his father with second sight, a loner and a wanderer by nature. A man of the woods and wilderness, silent when among others of his kind, skilled as any Indian with spear or bow, yet his reliance was upon the twin pistols made long ago by a superb Italian craftsman, and made by that man to demonstrate his skill to a great lord.

To Jubal Sackett, there was always another river to cross, another bend in the road, another hill to see beyond. His destiny was to be the first man west, yet was he? Had others gone before? Was there ever a *first*? There must have been, yet wherever he went there were signs that others had been before him.

KEOKOTAH: A Kickapoo; one of a nation of warriors and wanderers, known for their long, solitary treks into unknown lands. He found in Jubal, the son of Barnabas, a man to walk beside—a white man, but one of his own kind.

ITCHAKOMI ISHAIA: A daughter of the Great Sun, political and spiritual leader of the Natchez Indians of Louisiana and Mississippi. She was herself a Sun and a person of considerable importance in her village and tribe. She had been directed by the Great Sun to lead a small party west and locate a new place for them to move, as their wise men had foretold an end to the tribe if they remained where they now were.

KAPATA: Half Karankawa, who were cannibal Indians, he wished to wed Itchakomi, and aspired to leadership of the Natchez. He was a strong warrior, fiercely determined, and by marrying Itchakomi, a Sun, he would be in a position to maneuver for leadership. He immediately sensed a rival in Jubal, and intended to kill him.

NI'KWANA: The Master of Mysteries of the Natchez, a Medicine Man but more than that, for he was one of a mysterious people who merged with the Natchez in the distant past. A maker of magic, a man of wisdom and kindness.

THE COMANCHE OR KOMANTSI: A fierce and warlike tribe of horse-riding Indians who came down from the north destroying all in sight. During the course of a few years they wiped out most of the Plains Apache. At the time of this story they were just beginning to acquire horses by stealing them from the Spanish, but they and their associates, the Kiowa, were to become the finest horsemen of the plains. The Commanding General of the British forces, reviewing armies around the world, said they were the finest light cavalry he had ever seen.

For more than two hundred years they waged war with their relatives, the Utes, until finally they signed a formal Treaty of Peace at elaborate ceremonies to which I was an invited guest. It was the only formal treaty signing between two Indians tribes who had been at war. A Medicine Teepee was prepared and the elders of the tribes, after being purified by smoke from a cedar chip fire, wafted over them by an eagle's wing in the hands of a Medicine Man, entered the teepee for the formal signing. It was a most impressive ceremony at which I was honored to be present.

CONEJEROS: A branch of the Apache tribe, very active in eastern Colorado and neighboring areas, until finally destroyed by the Comanche.

GOMEZ: A renegade Spanish officer who tried to buy Itchakomi from Jubal; he had broken with his own unit but was hurrying back to Santa Fe to turn in the first report, to get his story on record first. A tough, ruthless, and dangerous man. A man without scruples and without a conscience.

DIEGO: The officer against whom Gomez rebelled; a good man, a sincere man. He warned Jubal the Spanish would not permit him to trade there, yet when Jubal explained the Spanish might need an ally as well as a supply point, he listened and seemed receptive.

UNSTWITA: A Natchez who had found the leader he wished to follow in Jubal, and with Jubal, a Sun. The Indians had no such role as "princess," yet had there been such a name, such a role, this Itchakomi Ishaia would have been.

We have much to learn about the American Indian, and unhappily many of the old men and women who knew the stories are gone. Such is often the case when there is no written language, for people are vulnerable and precious knowledge may be possessed by only one man, or at best a few.

A certain rite or ceremony, a dance, or a song, may have belonged to but one man. It may have been something he created as I would write a novel or someone would paint a picture. Perhaps that ceremony existed only in his own mind and he was the only one who could properly direct it, so if he dies the ritual dies with him. Others can often remember only fragments. But there is another thing: that song, that way, that dance *belonged* to the dead man, so it would not be used again. Feelings about such things vary from tribe to tribe.

Often the Indian does not wish to share those things sacred to him, and this I find easy to understand. The white man, not having the Indian background or early teaching or experience, can grasp only the superficial aspects of Indian culture. He may see the color and the movement without grasping any of the meaning it has for the Indian. Little as I know, I often listen to those who believe they know, and hear them expound at great length on what Indian lore is all about, and even to me it is apparent they have no idea of what they are talking about. The meaning has escaped them, as it well might escape anyone not an Indian. Some anthropologists have made mistakes in understanding as serious as those made by early missionaries.

At one time an Indian might be known by his costume but this is scarcely true today. At the various inter-tribal ceremonies, powwows, and such they have mingled and often have borrowed ideas for costume from each other, each seeking to add beauty or interest to his clothing, his headdress, his dancing.

It was much the same in the past. During the warfare between tribes young women were rarely killed. The Indian's idea of conservation in this respect could not have been improved, and these women were taken to wife by warriors of the victorious tribe and brought with them the stories and rituals they knew. Naturally, this was what they taught their children. A story that began as a Seneca story might be found among the Sioux or Blackfeet, or among any other tribe. Good stories have a way of traveling, and stories such as *Cinderella* or *Jack And The*

Beanstalk have been known in virtually every part of the world in one form or another.

We do not know the origin of all the American Indians or how much communication there might have been in times long past. Certainly many tribes migrated over the land-bridge from Asia. There is sufficient evidence for that, but many Indians have legends of arriving across the sea, and without a doubt there was much going and coming due to changes of climate, movements of game animals, and warfare, as well as population pressures.

As our archaeologists delve into the ruins left by primitive Indians here as well as in Central and South America, the picture of early American man is slowly taking shape. Pot hunters, seeking immediate profit, may destroy much that is vitally important. The particular clue that may open a door to unexpected knowledge may come from anywhere. We still are but scratching the surface insofar as ancient trade is concerned. A pot that cannot be dated according to its location has lost much of its value to the archaeologist and the historian.

We know there was trade and undoubtedly an exchange of ideas between the peoples of Central America and Mexico and those of our Southwest, and those of Louisiana such as the Natchez. How much of an exchange of ideas or what were the patterns of migration we do not know. It is at least possible that some of our Indians may have fled Mexico to escape the rising tide of human sacrifice by the Aztecs or those who preceded them.

One of the greatest joys of human life is that there is so much to be learned and gradually we are getting the tools with which to learn, and knowledge enough to know some of the questions that must be asked of the past.

The story of Jubal Sackett is but one chapter in the saga of the Sacketts, and a glance at what could have been a chapter in our history. My reason for writing it was threefold: first, to continue the story of the Sackett family; second, to explore a possible phase of our history; and last but perhaps most important, I have always wished I could have been the first man west, or one of the first to ride or walk into that country when only the Indians were there, to see it unblemished, unchanged, in all its original beauty. I came too late for that, so I wrote a story about a man who did.

RIDE
THE
RIVER

APPALACHIAN
MOUNTAINS

Scale of Miles

0   20   40   60   80   100

OHIO

Cincinnatti

Ohio River

WES

Greenbottom

VIRGIN

Louisa
Blaine Cr.
Paintsville

Big Sandy

Indian

Guyandot

KENTUCKY

SHAWNEE

Pikeville

Levisa Fk.

Tug Fork

ALLEGHEN

Pine Mt.

Russell
Fork

Cumberland River

Stone Mt.

Wallen Cr.

Clinch River

Old Boone Trail

Holston River

Nashville

Caney's Fork

Knoxville

French Broad R.

APPALACHIA

Crab Orchard

Grassy Cove

TENNESSEE

Blanket Mt.

Tuckalucky Cove

Thunderhead Mt.

Middle
Prong

MTS.

Clingman's Dome

Siler's Bald

CHEROKEE

GREAT SMOKY

Tennessee River

Shooting Creek

King's Mt.

GEORGIA

CREEK

SOUTH

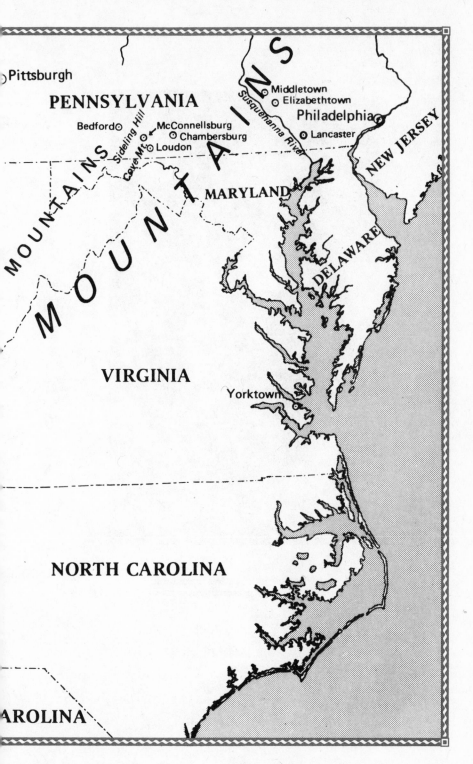

RIDE THE RIVER

First publication: Bantam Books paperback, July 1983
Narrator: Echo Sackett
Time Period: c. 1840s–1850s (before Civil War)

In which Echo Sackett goes from her mountain home in Tennessee to Philadelphia to collect an inheritance. There are others who plan to keep that inheritance for themselves and want no interference from some hillbilly girl who has just come down from the mountains.

Echo is small, dainty, and determined. Moreover, she is a Sackett, accustomed to taking care of herself, and she comes from an area where people are accustomed to doing just that. She is not about to be put down by any city thugs.

In Philadelphia she recognizes the name of Chantry, and seeks out Finian Chantry, who had fought in the War of the Revolution alongside Daubeny Sackett and has reason to remember the Sackett name. Now a distinguished lawyer, a man of great prestige as well as knowledge of the law, he wonders a little whether at eighty-odd years he can still handle himself when physical action appears. In his youth he had walked a quarter-deck on his own ship and handled some tough crews. Could he still do it?

He comes to Echo's aid, and then sends his nephew, Dorian Chantry, to follow her and see she gets home all right. Dorian is a young man with much to learn but he learns quickly when necessity demands.

Echo figures to take care of herself but if a handsome young city feller wishes to trail along, she's willing. What follows is what might be expected, but what the thugs sent by lawyer James White do not understand is that the mountains are filled with Sacketts.

Echo's Uncle Regal has been clawed by a bear and is out of action, but there are others, and when a Sackett is in trouble. . . .

Echo's brothers have gone west to the Shining Mountains where Ethan has become a trapper and free hunter (see BENDIGO SHAFTER) and Colborn has disappeared in the western mountains looking for treasure. Possibly he has been killed by Indians, but he has left behind a widow and several sons.

Trulove, all of six feet and six inches, with two hundred and fifty pounds of beef on him, is still around, as are Macon, and the weird one, Mordecai. Somehow or other they will have to cope with whatever comes.

Echo is a lady and comports herself as such, whether it is coping with the clumsy advances of White's clerk or going out to dinner with the distinguished lawyer, Finian Chantry. In the mountains people did things that needed doing when they had to be done, and of course, she has her pistols and best of all, her 'pick.

REGAL SACKETT: Echo's uncle, a stalwart, handsome young man who had a way with the ladies whether in the mountains or down to the Settlements. A hunter and a fighter, he was ready for anything from a hand-to-hand fight with a mountain lion or to dance a fandango. He took to singing, as mountain folks did, but he was a hard-working man who was usually a bit better off than most.

He knew where the best fur could be found, occasionally logged some timber, and had been known to pan a bit of gold from a mountain stream down Georgia way. He'd listened a lot at storytelling time and knows where a man might find a gemstone or two.

He'd been down to the Settlements and met some fancy ladies and some aristocratic ones, and they all had an eye for Regal.

FINIAN CHANTRY: Former seafaring man and soldier, a handsome elderly attorney in Philadelphia, respected by all. In his younger years a noted fighting man, now he wondered if he still had what it takes. He had been mentioned as a possible Justice of the Supreme Court, but with all this he looked back with some nostalgia to the days when he trod a quarter-deck and fought the Barbary Pirates.

DORIAN CHANTRY: His nephew; a young man about town in Philadelphia who suddenly found himself "protecting" a very pretty young lady who somehow did not seem to need much protection. He also found himself dealing with men who had no sense of gentlemanly behavior, and surprisingly, he found himself enjoying it. He had more of Finian in him than he had realized.

JOHNNY GIBBONS: A young Philadelphia lawyer who was writing a history of that city's waterfront. He knew his way around sailors' hang-outs, and knew a bit about lawyer James White, too.

THE DUTCHMAN'S: On Dock Street in Philadelphia; a waterfront dive, located in Gaff Tops'l Corner, a part of the waterfront just coming into its own. A tough place for tough men, with crimps about, ready to shanghai a crew for a price, and not a bit particular about whom they shanghaied. Everybody sailing the western ocean knew the Dutchman's. So did the police, so they avoided the place.

PENANG LAWYER: A strip of rattan used to encourage discipline on Far Eastern ships. A vicious kind of whip that could with only a few strokes leave a man's back lacerated and bloody.

KISSING THE GUNNER'S DAUGHTER: Bending a man over the barrel of a cannon before applying the Penang Lawyer or perhaps a rope's end.

DAUBENY SACKETT: Echo's grandfather; great-grandfather to Tell, Orrin, and Tyrel, among others. Fought at the Battle of King's Mountain and before that at the Second Battle of Saratoga and Sullivan's Raid on the Iroquois Villages. There will be much of him in my book on the American Revolution.

DAVY LEWIS: An historical character; an outlaw from the Dickey Mountains of Pennsylvania. Locally famous.

DOUNE: A type of pistol created in the Highlands of Scotland. John Murdoch made those carried by Echo. Good guns were treasured and passed down in the family.

JOHN McHENRY: An historical character; a famous hunter in the mountains.

TIM OATS: A former bare-knuckle prizefighter, thief, and thug. Employed by James White.

JAMES WHITE: A shyster lawyer, skirting the thin edge of crime, prepared to take any advantage, even if it meant a murder.

FELIX HORST: A thief, a murderer, and formerly one of those who haunted the Natchez Trace, murdering travelers along one of the most dangerous strips of road in America.

ELMER: A thin, pimply youth of no standards, moral or otherwise, who was traveling in dangerous company, a situation where he was expendable. For the first time he was out of the city and into the woods, walking forest trails, remembering what Echo was like, and gradually becoming uneasy about himself and his associates. The cheap, thieving, cocky notions have begun to seem just what they are, and for the first time he has begun to think of somebody other than himself. He discovered he was not happy with what he was doing. Despite himself, he found himself admiring Echo Sackett, appreciating her courage and shrewdness, and began to understand what the money would mean to her and hers.

ARCHIE: A free black man, former sailor, now a waiter; accompanied Dorian on his way west to watch over Echo.

LEW WETZEL: An historical character, also referred to by Zane Grey; a famous frontiersman and Indian fighter. Maintained a lifelong vendetta against Indians after they wiped out his family.

PATTON SARDUST: Another Natchez Trace outlaw, a tough, vicious man who, unfortunately for him, encountered Mordecai Sackett.

MACON SACKETT: Like Mordecai, a Clinch Mountain Sackett, descended from Yance. A ginseng hunter. Ginseng, a valuable plant for shipment to China or medicinal use here, grew in the

Carolina, Virginia, and Tennessee mountains. The hunters of 'seng or 'sang, as mountain folks called it, carefully guarded their sources which they gathered for sale. The market for 'seng was always a good one, and the hunters were usually solitary men given to spending months on end alone in the forest.

JOHN IRWIN'S ROPE-WALK: John Irwin established the first rope-walk (for making rope) west of the mountains. After his death, his son and mother continued the business until 1812. This was on Liberty and Third in Pittsburgh. After 1812 the rope-walk was removed to a new site near Irwin's home, and continued at that spot for many years.

GINERY WOOSTER: A somewhat fat, gray-haired man, his hair thinning. He took the news to the Sacketts that a Sackett girl left the steamboat at the mouth of the Big Sandy and seemed to be in trouble.

SIDELONG OR SIDELING HILL: In the Tuscaroras of Pennsylvania. A steep and difficult hill in those years.

NOBLE'S TAVERN: A well-known stopping place on the westward route in Pennsylvania.

GINSENG: A most valuable herb; tea has been made from its leaves but it was the root that was most eagerly sought. In China it is the most valued herb, considered an aphrodisiac. From the time it was first discovered in the eastern mountains it has been hunted for use and for profit.

BIG SANDY: A tributary of the Ohio River, and at the time it was Indian country. The red man loved it and with reason, for there was plenty of game, and there were salt licks. The Levisa Fork was especially attractive. Most of the tall hats worn by the grenadiers of Napoleon were made from bear skins taken along the Big Sandy and the Levisa. The skins were taken down the river to New Orleans and shipped to France.

There were fine forests there, and some beautiful valleys, loved by the Indians and by those who replaced them.

CLINGMAN'S DOME: One of the highest peaks in the Smoky Mountains, over sixty-six hundred feet. A noted landmark.

SILER'S BALD: Roughly four miles west of the Dome and 1,000 feet less in altitude, it is a difficult climb over slippery rocks for a part of the way. It has a beautiful growth of rhododendrons, and a superb view toward North Carolina, if the weather is clear.

MORDECAI SACKETT: A long hunter, a man of the woods, rarely seeing other people, living off the country. Occasionally he visited his people, then was gone again for months, nobody knew where. Perhaps the most dangerous of all the Sacketts, friendly to the Indians, wise in the ways of birds and animals, living among them but leaving no traces behind. A man with no need for any of the things upon which most people base their lives. He still used the wild, wavering cry adopted by the first of the Clinch Mountain Sacketts when they discovered how far such a cry could be heard when in the mountains.

TRULOVE SACKETT: A big man, roughly handsome, a hand-logger and hunter. Skilled at handling unwieldy logs in rough country. From trial and error and much work alone he had learned how to use leverage and balance and many sleights in getting his logs to rivers where they could be floated down stream. Much of his logging was for special timbers, huge maples and oaks that were fine timber for the making of furniture. For years, since he was a small boy, he had been roaming the forest and knew where to find the kind of logs he wanted. Wherever he went he was studying not only where the right timber could be found but how to get it to water where it could be floated. Some of the huge logs were immensely valuable in themselves, eagerly sought after by builders of fine panels or furniture.

He, Mordecai, and Macon exchanged ideas and information, and the other Sacketts, woodsmen all, added what they discovered to the total of their knowledge of timber land and forest. Meeting occasionally, they could talk with knowledge of the mountain areas.

Often, returning to his cabin after an absence Trulove would discover on his table a crudely drawn map on birchbark showing him where a fine maple had been seen, or a stand of chestnut still untouched by blight.

The wilderness, be it desert, plains or forest, will take care of man, if man will but care for it. There is beauty there, but there is life, and a living for many, but there is death, too, if one becomes too casual. The wilderness is waiting, but one must live with it, and not against it.

If we strip away the forests, man will die, and the wild life will die. Man needs the forest, for it gives us the oxygen by which we survive. It cleanses the air we breathe so we can breathe, it removes impurities and leaves the air clear for far-seeing men.

And that is what we need, what we need desperately, those far-seeing men.

How small a man are you? Or how big?

THE
DAYBREAKERS

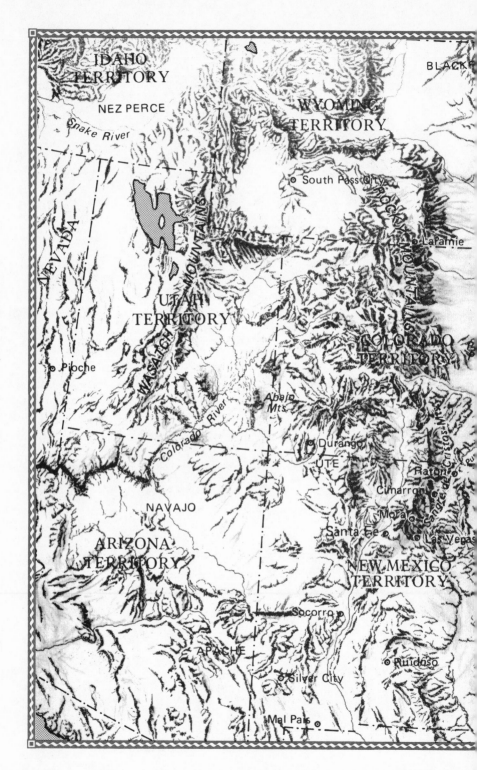

UNITED STATES, 1867

MILES

0   50   100   150   200

DAKOTA
TERRITORY

NEBRASKA

SIOUX

Platte River

CHEYENNE

Nebraska R.

KANSAS

Abilene

PAWNEE

Great Bend

Pawnee Rock

Arkansas

River

Dodge

Fort Dodge

Little Arkansas R

Cow Creek

Independence

MISSOURI

KIOWA

BLIC LAND

Cimarron River

Baxter Springs

Ozark Mts.

COMANCHE

INDIAN TERRITORY

ARKANSAS

TEXAS

97

THE DAYBREAKERS

First publication: Bantam Books paperback, February
1960
Narrator: Tyrel Sackett
Time Period: c. 1870–1872

This is the story of Tyrel and Orrin Sackett, who went west after the War Between the States, and what happened to them in that new land where they went to find a home for Ma. Somehow, Tyrel believed, Ma figured if she was west she would somehow be closer to Pa, who died or was killed out there a long time ago.

There were stories in the family, too, of another of them; Jubal Sackett to be exact, who had gone west away back before anybody else. They had heard stories that he married an Indian girl out there and had been trading with Spanish folks, but that was all a flimsy rumor from an Indian who told another Indian.

Orrin was fixing to get married when trouble came. The trouble was Long Higgins. Now they'd fought and feuded with the Higginses for quite a spell, and good, tough men they were, and they salted away some good Sackett men before they tapered them down to size. Long, he was the mean one. He knew Orrin was shapin' up to marry and figured he'd not be armed. What he didn't figure on was Tyrel.

So when they buried Long Higgins Tyrel had nothing to do but get out of there because the law was Ollie Shaddock and Tyrel did not want to confront him. Away back somewhere Shaddock and the Sacketts were kinfolk. The Sacketts feuded some but never faced up to the law.

"Pa taught us respect for the law so I hit the trail for the western lands."

Those last words were Tyrel himself speaking, but Orrin had started west, too, and not far behind him, for Long Higgins's bullet had killed Mary Tripp, the woman who was to be his wife. Without her, he figured why not go, and started west following Tyrel, and trying to catch up.

What happened after that the stories will tell you, but it was what was happening to many men headed west. Most of them weren't holding anything. I mean they didn't have cash money, so they tied their rope on the first job that showed itself, no matter what the brand, so long as it was honest.

Their first job was driving cattle, and living in the mountains since they were boys, they'd herded cows from time to time, and even flocks of turkeys and sometimes hogs. Back yonder whatever they had to sell had to get to market on its own legs. A body can pack only so much. Driving cattle was easy enough after what they'd been doing. Learning to rope was something else, but all their lives they had been adapting themselves to work of one kind or another. They learned quickly.

CAP ROUNTREE: He looked as old as the mountains around him and just as tough. He'd been over the Santa Fe Trail as a boy, had trapped for fur, hunted buffalo, and prospected some. He'd been up the creek and over the mountain, probably all of them. He had lived through border troubles, Indian fights, and whatever was happening where he was. He had lived with the Sioux and the Nez Perce. He never looked for trouble but he could handle it.

TOM SUNDAY: Foreman for Belden when he met the Sacketts, a disbarred lawyer who had killed man in a gun duel in Louisiana and gone to prison for it. Well-educated, and a gentleman born, but the years had used him hard. Very good with a gun. A man going west to begin again, to find a place for himself in the political life of the West where it did not matter what you had been or had done, but only that you did your part wherever you were and could stand the rough going. It was what you did now that mattered, and what you were now. Too many men had pasts they had ridden away from but the West was a place to start over.

ORRIN SACKETT: Six years older than Tyrel; a handsome man with a fine speaking and singing voice, appealing to women. He liked people, mixed well, and had a way with words. He decided to study law, partly inspired by Tom Sunday, and to enter politics. He wanted a home of his own, and deeply regretted the loss of Mary Tripp, a childhood sweetheart who had died for him.

TYREL SACKETT: You had to push to start a fight with Orrin, but not with Tyrel. Boyish in appearance, although lean and dark as Sacketts were inclined to be, there was something cold and still inside him when trouble started. Never wanting trouble, he had grown up in the midst of a feud and the bushwhacking guerrillas of the Civil War period, and he was ready, always ready. The Sacketts had been raised to respect the law, God, and their country, as well as the equal rights of others.

REED CARNEY: He wanted to be known as a gunfighter; he believed he was a tough man. He swaggered a little, chose the company of men he thought were tough, and some of them were. It was easy to fantasize, easy to imagine. Then the day came when suddenly he was faced with the harsh reality. That despised "farmer," as he called him, was facing him in the street, and he had a gun, too, and he was obviously ready, so very, very ready. Suddenly, the fantasy turned grim. The street was dusty, hot, and he was alone. Now he had it to do, but he was going to be shot at, perhaps killed. His mouth was dry and his knees felt like water. Suddenly he wanted to be away, far away, he wanted to be anywhere but here. Tyrel Sackett was letting him off the hook, he was getting a break, but should he? Was being known as a dangerous man worth the danger?

DON LUIS ALVARADO: A Spanish gentleman, ranching in New Mexico. A man who wanted only peace and time to develop his ranch and raise better cattle.

DRUSILLA ALVARADO: Don Luis's daughter, and a girl who knew a good man when she saw one, even though he was not of her blood or her kind, not even of her religion.

MARTIN BRADY: A saloon-keeper, a man willing to murder or to have a man murdered, a man who changed because of what he saw in another man. His kind, too, helped to open the West, to blaze the trails and to open a business, even if it was a crooked one. But his kind did not last unless they changed with the times, as Martin Brady was to change.

CHICO CRUZ: Dangerous as a coiled rattler and just as remorseless, a man tight as a coiled spring and with a streak of madness in him.

JONATHAN PRITTS: A man with great pride in himself and a contempt for others. He had come west with the idea of taking land from the Spanish who owned most of the grants. He intended to do this by political means if possible, by force if necessary, yet as the moment neared he thought less and less of politics and more of guns. Wealth came slowly in the East, and men of older families held the offices he craved. In the West, it seemed, a strong man might take what he wanted. The Spanish he believed were to be dispossessed and he planned to be the first in line. He had prepared his political situation very well before going west and was sure that once in the saddle all would go well. He was used to using men; the trouble was that the Sacketts were not there to be used.

LAURA PRITTS: Jonathan's daughter, a beautiful girl at first sight; at closer range, less beautiful. But she was a city girl from a background Orrin had never seen. It was as Tyrel had warned. He was seeing his dream, not the girl who was really there. She thought her father was the greatest of men, and wished to see him succeed in his endeavors, which he had convinced her were right and just. She despised the Spanish, the Indians, and most of the Anglo citizens, whom she considered trash. At first, she was much taken with Orrin, a handsome, dynamic man, but even in this she was influenced by her father's wishes.

OLLIE SHADDOCK: From Tennessee; distant relative by marriage of the Sacketts; briefly an officer of the law in Tennessee.

DROVER'S COTTAGE: A restaurant in Abilene well-known all up and down the trail; a place for the big cattlemen to gather after cattle sales. Served excellent food; often as good as could be had in any big city cafe or hotel.

FETTERSON: A very tough man, rider for Jonathan Pritts, and his second-in-command, holding the job Pritts had planned for Orrin Sackett. Not above hiring a killing for Pritts, he could do his own shooting when need be. A tall, blond man with a twisted look to his mouth caused by an old scar.

SANDY: One of three who wanted to kill the wounded Miguel, and fancied himself as a gunfighter until he caught two slugs from Tyrel Sackett. He didn't last long enough to realize his mistake.

BACK RAND: A would-be herdcutter who lived beyond expectation because one of the men riding with him was Aiken, from the Tennessee Mountains, who recognized Tyrel Sackett. Back Rand decided not to try cutting the herd.

JUAN TORRES: Foreman for Alvarado; a good man, wise in the ways of range cattle and horses. Jonathan Pritts wanted him dead.

BULLY BEN BAKER: A former keelboat man, a brawler and a tough, skeptical of Orrin Sackett, the new marshal. Some men took a lot of convincing.

CERAN ST. VRAIN: A former mountain man, trapper, and associate of Kit Carson. Highly respected in Mora, Santa Fe, and by all who knew him. An historical personage.

VINCENTE ROMERO: Another distinguished citizen; well-known, well-liked, equally respected in both Spanish and Anglo communities.

ANTONIO BACA: One of Alvarado's men but one with no liking for Tyrel Sackett, and jealous of his relationship with Drusilla.

The Sacketts brought their mother west and found a home for her in the new lands where life would be easier and where her family would not be far away. Somewhere in those southern Rockies was where her beloved husband had disappeared, and she felt closer to him in Mora (New Mexico—see page 111).

In most western communities, whether in mining or cattle country, there was a beginning when the country and the towns themselves were rough and wild, but not long after the first saloon and general store a church would be built, and then a school. The shootings, when they took place, were usually on the wrong side of town and interfered but little in the daily life of its most reputable citizens. And the shootings were a passing phase, a time of growing up, of shaking down, of getting the country settled, and the wild bunch either reformed or found their places on Boot Hill.

SACKETT

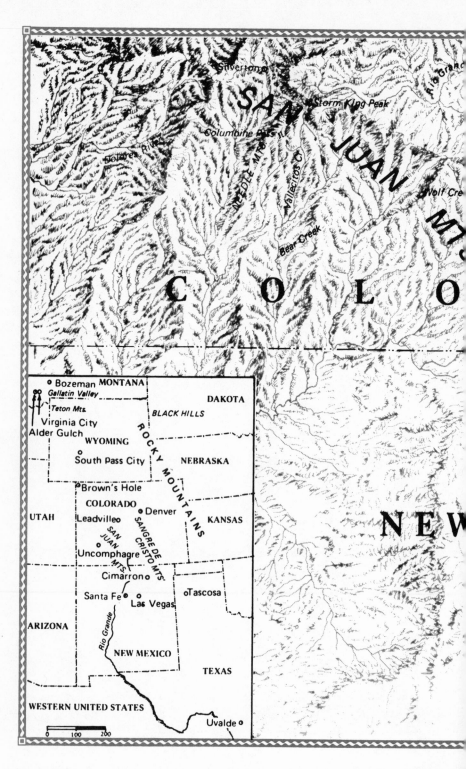

Silverton

SAN JUAN

Rio Grand

Storm King Peak

Columbine Pass

NEEDLE Mts

Vallecitos C.

Wolf Cre

Bear Creek

MTS

C O L O

Dolores River

Bozeman MONTANA
Gallatin Valley
Teton Mts.   DAKOTA
Virginia City   BLACK HILLS
Alder Gulch
        WYOMING
        South Pass City   NEBRASKA

Brown's Hole

COLORADO
Leadville   o Denver   KANSAS
         SAN
         JUAN   SANGRE DE CRISTO MTS.
Uncomphagre
         MTS.

UTAH

Cimarron o

Santa Fe o o
         Las Vegas   o Tascosa

ARIZONA
         Rio Grande

         NEW MEXICO

                              TEXAS

WESTERN UNITED STATES

         0   100   200   Uvalde o

ROCKY MOUNTAINS

NEW

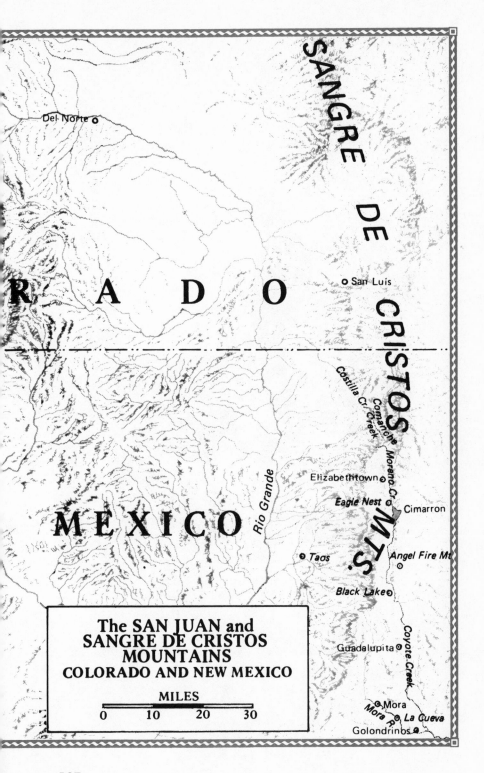

The SAN JUAN and
SANGRE DE CRISTOS
MOUNTAINS
COLORADO AND NEW MEXICO

MILES

| 0 | 10 | 20 | 30 |

SACKETT

First publication: Bantam Books paperback, May 1961
Narrator: William Tell Sackett
Time Period: c. 1874–1875

In which William Tell Sackett finds a trail unlike any trail he had ever seen before, and he follows it to gold and a girl, in that order. Other men come to claim the gold but not to mine it. They come to cheat and steal, to reap the benefits without enduring the hard labor and the sweat needed to bring it from the ground.

If one rides the Durango to Silverton Railroad, as many do these days, he will find himself winding through a narrow and picturesque gorge with towering peaks above the rushing waters of the Animas River below or alongside. Waterfalls will tumble over the rocks beside the train and occasionally deer will be seen. Every bend of the track will offer some new insight into the West as it was, for the gorge can only be reached by the narrow-gauge train or a helicopter. Unless, of course, one wishes to hike in.

When nearing the end of the trip through the canyon one comes to Needleton. There some will leave the train to back-pack through the Chicago Basin and over Columbine Pass into Vallecito Canyon. The scene of most of the events of this story take place in the upper Vallecito, above Johnson Creek.

Today that train is loaded with tourists seeing the canyon and visiting Silverton at the end of the run. Many years ago, when I first made the trip, it was aboard a mixed train carrying a few passengers, a couple of cars of freight, and I believe at least one flatcar, but of that I cannot be sure. It was long ago and I had no particular reason to notice. I was riding the train to Silverton with the idea that I might obtain a job in one of the mines. I had no such luck, but on the return trip we left the train at Needleton, and back-packed through Chicago Basin and over Columbine Pass. If I recall correctly there were several prospects in the Basin being worked at the time.

Only a week or ten days before I'd been paid off at the mine where my friend and I had worked together. He was a machineman, I was a mucker and trammer, and I had some money, I believe something over two hundred dollars, so there was no pressing need that I go back to work.

Once arrived at his claim I helped a little with the assessment work but most of the time was spent in hiking around the country. My friend was in no hurry, either, working a little and loafing about enjoying the warm afternoon sun, the fishing and the mountains.

If memory serves there were two or three men holed up at Logtown but we saw little of them. Most of the time I hiked the mountains, climbing into some relatively inaccessible places, spots I would eventually write about in SACKETT.

Aside from Vallecito Canyon I prowled around Mt. Oso, Irving Peak, Half Moon, and Hidden Lakes. Much of it was rugged travel but I'd always liked high mountain country and this was my first opportunity to really indulge myself. Before I had been working for somebody or under the necessity to get someplace. Much of the time I did not know exactly where I was, only where camp was, and several times I stayed out all night because it was easier to hole up in some cave, overhang, or under a fallen tree than to hike back to camp. My friend was not a worrier and for all I knew he didn't give a damn.

What I refer to in the story as the ghost lake was just a large pool of melted snow-water, probably only inches deep, but I never checked to find out. Several times I saw bears, one digging for a marmot, another turning over dead logs to look for grubs or whatever. I had good binoculars with me that I'd borrowed from my friend, and often I'd sit for a half hour or so just studying the country, watching the animals, and seeking out trails or possible routes. However, in that high country, as in many such places, following trails was always good business. Somebody had gone that way, and if it was worn, many people had, so it was possible. Many routes that seem good end in steep drop-offs and one has to climb all the way back. If there is a trail, stay with it. That's my advice. Look around if you like but when you move on, stick to the trail.

It was the first time in my life that I had leisure a
made the most of it. I doubt if I was ever more than seve.. ᴜ
eight miles from camp but it was mostly up, choosing my way
with care.

In my years of wandering about in wild places, often
alone, I have never taken unnecessary chances, and anyone who
does is a fool. Recklessness is not bravery. I am inclined to
agree with the explorer Roald Amundsen that what we call
adventure is simply bad planning.

WILLIAM TELL SACKETT: The eldest of the five Sackett
brothers of his family, he grew up in the Tennessee-North
Carolina Mountains, joined the Union Army in the Civil War
and rode most of the time with the Sixth Cavalry. He fought
Indians in Dakota and Montana and rode on a cattle drive from
Texas to Montana. The great love of his life was in his Civil
War period, a tale yet to be told. He also appears in THE
SACKETT BRAND, MOJAVE CROSSING, THE LONELY MEN, TREA-
SURE MOUNTAIN, LONELY ON THE MOUNTAIN, and as just an-
other working cowboy in DARK CANYON.

ANGE KERRY: An Irish-Spanish mixture; Tell found her in a
cave high in the mountains above Vallecito Canyon. Discovered
her, almost lost her, but eventually married her. It just goes to
show you a man's not safe anywhere, even at the end of a ghost
trail past a ghost lake in a place where no one is likely to be.

CAP ROUNTREE: Mountain man, cowpuncher, stage driver,
he's done it all and carries the scars to prove it. Nobody knows
how old he is and he isn't talking. Some say that Pikes Peak
was a mere hole in the ground when he first came west. He also
appears in THE DAYBREAKERS, THE SACKETT BRAND, and LONELY
ON THE MOUNTAIN.

MORA, NEW MEXICO: On the Mora River, in Mora County.
The name's origin has been credited to several sources. Some say
it was named for the mulberry, some for a dead man found by
Ceran St. Vrain, but it was probably a surname.

ELIZABETHTOWN: A onetime copper and gold mining town, about 5 miles east of Eagle Nest, in Colfax County. First settled about 1865. Prospectors found gold on Willow Creek. Town named for a daughter of John W. Moore. Now almost a ghost town.

WILL BOYD: Gambler, gunman; he loses a mustache under peculiar circumstances not altogether related to cosmetics.

JOHN TUTHILL: A banker whose interests ran beyond interest. He knew that gold was where you found it and he didn't mind one bit if the gold belonged to somebody else. John Tuthill knew a lot about gold and even where gold was likely to be found. What he didn't know was a lot about mountains when the weather has been nice in the late fall. He didn't know much about weather in a country where if you don't like the weather you just wait five minutes.

JOE RUGGER: A good man in bad company; he knew when to throw in his hand and draw fresh cards.

THE BIGELOWS: A group of very rough brothers with plenty of nerve but very poor judgment. One of them had no more sense than to try a bottom deal on a man whose father began teaching him about cards and crooked gamblers when he was five.

KID NEWTON: A would-be badman traveling in the wrong company.

BEN HOBES: Wanted in Texas and a few other places but not wanted in many more. A wise man in the ways of the wilderness, he gambled on the weather and came up the loser. Or did he? A tough man might make it, particularly if he had some Al Packer in him.

BENSON BIGELOW: The old he-coon of the Bigelow tribe; he had it made and could have walked away, only at the last he couldn't leave it at that.

No Boot Hill graves are in sight, and those who lie there were buried deep and the ground smoothed out and the grass grows green where they lie.

There were no foundations laid for the buildings there, only timbers laid on the bare ground, and time and decay have done for them. Where they stood, wind blows through the grass and a few aspen have come up, and here and there a spruce among them. Only sometimes when hiking in the high-up mountains above Vallecito Canyon, up where the gray rock is splashed with leftover winter snow, sometimes, if you listen, you can hear a sound like a woman crying in the night.

She did not die there but her ghost came back to the place where she lost a grandfather, almost died alone, and then found for her own brief while happiness with a man she loved.

LANDO

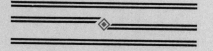

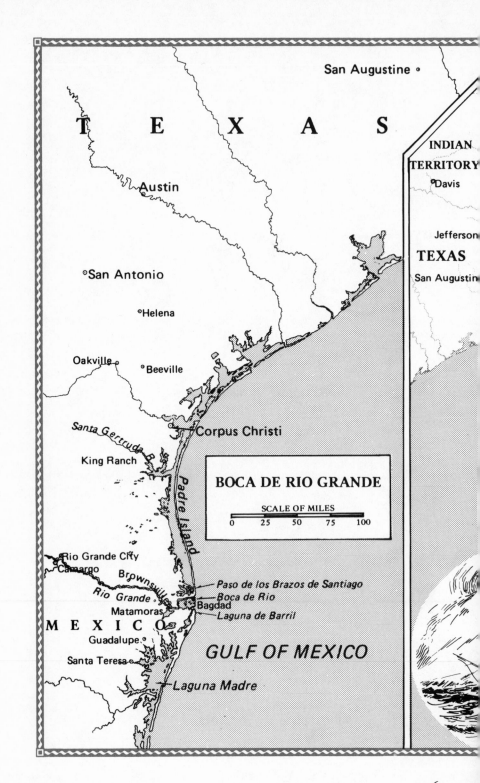

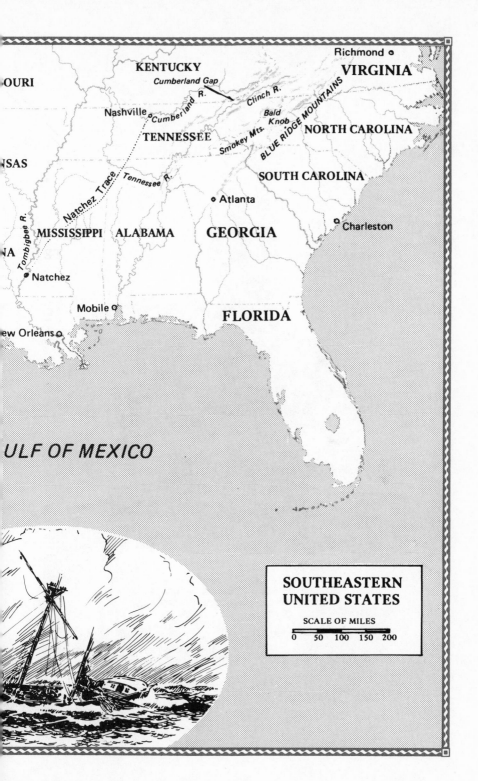

KENTUCKY

Richmond ○

VIRGINIA

○URI

Cumberland Gap

Cumberland R.

Clinch R.

Nashville ○ *Cumberland*

Bald
Knob

Smokey Mts.

BLUE RIDGE MOUNTAINS

NORTH CAROLINA

TENNESSEE

○SAS

Natchez Trace

Tennessee R.

SOUTH CAROLINA

○ Atlanta

Tombigbee R.

MISSISSIPPI ALABAMA GEORGIA

○ Charleston

Natchez

Mobile ○

FLORIDA

ew Orleans ○

ULF OF MEXICO

SOUTHEASTERN
UNITED STATES

SCALE OF MILES

0   50   100   150   200

LANDO

First publication: Bantam Books paperback, December
1962
Narrator: Orlando Sackett
Time Period: c. 1873–1875

This is the story of Orlando Sackett and his racing mule; it is also the story of the Tinker, who was a tinker but also a pack peddler, once a pirate, and whatever else it took to pick up the loose chips.

When Orlando leaves the mountains on a quest for something better than he has, he does not know that he is also embarking on a quest for hidden treasure on which several relatives are also engaged, a trek that takes him south as well as west and eventually into Mexico and behind the walls of a Mexican prison.

He becomes a bare-knuckle prizefighter and meets an old enemy inside the squared circle, but along the way he encounters several very lovely ladies, and at the end has a six-shooter arbitration with some enemies of his own and some he inherited.

THE TINKER: A gypsy, of mysterious background; a pack peddler in the Blue Ridge and Smoky Mountains who came from—who knows? Real name: Cosmo Lengro. His origin a mystery, his reasons for becoming a pack peddler even more so, except . . . a pack peddler, sooner or later, hears everything. People like to talk to a friendly stranger who is gone tomorrow, and often they tell him things in their quiet talk over a jug of 'shine or over a cup of coffee, things they would not tell their next door neighbor.

A wily young man with a gift for making things work, a man who makes knives of a quality unknown elsewhere and of a kind of steel possessed by no one, a steel that will cut through anything. His knives are sought by everyone but made for a chosen few. Even Lando, his friend, does not have one.

Mountain people eagerly await his coming. He has dress goods, needles, and all sorts of necessities, but he also has little gimcracks of gifty things that arouse eager interest. He also has news, the most precious of items, and gossip about what is happening elsewhere in the mountains and what women are wearing in the Settlements.

THE KURBISHAWS: Lando's mother's family; Aleyne Kurbishaw married his father contrary to her family's wishes and there was hatred on the Kurbishaw side for Falcon, Lando's father.

The Kurbishaws had a dark side of anger and bitterness. They thought much of themselves, and believed by rights they should have wealth except they considered themselves above the need to work for it. Work was for peasants, for common men, not for those of their presence, their family, their importance. And then to have one of the family marry a Sackett when she could have married money! It was too much.

WILL CAFFREY: Falcon Sackett left his son to be cared for by Will Caffrey, and a considerable sum of money to pay for it, and provide for his schooling. Caffrey used the money for his own purposes and to educate his own son, Duncan. Lando was forced to work, but when they tried to beat him, he ran away and went back to the deeper woods and the cabin in which they had lived when he was born. Lando left with Will Caffrey hating him both for the injury Will had done him in appropriating his money and for the beating Lando had given his son.

DUNCAN CAFFREY: Gambler, prizefighter, and boyhood enemy of Lando, but a fighter of brawn and skill.

HIGHLAND BAY: A noted racehorse with many victories behind him. Owned by Will Caffrey.

JEM MACE: An English prizefighter, said to have been a gypsy, and once bare-knuckle champion of the world. One of the very first scientific boxers. That he was an able and successful fighter, there is no doubt, although he boxed at a time when the gentry was less involved and the gamblers more so. His fistic career covered the years from 1855–1864, with most of his fights taking place in England before he came to America. Mace was born in 1831 at Beeston in Norfolk. There were no weight divisions in his period and his best fighting weight seems to have been one hundred and fifty pounds, although he often weighed less. Today he would be classed as a welterweight.

Jem Mace often fought men we would classify as heavy-weights or light-heavyweights today. He fought under the London Prize-Ring rules which meant a knockdown was the end of a round. The term "knockdown" was loosely interpreted and meant any time a man went to the ground. It was perfectly permissible to throw a man down or trip him. A round might be ten minutes or it might be ten seconds, ending whenever a fighter went down.

Present-day fights are fought, as they have been for many years, under the Marquis of Queensbury Rules, and a round is three minutes, the rest between rounds one minute.

CULLEN BAKER: My novel THE FIRST FAST DRAW deals with him. To some he was a hero, to others an outlaw and a killer. What you believe often depends on your source of information. His activities were largely confined to the area around Jefferson, Texarkana, the Sulphur River area, and Caddo Lake, yet there are stories that he went west as far as Salt Lake and even that he was associated for a time with Brigham Young's so-called Destroying Angels.

He was, as in this story, associated for a time with Bill Longley and Bob Lee. Longley was only briefly associated with Baker and was later hanged. Bob Lee was a Southerner who continued to wage war after the surrender to Grant. A man of good family, he was also a good man with a gun. The title of his story comes from the fact that until the 1850s the pistols generally available were too cumbersome for a fast draw and were seldom carried on the person.

GOVERNOR EDMUND JACKSON DAVIS: A Reconstruction governor in a state needing no reconstruction, as the war had done no damage there. An honest, decent man in a very unpopular job, a Republican governor in Texas, a largely Democratic state. His black police force was extremely unpopular. Most of the better class of black men would have nothing to do with the police force and those recruited often invited trouble in a situation that demanded the utmost in tact and consideration. During the last days of the Civil War and for at least ten years after there was much feuding and fighting among the white population as the various factions tried to settle their difficulties by direct action.

The Davis police got very little cooperation, and in any event were incapable of coping with it. Davis was defeated in his bid for re-election but refused to give up the office until assured he would get no support from President Grant.

FRANKLYN DECKROW: A man of pride but in all the wrong things. A planner and a conniver, but a man of whom to beware. He would destroy a man, not with a gun but with ink, usually red ink.

MARSHA DECKROW: His daughter, and a niece of Jonas Locklear. Very pretty, but pretty is as pretty does, as they used to say in the mountains and elsewhere.

JONAS LOCKLEAR: A former ship's captain who came up the hard way; a tough man but a just one. Franklyn Deckrow believed him gone for good, which left Deckrow in charge, but Jonas returned. For how long?

LILY ANNE DECKROW: Sister to Jonas, wife to Franklyn Deckrow; a lovely but unhappy woman.

VIRGINIA LOCKLEAR: Called Gin; a woman of intelligence and courage with much of her brother's strength and vitality. A beautiful, seductive woman who could ride as well as any vaquero. A very cool lady, indeed.

JEAN LAFITTE: A pirate, smuggler, slave dealer and patriot, owner with his brother, Pierre, of a blacksmith shop (where the work was done by slaves) in New Orleans. This shop became a center for plotting and piratical activities. The brothers LaFitte seemed to have a hand in much that was taking place and owned shares in several privateers operating out of New Orleans or their bases at Galveston or Barataria. At one time they were engaged in a plot to seize Texas.

Believed born in 1781 in Bayonne, France, Jean later moved to an island in the Caribbean. After revolts there, the family moved on to New Orleans.

There is a story that a British agent tried to bribe him to show them the secret route through the bayous from the Gulf to New Orleans used by the smugglers. The offer was said to have been made in the Old Absinthe House (which still exists) and that Jean LaFitte was offered a handful of gold. His reply was to pin the hand to the bar with a dagger. True or not, the story is typical of many told about LaFitte. During the Battle of New Orleans, when the city was attacked by the British, LaFitte supplied artillery and gunners for the defense, and thus was a major factor in the United States winning the Battle of New Orleans.

ERIC STOUTEN: Killed by the Kurbishaws; he knew the location of the treasure. A seaman and fisherman in the past, Stouten came to Mexico as a cavalryman in the command of Captain Elam Kurbishaw, but he had visited Mexico before.

JEFFERSON: In Marion County, Texas. Built along Big Cypress Bayou. It was for a time the principal port of Texas and a prosperous city. A number of the old homes and other buildings still exist from those earlier years when Jefferson was a booming town with what seemed a glowing future. The destruction of the Red River Raft lowered the water and killed the town as a major seaport. The construction of the railroad to Texarkana was the final blow. Jefferson remains a pleasant town, well worth a visit.

SAN AUGUSTINE: Site of a mission found in 1716. Philip Nolan held horses there when making a gather for the Louisiana troops. At that time corrals and a cabin were constructed. The town of San Augustine developed on the site and some fine old mansions remain. These towns in northeast Texas are more "southern" in nature than what is usually considered western.

JUAN CORTINA: Born in Mexico on May 16, 1824. Owner of considerable property on both sides of the border, Cortina was a natural leader and a champion of the rights of his people. On the Texas side of the Rio Grande, his main ranch was at Santa Rita near Brownsville. Considered a bandit by some, he acquired stock where he found it, driving cattle across the Rio Grande on many occasions. He was indicted on at least one occasion but never brought to trial. On another occasion he captured the town of Brownsville after the local marshal had beaten a Mexican prisoner, and took the prisoner from the marshal.

Several forces were sent against him, some including Mexicans of Texas ancestry, but he defeated these attempts until he was himself defeated in a battle fought near Rio Grande City. His activities continued on both sides of the border where he had friends among the Anglos as well as the Mexicans. On another occasion his troops were routed by Major John S. Ford of the Texas Rangers. Finally, Colonel Robert E. Lee was appointed commandant of the district with instructions to pursue into Mexico if necessary.

Cortina remained a power in the area south of the border for many years and was acting governor of Tamaulipas under Benito Juarez. He continued some of his extra-legal activities until his own government intervened and he was removed to Mexico City. He died there in 1894, certainly one of the most interesting and exciting personalities along the border. Although he was never known to hesitate in appropriating any loose cattle, horses or mules, there was little he would not do for a friend, an abused Mexican, or anyone who appealed to his sense of justice or gallantry. Known to his intimates as Cheno.

MAJOR L.H. McNELLY: Captain of the Texas Rangers, soldier in the Civil War, and farmer. He was a quiet man, slender of build, and soft-voiced. He served with the hated Davis police for a time but seems to have emerged from that experience a man respected and trusted insofar as his own activities were concerned. Later, with the Texas Rangers, he proved to be one of their most able commanders, although weakened by tuberculosis.

BEEVILLE: Settled by Irish immigrants in the 1830s, it was for a time a wild town with many gamblers, much footracing, horseracing, and such. Ed Singleton, a notorious outlaw, was hanged there in 1877. It is said he left his skin to the local law officers to be stretched over a drumhead, the drum to be beaten on each anniversary of his death as a warning to others who might wish to follow in his footsteps.

OAKVILLE: For a number of years this quiet little town was the hang-out for a number of outlaws and would-be outlaws, and the scene of several gun battles, a place where law officers were unwelcome. Capt. L.H. McNelly finally moved in and cleaned the place up in 1876. There, as elsewhere in the West, the outlaws and their women usually kept to their own side of town and their own places of resort, interfering very little with the schools and churches around which the town's social life revolved.

MANUEL: A boy who loved a mule, and who went away to ride it in races.

DOC HALLORAN: Occasional horse trader; a long, thin man with thin reddish hair. His kind was to be found in every western town, and that is still the case.

BALD KNOBBERS: A group of vigilantes around Forsyth, Missouri, they were originally organized to cope with a growing crime problem, but at the request of state authorities, the responsible citizens withdrew. The group was then taken over by a bunch of ruffians who were responsible for attacks upon squatters, tie-cutters, and various others until, in 1887, the citizens arose, hanged three of them, and arrested two dozen others. Some escaped to carry on their criminal activities in a more comfortable climate. The name "Bald Knobbers" was given them because of their meetings on Bald Jess, a summit overlooking Forsyth. Several former members of the group became well-known further west, but the term was often applied to others from Missouri or Arkansas who had no connection with the original group.

THE HENRY RIFLE: Perfected by B. Tyler Henry, a .44 calibre repeating rifle produced at the old Volcanic plant in New Haven, Connecticut. Aside from the Spencer, it was the only successful repeating rifle on the market in the United States. It was the forerunner of the Winchester, which was developed from the Henry in the late 1860s.

The Henry appeared during the Civil War and a few of the rifles saw service in that conflict, although its distribution was limited at first. It carried fifteen shots in a magazine tube under the barrel.

OTHER WEAPONS: During the period immediately before and following the Civil War, many kinds of guns appeared on the frontier. For a time almost any pistol was called a "Colt," almost any rifle a "Winchester." The two types became so common that the brand names became synonyms for those types of weapons.

The men who came west often brought with them the weapons they had used during the war. A frontiersman himself, Lincoln knew a man could scarcely exist or keep his family alive without a horse and a rifle, so the discharged Confederates were allowed to keep their weapons.

The men and women who came west were from a variety of backgrounds and so the weapons they brought with them varied too. The Hawken, the Sharps, Spencer, Henry, and Winchester were all well-known, and the Ballard as well, but at least fifty other types of rifles might be found on the frontier, and as many pistols. These included: the Le Mat, a pistol with two barrels, one firing a .36 caliber shell, the other a shotgun shell; the Dancer; Whitney; Griswold & Gunnison; Spiller & Burr; Merwin & Hurlburt; and many another. Some men in the

West bought weapons there but many inherited them from older members of the family or from friends.

Many varieties of derringers (named after Henry Derringer) were produced, and pistols combined with knuckle-dusters or knives were common. There were canes as well as umbrellas that carried gun barrels.

However, next to the Colt, the most popular pistol was the Remington. Smith & Wesson won a contract to supply 250,000 pistols for the Russian Army after the Grand Duke Alexis saw what Buffalo Bill Cody could do with one. That kept them from supplying many guns to the western market.

Colt revolving rifles and shotguns were also generally available. My great-grandfather was carrying the former when killed by the Sioux in Dakota. Those who knew him said he was seldom known to miss his target.

WALCH NAVY: A pistol firing twelve shots; there was also a Walch that fired ten shots. Yet these were not exceptional, for pistols were made at the time capable of firing eighteen or twenty shots. I have not heard of one of these on the frontier but everything else wound up there, so why not?

ORLANDO SACKETT: A son of Falcon Sackett and Aleyne Kurbishaw, he was five feet ten inches in height and usually weighed about one-hundred eighty pounds, but was unusually strong. This was partly a matter of heritage, but even more due to the very hard work he did as a boy and young man. He grew up, like most of the Sacketts, in the mountain country of Tennessee, where a major part of their living depended on their hunting and trapping ability.

Among their neighbors were the Cherokee Indians, and a bit further away the Choctaw, Chickasaw, Creek, and Seminole Indians. The Sacketts hunted with the Indians, shared a part of their lives, and learned much from them.

He also appears in THE SACKETT BRAND.

MOJAVE
CROSSING

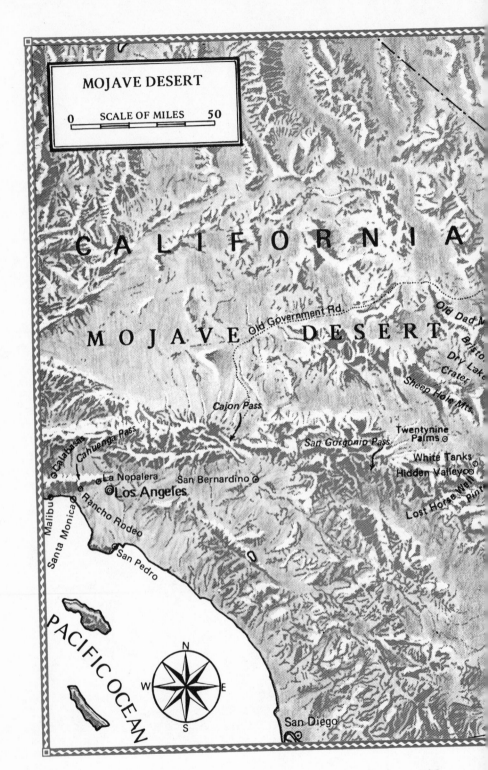

MOJAVE DESERT

0   SCALE OF MILES   50

CALIFORNIA

MOJAVE   DESERT

Old Government Rd.

Old Dad M

Bristo

Dry Lake

Crater

Sheep Hole Mts

Cajon Pass

San Gorgonio Pass

Twentynine Palms ⊙

White Tanks

Hidden Valley ⊙

Calabasas

Cahuenga Pass

La Nopalera

San Bernardino ⊙

Los Angeles

Lost Horse Well

Pint

Malibu

Santa Monica

Rancho Rodeo

San Pedro

PACIFIC OCEAN

N

W   E

S

San Diego

Callville

VADA

Hualapai Indian
Reservation

ldorado Canyon

Secret Spring

Union Pass

g

Black Canyon

Rock Spring

Dead Mts.

Sacramento Wash

Hualapai Mts.

nite
ell

Piute Wash

Hardyville

Fort Majave

Prescott

Piute Mts.

Cottonwood

oring

Chemehuevi
Indian Reservation

La Paz

A R I Z O N A

Colorado River

MOJAVE CROSSING

First publication: Bantam Books paperback, July 1964
Narrator: William Tell Sackett
Time Period: c. 1875–1879

In which William Tell Sackett meets a beautiful woman. It so happens he is carrying thirty pounds of gold. Is the meeting coincidence? Even a young man raised in the mountains can begin to wonder, especially when the woman convinces him he should guide her to Los Angeles, across the desert.

Tell knows a lot about the desert but how much does he know about women? Or can one woman make him forget what he knows?

HARDYVILLE: Near the present site of Bullhead City and Davis Dam, not far from the site of the old Katherine Mine where this writer put in several months underground, and near the area where Johannes crossed the Colorado in my book THE LONESOME GODS.

Hardyville was for many years the head of navigation on the Colorado. Steamboats from Yuma came up the river and occasionally, when the water was high, continued on to Callville, now under the waters of Lake Mead. Hardyville was the creation of William Hardy, who established a trading post, saloon and other structures at that point on the river. He helped build the road east to Beale Springs (now Kingman) and thence to Prescott and Fort Whipple.

For a number of years the Beale Road was constantly under attack by small parties of Indians. Through the 1860s there were continual reports of attacks along the road, and a number were killed on both sides.

CALLVILLE: Now buried under the waters of Lake Mead, this was the final possible port on the Colorado, but could only be reached when the season was right. This station was founded and held by Jacob Hamblin, a well-known Mormon pioneer who explored much of the region north of the Colorado. Born at Salem, Ohio in 1819, he emigrated to Utah in 1850, and devoted himself to establishing and maintaining peace between the Indian and the white man. In his areas he succeeded very well. Hamblin, for a time missionary to the Hopi, investigated the area of Bluff, Utah in 1879.

TRELAWNEY GIRLS: They lived in the mountains from which the Sacketts came and, like the Sacketts, were a very special breed. Wild, beautiful girls who occasionally left the mountains for the "Settlements," they were as expert with rifles as most mountain men, and needed protection from no one.

DEAD MOUNTAINS: On the Colorado; a small, very rugged range, and not as dead as they at first appear.

BEALE: A former Naval officer from whom Beale Springs was named. He carried the news of the gold discovery to Washington, D.C., and some of the gold. The news had reached Washington before his arrival, but the gold itself was most convincing. Beale also advocated the use of camels in western transportation and some were imported, along with camel drivers. The experiment was written off as unsuccessful despite the loads the camels could carry, but much of this was because the soldiers simply did not like them (there's not much to love about a camel!) and they frightened the horses, causing runaways and stampedes. One argument given was that the sharp rocks in our deserts cut their feet, though it may not have been realized that many Asiatic and African deserts are similar to ours.

However, other camels were imported and were used to transport salt from Walker Lake to Austin, in Nevada, for some time. By and large, though, westerners did not take to them and the effort petered out. Some of the camel drivers became quite well known in their own way. Hadji Ali, known in the West as Hi Jolly, was a favorite character. And it was at the home of Greek George, another camel driver, that Tiburcio Vasquez, the famous California outlaw, was captured.

SECRET PASS: An abandoned stage route west of Kingman to the Colorado and beyond. Winding through a maze of rock formations, it offered unique opportunities for ambush.

SECRET SPRING: A spring of good water near the old stage line.

SACRAMENTO WASH: The valley west of Kingman that lies between the Cerbat and the Black Mountains. The road crossed by Union Pass, slightly changed from the old route, possibly because of a somewhat embarrassing rock formation. Close by the old route lay the old Frisco and Arabian mines, now forgotten except by history.

PIUTE OR PAH-UTE SPRING: A desert watering place about twenty-two miles west of the Colorado. In the early days there was good grass on the hills to the right of the spring and a patch of grass below the spring. This was a station on the old Government Road (also referred to in my novel CALLAGHEN) and a small fort was built there. Usually four soldiers stood guard.

ROCK SPRING: Twenty miles west; usually guarded. A stopping place for mail riders. Considerable grass nearby in those days.

MARL SPRING: Well back in the country now, another station on the old Government Road. The water used to come from tunnels in the hillside; now it issues from a pipe and is used by cattlemen. It is twenty miles further west. Remains of the small fort can be found. In July of 1866 a small band of Piutes attacked the last wagon of a small train and killed a teamster named Leonard Taylor, shot him through with arrows. The other teamsters opened fire and drove off the attackers.

Such attacks took place at intervals all along the old Government Road from San Bernardino to Prescott.

DORINDA ROBISEAU: A traveling lady of wit and nerve. As Tell Sackett said, "When I saw the black-eyed woman a-looking at me I wished I had a Bible."

COOK'S WELL: East of the Providence Mountains in the Mojave Desert. Off any known trail when I was last there, but a few miles southeast of the Old Domingo Ranch. Flowed into a trough built for range cattle.

BLIND SPRING: This one is tough to find. Four miles or so south of Cook's Well. A watering place for stock, off the beaten track. (Readers must understand that in some cases I have not visited these spots in forty to fifty years. I could go right to them, but in that intervening period some springs may have ceased to exist, while others may have only occasional supplies of water.) The only trails have probably now been overrun by motorcycles or four-wheel-drive vehicles.

PROVIDENCE MOUNTAINS: Probably so-called because in this desert region the pioneers found springs where they expected none. Several peaks are over five thousand feet. The Mitchell Caverns are here.

HIDDEN VALLEY: Formerly one had to get down and crawl under some rocks to enter, but now the park rangers have created steps so anyone may climb easily over the rocks and go inside. Stolen horses were once hidden here until the chase was over, and then driven on to be sold. How they got into the valley is still a mystery, although possibly a huge boulder has blocked the entrance they once used. A search might require months, and prying into every nook and cranny in a place where there are thousands of them. An interesting visit.

PEG-LEG SMITH: An historical character; a trapper, horse thief, and whatever it took to get whiskey money. Famous for claiming a lost "mine" that never existed. Peg-Leg stole some mules and murdered their drivers, and knowing nothing of gold ore, he emptied the sacks they were carrying on the ground, wanting the sacks. Later, when he discovered what he had dumped out, he could not find the place again. There is a story that the gold was found just a few years ago, and I believe it possible.

BUFFUM'S: The best saloon and gambling house in Los Angeles during those wild days when the town was ceasing to be just a cattle town and supply center, and moving to become a city.

LA NOPALERA: Literally, The Cactus Patch. Now Hollywood. In those early years a sea of prickly pear.

TIBURCIO VASQUEZ: Mentioned earlier; California's most noted outlaw, and from whom some of the details were taken to garnish the story of the fictional outlaw, Joaquin Murietta. The latter was a creation of a Cherokee Indian writer, John Rollin Ridge, who did a fictional piece for the old *Police Gazette*, which many believed, and still believe, was factual.

Vasquez Rocks, seen in many movies and now in commercials, were named for him. He had a hide-out in a canyon close by but often kept a man up in the rocks to watch for prospective "customers" or the posses that often hunted him. He was for a few years a very busy outlaw, robbing Anglos and Hispanics alike until captured just off what is now the Sunset Strip in Los Angeles. He was hanged at San Jose.

WASHINGTON GARDENS: An amusement park, zoo, and picnic grounds, very popular in Los Angeles, for a number of years. Long forgotten now.

CALLE DE LOS NEGROS: Then called "Nigger Alley," and the toughest street in the toughest section of Los Angeles, although the people who lived there were largely Chinese or a mixed lot from the rougher side of things.

RANCHO RODEO DE LAS AGUAS: The area now known as Beverly Hills, California.

BEN MANDRIN: He had been a pirate once, and he still had in him what it took to make men walk the plank. He also still had some of his ill-gotten gains stashed in the mountains that overlook Malibu and divide it from Hidden Valley. His friends did not know that, nor did his enemies.

SANDEMAN DYER: He had been a coldblooded killer during the Civil War and why should he have changed? Tell Sackett had known him at Shiloh, and he wasn't a man you forgot.

NOLAN SACKETT: He was one of the so-called outlaw Sacketts, a descendant of Yance who settled in the Clinch Mountains. Was blood thicker than branch water? What would happen when Sackett found Sackett?

WILLIE AND CHARLIE BUTTON: They were known men, horse thieves by reputation, hiding their stolen stock in Hidden Valley in what is now Joshua National Park. Well-known characters in their time and place.

PICO HOUSE: It still stands in Los Angeles, once its best hotel, and built by Pio Pico, the provincial governor at Los Angeles, in 1870. In his time everybody in Los Angeles knew Pio.

DAYTON AND OLIPHANT: The sort of men every town has to deal with, briefly at least. Supposed businessmen but prepared to cheat anyone for a dishonest dollar. They come and they go and usually the only ones who remember them are those they cheated or tried to cheat. They call it business but legitimate businessmen soon learn to recognize their kind.

RODERIGO ENRIQUEZ: A grandson of old Ben Mandrin, a gentleman and a brave man.

JOSEPH CHAPMAN: Only mentioned here; he came ashore from a pirate ship, was wounded and captured. Nursed back to health, he married, in the most romantic tradition, the girl who did the nursing. He was California's first Anglo citizen, built a mill, and had a hand in building much else. He proved himself a good citizen and an honorable man.

LOS ANGELES: A wild little town on the Los Angeles River, founded by the Spanish in 1781. It has since become a city. In the early days it was rough as Dodge City or Abilene or Tombstone. It had more than its share of "western"-type characters, and some famous gun battles, with the Carlisle-King fight being the most notorious. Several of its leading citizens were former mountain men who came west to develop cities after the price of beaver dropped due to the change in fashion that replaced the beaver hat with the silk hat. They were men with ideas who knew opportunity when they saw it. At one time they owned much of what is now the western part of the city.

MUSTANG
MAN

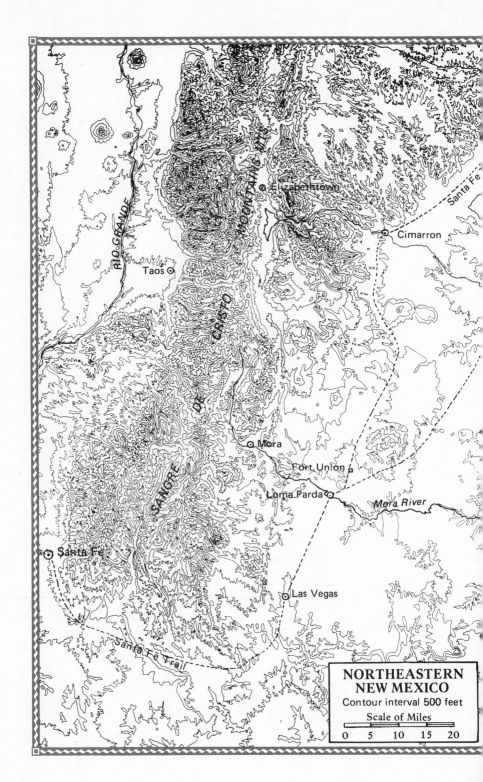

NORTHEASTERN
NEW MEXICO
Contour interval 500 feet
Scale of Miles
0   5   10   15   20

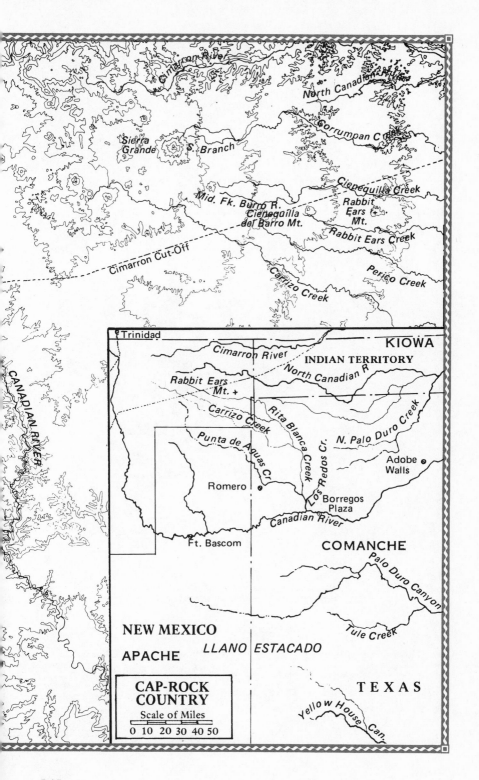

Cimarron River

North Canadian

Corrumpan Cr.

Sierra
Grande   S. Branch

Cienequilla Creek

Mid. Fk. Burro R.   Rabbit
Cienequilla   Ears
del Barro Mt.   Mt.

Rabbit Ears Creek

Cimarron Cut-Off   Perico Creek

Carrizo Creek

CANADIAN RIVER

Trinidad   KIOWA

Cimarron River   INDIAN TERRITORY

North Canadian R.

Rabbit Ears
Mt.

Carrizo Creek   Rita Blanca Creek   N. Palo Duro Creek

Los Redos Cr.

Punta de Aquas Cr.   Adobe
Walls

Romero   Borregos
Plaza

Canadian River

Ft. Bascom   COMANCHE

Palo Duro Canyon

NEW MEXICO

APACHE   LLANO ESTACADO

Tule Creek

TEXAS

CAP-ROCK
COUNTRY
Scale of Miles
0 10 20 30 40 50

Yellow House Can.

MUSTANG MAN

First publication: Bantam Books paperback, May 1966
Narrator: Nolan Sackett
Time Period: c. 1875–1879

Nolan Sackett was one of the fighting twins from the Clinch Mountain country of Tennessee. His branch of the Sackett family had been founded by Yance, to whom living in the mountains was like cider in the jug. He liked nothing better.

When rich land down in the bottoms was being settled by late-comers, Yance and his descendants kept to the high country where the hunting was good. The Clinch Mountain Sacketts never did take to towns and hi-falutin' ways. They took to long rifles and hound dogs.

They were lion and bear hunters, but coon hunters, too. Generally speaking, when it came to the world's goods, they were poor folks. Now and again they'd be scrapin' the bottom of the cornflour barrel, but there was always meat on the table.

When they needed cash money they hunted ginseng, " 'sang" to mountain folks. Knowing the mountains the way they did, it was easy for them to come upon a patch of ginseng, which was worth real money down to the Settlements.

Their feet were clever for dancing but usually they sat out the dances waiting for the fighting to begin. As soon as the 'shine had been circulating long enough to generate differences of opinion, there would be fighting.

Nolan and Logan were never strong for dancing, or maybe they were too strong for it. They ate ramps.

When a body eats ramps that keeps his dancing partners down to a minimum. Ramp-eaters are a special breed of folk. Nobody has ever discovered whether they make good neighbors or not because nobody ever gets that close unless it's another ramp-eater. Back in the coves and hollows folks say a ramp-eater can take a bear just by breathin' at him. I hold that to be an exaggeration. Maybe sometimes a coon, but not a bear.

Wild onions and garlic will make for space around a man, but ramps? They'll empty a room.

The Clinch Mountain Sacketts were workers with wood. When they weren't hunting or fighting or farming their side-hill acres they were making things. Of an evening they'd sit by the fire, talk to family or neighbors while they whittled and polished on axe handles, gunstocks, or shoe trees. Not that they ever used a shoe tree but down at the Settlements they brought a good price.

It was not an easy thing to pin them down to it but they made the best cradles in the mountains and there were a lot of good cradlemakers around, as well as men willing to fill them.

MUSIC IN THE HILLS: Back in the high-up hills in those days there was singing in the mountains, and folks made their own instruments or had them made by somebody close by who was handy at it. They made fiddles, dulcimers, and banjos, or whatever was needed to make music.

A fiddle had to stand the gaff. When they made music for dancing it was a boot-stomping, swing-your-partner sort of music, and a fiddle had to stand up to hard use.

A big thing in those days was a "sing." Word would get about that somebody was having a sing and folks would come from miles around to take part and to listen. Sometimes a fat hog was the prize, or a heifer, but it was not the prizes folks came for, but the music. Often they'd drive in a spring wagon or ride horse- or mule-back thirty or forty miles to take part, and just as often they'd been rehearsing and singing to be ready when the time came. Some made their own music to sing by, but often enough they just sang.

Mostly it was ballads from the old country, dating back to Elizabethan times, or versions of their own built on the same tunes. They made songs of people they knew who were legends in the mountains, or about Andy Jackson, Davy Crockett, or somebody like Floyd Collins. If something happened, like a train wreck or a ship sinking or a gunfight, there'd be a song about it within the week.

FLOYD COLLINS: He was a Kentuckian who found a cave on his property. He had known of it for years but believed it to be just a small sinkhole. One story is that he dropped his jackknife into the hole and went down to retrieve it, discovering an opening leading off from the hole. Hoping to have a cave that could be exploited, he began exploring and was trapped by a falling boulder.

Efforts were immediately organized to get him out, but the affair turned into a three-ring circus with crowds gathering, and hotdog and balloon vendors making a killing. Some say the efforts to save Collins were deliberately stalled to keep the gravy train rolling for the vendors. In any event, Floyd Collins died in that cave.

The story has been made into a movie with Kirk Douglas called *Ace In The Hole* and it was almost immediately made into a song called *The Death of Floyd Collins*. An almost forgotten chapter of the Nashville music business is that for a time they put out instant records. No sooner was there a disaster than a song was written about it and a recording on sale. It was so with the death of Floyd Collins, and with the sinking of the *Vestris*.

I was in Oregon at the time, if I recall correctly, and remember that the record of the *Death of Floyd Collins* was being played on many music boxes or wherever there was a record player.

Times have changed. The hills don't sound with music as they once did and the singers have gone down to the Settlements like Nashville to make music or to listen. In the old days a boy or girl just couldn't wait to have a broken heart just so he or she could make up a song about it.

It's like the coffee. Nobody parches their own coffee any more, and a good cup of coffee is hard to find. Why, the coffee you find these days won't even take the silver off a spoon! Maybe that's why the Sackett boys went west. They'd heard those cowboys out yonder drank good coffee.

There was a song they used to sing in the mountains about "Black, black, black was my true love's hair."

That was the way they liked their coffee, Black, Black, Black!

NOLAN SACKETT: He wasn't headed anywhere but away when he saw that wagon out in the middle of nowhere, and he didn't quite like the look of things, but one of them was a right handsome woman, so he stopped. That was when his trouble began, and it carried him on for some distance. It seemed like a man couldn't even ride across country without running into some kind of a difficulty.

When he heard there was gold left near Rabbit Ears and that there were women involved, he knew he was riding right for trouble.

YELLOW HOUSE CANYON: One of a series of canyons, including the larger Palo Duro Canyon, that stretch down the Panhandle of Texas. From some distance off there was, in the old days, no indication of their existence, the plains seemingly unbroken to the horizon. This was Comanche-Kiowa country for many years. Go to Lubbock, Texas, in the Panhandle. They will show it to you.

PALO DURO CANYON: The bleak plains of the Panhandle are slashed suddenly by a truly amazing canyon. In the first place, you don't expect it to be there. Indians used to raid and rob and then ride away. The soldiers following would see them and then they would vanish, dropping into their canyon hideout that the Army was some time in finding. Almost a thousand feet deep, it is anywhere from a few hundred yards wide to more than ten miles.

Charlie Goodnight, one of the greatest of the cattle drivers and inventor of the chuck wagon, brought cattle to the canyon and established the JA Ranch. The main canyon was well-watered, as were most of the branch canyons; there was standing timber; and little fencing was needed. For generations the Comanches had come to the Palo Duro, fattening their ponies on the rich grass and hunting the buffalo that also made the canyons their home.

JIM CATOR: An historical character who had his buffalo camp on the North Palo Duro, a three- or four-day ride from where Goodnight located. There was no town nearer than one hundred miles in any direction.

146

SOSTENES L'ARCHEVEQUE: An outlaw and gunman, reported to have killed twenty-three men. When the Casners moved sheep into the area, some outlaws conspired to steal the flock and Sostenes was sent to kill them. Maneuvering one of the Casners into hunting with him, Sostenes shot him in the back of his head, then returned to camp and murdered the man's brother. He was apparently working with outlaws from the Robbers' Roost, off to the north. Sostenes was later killed by his brother-in-law simply to rid the country of a coldblooded killer. Goodnight and the Casners got along well and had established a good relationship with the Mexicans at Borrego Plaza and Romero. Goodnight had been assured that if Sostenes made trouble they would take care of him. He did, and they did.

FORT GRIFFIN: A small military post and a town close by, the latter a supply point for buffalo hunters. The town catered to a rough, independent lot, and a great many of the men who became noted gunfighters first served their apprenticeship as hunters of the buffalo. Many renowned western characters passed through Fort Griffin at one time or another. One story has it that it was here that Wyatt Earp first met Doc Holliday, and Pat Garrett outfitted there for buffalo hunting.

COMANCHEROS: New Mexicans who traded with the Comanches, supplying them with arms and ammunition and taking in exchanges horses, cattle, or other loot taken from Texas homes the Comanches had raided. A trade disapproved of by most New Mexicans, but one highly profitable at times.

BORREGOS PLAZA: On the south bank of the Canadian River, roughly a mile from the site of Tascosa, which was built later. Borregos Plaza had been settled by former Comancheros led by Colas Martinez, a friend of Charlie Goodnight. It was a small, pleasant village inhabited by friendly people and strangers were welcome as long as they behaved themselves. There are several versions of the death of Sostenes l'Archeveque other than the one given here but the purpose was the same. The community wished to rid itself of a troublemaker.

ADOBE WALLS: This spot is referred to in several of my stories and is without doubt one of the best-known places in Texas, although visited by few, comparatively speaking. It was the site of two battles with Indians, both decisive.

Originally a trading post built by William Bent about 1842–43, it was eighty feet square with adobe walls nine feet high, and was situated in what is now Hutchinson County, Texas. The original fort was built under the directions of William Bent and Ceran St. Vrain in an area where the Kiowa, Comanche, Arapahoe, and Cheyenne were sure to be found, and the traders made periodic trips to the site for trading purposes.

The First Battle of Adobe Walls took place on November 26, 1864. Colonel Kit Carson, leading the 1st Cavalry, New Mexico Volunteers, moved to attack a Kiowa village of some 150 lodges after a series of raids on outlying ranches and towns.

Carson's command consisted of 14 officers, 321 enlisted men accompanied by 78 Indians and 2 howitzer cannons. Upon nearing the village, Carson left his wagons, guarded by infantry, to follow, and advanced to the attack. They scattered the Kiowa and burned their village, but the Kiowa alerted several Comanche villages that were also in the vicinity.

Carson moved into the ruins of the trading post, underestimating the size of the force, which numbered several thousand Indians, that opposed him. There was sporadic fighting throughout the day and then Carson withdrew to protect his oncoming supply train. Despite the retreat, however, Carson had won a decisive victory.

However, as Custer would do twelve years later, Carson seriously underestimated the size of the force that could be brought against him. Logic was on his side, but on this occasion, as with Custer, logic did not conform to the facts.

Carson knew, as did Custer, that maintaining a large force of Indians in the field was beyond the abilities of the Indian. The American Indian had never thought of war in terms of a campaign, of a series of battles leading to a final victory. He thought in terms of raids or single battles, so had never organized a supply system. What food they had was carried with them or taken by hunting as they traveled, but when a large body of Indians came into an area all the game promptly left the vicinity and took to the hills for protection. Custer's scouts had warned him of the size of the pony herd, judging by the dust cloud, but that dust might be accounted for in other ways and so he doubted the presence of so many Indians. With adequate reason he discounted the reports brought by his scouts. Carson had no such reports but had the same reasons for doubting the presence in the area of a greater number of Indians than those in the village he attacked.

After both battles, the parties of Indians broke up and went their ways to hunt for meat.

The Second Battle of Adobe Walls was ten years later, and seldom in history have so few men fought a battle more decisive.

To be closer to the market, store owners Rath and Wright moved out from Dodge City a supply of ammunition, whiskey, and such other supplies as buffalo hunters might need, and located a store at Adobe Walls in the heart of the buffalo hunting country. There were several buildings, and outside the buildings was a covered wagon in which two men were sleeping. In all, on that fateful morning of June 27, 1874, there were twenty-eight men and one woman present at Adobe Walls. The one woman was Mrs. Olds, wife of a storekeeper.

Actually, the men were scattered in three buildings: in Jim Hanrahan's saloon and in the two stores, that of Rath & Wright, and another operated by Myers and Leonard.

The attacking Indians were largely Kiowa, Comanche, and Cheyenne, led by Quanah Parker and Lone Wolf. The one who instigated the attack was a medicine man called Isatai, and Isatai had been making big medicine. His idea was to gather all the Indians together and drive the white man east of the Mississippi, out of Indian country forever.

He claimed his medicine was good, that he could protect the others from injury, and that the time had come.

Many Indians were skeptical. They then suggested that if the attacking party, variously estimated at seven hundred to onethousand men, could wipe out the buffalo hunters at Adobe Walls, the rest of them would join in the drive to sweep the country of white men. First, though, Isatai had to prove his medicine was good. When the fight began nearly one thousand Indians attacked, with probably twice that number as spectators.

In the stores and the saloon at the time were thousands of rounds of ammunition, food supplies, and whiskey enough to last for a month or more.

What happened next has never been fully explained. In one of the stores where a number of men were sleeping, there was a sharp report. It awakened everybody, who believed the ridgepole had cracked. By the time they discovered that nothing was wrong, Billy Dixon, then twenty-three years old, decided it was no use trying to get back to sleep when no more than an hour later he would be packing to leave for the hunting grounds. He decided to get his picketed horses, pack up, and be ready to leave at daylight. He went outside and walked to where his horses were. He was leading them back when his eye caught a hint of movement. He glanced around and against the first gray light of dawn he glimpsed a long line of charging Indians, still some distance off but coming at a dead run. Dixon dropped the lead ropes and leaped for the door. He made it just in time.

The Indians swept around and among the buildings. The two men asleep in their wagon were killed as they grabbed for their rifles. A large dog was also killed, and then the fight began.

Isatai could not have chosen a worse spot to begin his attack. The twenty-eight men at Adobe Walls were all dead shots. Most of them had already put in two or more seasons on the buffalo prairies firing thousands of rounds in the killing of buffalo. Most of them were veterans of other Indian battles and several were men whose names would make western history, such as Billy Dixon himself and Bat Masterson, then just seventeen. They were securely lodged behind log or sod walls and their firing was done from rests where they could take their time and pick their targets.

The shooting continued for several days but the riflemen were too good and their position too secure. The event that may well have broken the back of the effort took place on the second day, when a party of Indians appeared on a ridge some distance away and Billy Dixon was asked to see what he could do. Using his Sharps Big Fifty buffalo gun Billy knocked an Indian from his horse at a distance, checked a few days later by an Army officer, of seven-eighths of a mile.

By the middle of the fifth day hunters were gathering from all over the area, and over a hundred of them had come to the aid of the men at Adobe Walls. By the time the Army arrived, the fight was over.

The casualties among the hunters amounted to four men and a dog: the two Shadler brothers, killed in the first attack; one man killed later; and the last was the husband of Mrs. Olds, killed when his own gun discharged accidentally.

CROSS TIMBERS: Two remarkable belts of timber beginning in Oklahoma and running south to the middle of Texas. Dense stands of timber, they were some distance apart, each varying in width. As they were often as much as fifteen miles in width they presented a formidable obstacle to travel. They were a haven for much wildlife, including some of the last grizzlies found in Texas. They were famous landmarks both for the Indian and the white man. In the eastern Cross Timbers the trees were larger, the growth more dense. A good part of the timber was blackjack or post oak.

LLANO ESTACADO: The so-called Stake Plain. Literally, it includes most of the Panhandle of Texas, a vast uplift protected from erosion by the Cap-Rock. Flat as a floor for many miles, it was in the beginning virtually without water, hence uninhabited and rarely visited by either Indian or buffalo. The origin of the name has been much debated. One quite logical explanation is that it was so named because of the necessity of staking one's horse as there was no tree or shrub to which a horse could be tied. Another explanation is that the earliest travelers placed occasional sighting stakes so they could maintain their direction. A dozen other explanations have been offered. Read them all and take your pick. You are as likely to be right as anyone else.

SERBIN, TEXAS: In Lee County, a town founded by Wendish Lutherans in 1854. John Kilian was the leader of a group of some five hundred of the Wends who settled there and built a rock church that was still standing when I last was there. The church was built before the Civil War. Nolan Sackett was jailed there for a shooting, but the Wendish folk had reason to favor him and he was allowed to escape.

RABBIT EAR MOUNTAIN: An important landmark on the Santa Fe Trail. The peaks give the impression of rabbit ears from a distance, but it is also said that a Cheyenne chief called Rabbit Ears was killed near there and buried on the mountain, if such it could be called. The mounds are situated in Union County, New Mexico, north of Clayton.

Just north of the mountain in a box canyon is a green pool covered with a thick scum. The walls of the canyon have been blackened by fire, and there is an opening, very uninviting, about three to three-and-a-half feet in diameter. It is possible there was oil or gas here that may have been set afire by lightning or some other cause. The situation is virtually as related in the story.

RABBIT EARS CREEK: Creek heads up near Rabbit Ears, flows through a part of Texas and into Oklahoma. Gregg lists it as a stopping place on the Santa Fe Trail.

SLANTING ANNIE: A frontier prostitute who followed the boom camps. So-called because one leg was shorter than the other. An historical character.

OLLIE SHADDOCK: A freighter at this period; kin to the Sacketts; he appears in THE DAYBREAKERS.

MORA: A pleasant town in New Mexico; Tyrel Sackett located there, and it was visited by Tell Sackett. Orrin came here with Tyrel. It was the town where the mountain man Ceran St. Vrain, partner of Kit Carson, located.

ROMERO, TEXAS: Settled by Casimero Romero, a sheepman; an area where Comancheros operated. Just a few miles from the New Mexico border.

LOMA PARDA: Now a ghost town; a drinking town for soldiers from Fort Union. On the Mora River, and a rough place in its day. Usually off-limits to soldiers. It was a hang-out for thieves, gamblers, and formerly a base for Comancheros.

TINKER KNIFE: A knife made by the Tinker, a pack peddler in the Tennessee Mountains. Made from a variety of steel known only to the Tinker, but derived from the same steel used in the Toledo and Damascus blades. Most of the steel in those famous swords and scimitars was imported from India. The Tinker made few knives and only for close friends or someone he admired.

NATHAN HUME: A trader to Santa Fe who, when his wagon train was attacked, buried the gold he carried. He was killed, but two others escaped.

THE KARNES, SYLVIE, RALPH, AND ANDREW: Connections by marriage to Nathan and Penelope Hume. Sylvie was a woman who knew what she wanted and would stop at nothing to get it. A woman totally without conscience, she was perfectly prepared to murder anyone who got in the way.

Ralph, her older but subordinate brother, was cut from the same pattern but a follower rather than a leader. Andrew was younger, not very bright, ready to do what Sylvie suggested.

STEVE HOOKER: A small time crook; worked at something most of the time but was simply watching for a chance to steal.

TEX PARKER, CHARLIE HURST: Allies of Hooker, and of the same type. Stole horses, cattle, or anything lying loose, and candidates for a necktie party.

TOM FRYER, NOBLE BISHOP, AND FERRARA: Outlaws of another sort. Tough, capable and dangerous, but careful.

PENELOPE HUME: Nathan was her grandfather, and she inherited the papers that told where the gold could be found. A determined young lady whose future rested with that gold. She was alone in the world, and in the West of the 1870s there were few jobs for women of any age. What little she had was invested in this trip west and the effort to find the gold. Jacob Loomis was riding with her, but could he be trusted?

BOGGY DEPOT: In southeastern Oklahoma near the towns of Atoka and Caddo. It was an important town, growing from a log house into an important trading post and a Civil War army station. It was a Choctaw-Chickasaw town settled about 1837 after the move of the Indians from the Georgia-North Carolina-Tennessee area. The town became a post office in 1849. The home of Chief Allen Wright was destroyed by fire in 1952, and it was he who named Oklahoma. His granddaughter, Muriel Wright, was an Oklahoma historian and a remarkable woman whom I was proud to know as a friend.

Chief Wright translated several books into the Choctaw language and contributed much to his people and to the state of Oklahoma.

The present town is located a couple of miles from the original site of Boggy Depot. During the Civil War, Confederate troops were stationed there, and the town is referred to many times in early western literature. The town was named for Clear Boggy Creek.

INDIAN TERRITORY: After the removal of the Five Civilized Tribes from their homeland, much of Oklahoma was designated as Indian Territory. Influenced by Scottish and Irish traders who came among them in the early years, the Indians of the Five Civilized Tribes—the Cherokee, Choctaw, Chickasaw, Creek, and Seminole—had become so successful as to arouse jealousy of some of their less ambitious neighbors. The Indians owned mills, mines, steamboats on the rivers, and some of them had most beautiful homes. They also had plantations and farms, and owned a considerable number of slaves.

Gold had been discovered some time previously but the find was kept quiet until much later. When the news got out, it led to further agitation to move the Indians out of the country. In a tragic journey over the Trail of Tears, the Indians were removed to Oklahoma, permitted to take only what they could easily carry.

By this time they had their own written language and a newspaper printed in both English and Cherokee. The gold discovery came to nothing but the area lost some valuable citizens who were to contribute much to art, literature, business, and politics.

A minor but interesting story was that of John Rollin Ridge, a Cherokee, who created the story and the character known as Joaquin Murietta, taking several of the members of Murietta's band from the names of actual persons associated with Tiburcio Vasquez, an outlaw who was the real thing.

BILL COE: An outlaw, horse thief, and cattle thief. A good-looking man, and game. He operated an outlaw gang from a rock fortress built near the border of Colorado and New Mexico, and his gang raided and robbed with impunity. Charlie Goodnight looked on them with some disfavor and there were reports that Coe intended to kill him. For three years or so they operated from the house on the Cimarron, ignoring the vigilantes organized to handle just such problems. Coe was captured by soldiers who delivered him to a jail. During the night vigilantes took Coe from the jail to a nearby tree. When he was taken from the jail, somebody offered him a blanket but he refused and suggested, "Somehow I don't think I'll be needing it."

A few weeks later some of the other members of the gang also encountered a Reform Society with a rope and the Coe house became a roost for owls.

FLINCH: A tough Indian who could wait until the time was right.

JACOB LOOMIS: Who was to know what happened to Penelope? Who would there be even to ask questions? And with the gold he could go where he wished, live as he wanted. It all seemed very simple. It seemed foolproof. The trouble was that all such plans look good until the imponderables appear, those little things you didn't expect. And the man with a criminal mind is an incurable optimist. He always believes things are going to turn out right for him.

HARRY MIMS: A tough, salty old man who knew more than anyone believed.

OSCAR REINHARDT: A teamster, and a substantial citizen skilled at his job.

THE GENERAL AREA: This corner of New Mexico shows much evidence of ancient occupation. Spear heads have been found in close proximity to the bones of mammoths, and there are many indications that Indians of all periods found this a good hunting ground, through several changes of climate. Folsom points, one of the oldest varieties found on the continent, were discovered near here.

Buffalo roamed here in the thousands and even today antelope can be seen.

Uncle Dick Wootton, mountain man, established his station and toll road at Raton, and Governor de Anza pursued Cuerno Verde, the Comanche chief, through here and won a great battle near Ojo Caliente.

Not far to the north is Wet Mountain Valley where Jubal Sackett located his trading post, and the Greenhorn Mountains close by are named for that Comanche chief, Cuerno Verde. This area was also traveled by Flagan and Galloway Sackett. Their story is told in THE SKY-LINERS.

THE
LONELY
MEN

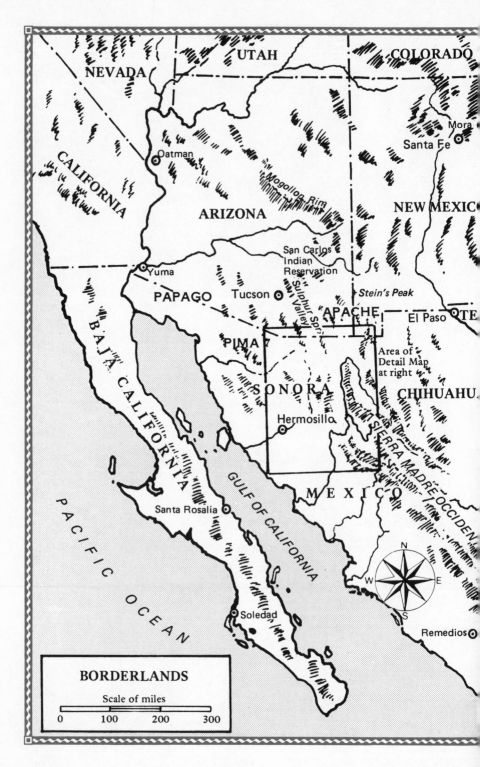

BORDERLANDS

Scale of miles

0   100   200   300

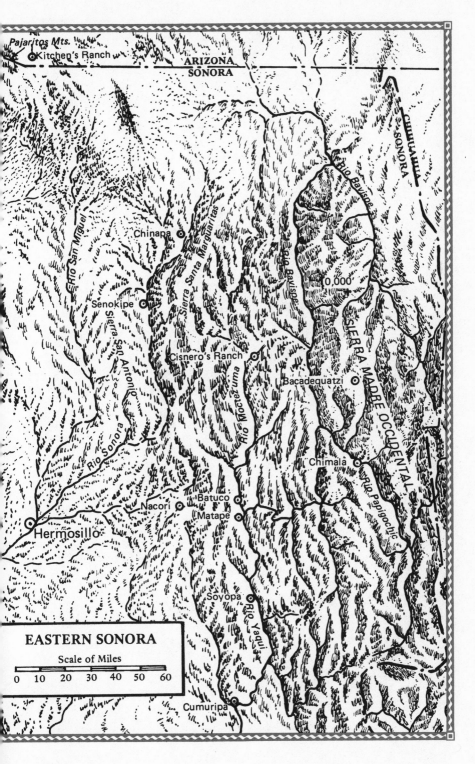

Pajaritos Mts.
Kitchen's Ranch
ARIZONA
SONORA

CHIHUAHUA
SONORA

Rio San Miguel

Rio Bavispe

Chinapa

Rio Bavispe

0,000

Sierra Santa Margaritas

Senokipe

Sierra San Antonio

Cisnero's Ranch

SIERRA MADRE OCCIDENTAL

Bacadequatzi

Rio Moctezuma

Rio Sonora

Chimala

Rio Papigochic

Batuco

Nacori

Matape

Hermosillo

Soyopa

Rio Yaqui

EASTERN SONORA

Scale of Miles

0   10   20   30   40   50   60

Cumuripa

159

THE LONELY MEN

First publication: Bantam Books paperback, May 1969
Narrator: William Tell Sackett
Time Period: c. 1875–1879

When Tell Sackett rode into Mexico he believed he was riding to rescue young Orry Sackett from the Apaches, risking his life and the lives of his companions in the effort.

He had not known Orrin had a son until Laura Pritts Sackett told him so, but he knew of the marriage. Orrin was in Washington, D.C. and if anybody was going to rescue the boy it was up to him.

What he did not know was that he was about to become a victim of a woman's hatred, a woman who plotted to kill him because he was Orrin's beloved brother, and who cared not in the least that others might die as well.

Tampico Rocca, Spanish Murphy, and John J. Battles were the kind of men one was likely to find in places like Tucson, El Paso, or the border towns. Their kind might be found anywhere in the West, driving stage, serving in the army, prospecting for gold, or herding cattle. They had gotten together in Yuma and rode east for mutual protection, now that their casual meeting had been cemented by the smoke and blood of battle, and each had found much to respect in the others. When Tell Sackett announced his intention of riding into Mexico to find his nephew, they had no other thought than to go with him. His trouble was their trouble.

WILLIAM TELL SACKETT: Left the mountains of Tennessee to take part in the Civil War. Joined the Sixth Cavalry of the Union, served on detached service in other areas. Also in SACKETT'S LAND, MOJAVE CROSSING, THE SACKETT BRAND, TREASURE MOUNTAIN, and LONELY ON THE MOUNTAIN, and briefly, as just another working cowboy, in DARK CANYON.

He could barely read and write, having attended school for only a few months on several different occasions. He could ride, rope, shoot any kind of a gun, and was skilled with stock. He grew up hunting, trapping, and fighting. Six feet three inches, he was lean, but broad-shouldered. Essentially a lonely man, he was shy with strangers. Accustomed to hard work, he preferred to be let alone to work at whatever he was doing, from punching cows to mining.

He liked women but was uncomfortable around them. At dances or parties he could usually be found somewhere in the background, simply enjoying the music and watching the others, and was content to have it so.

Of the great love of his life he rarely spoke, and even his brothers knew nothing of her. He met her and lost her during his Civil War days.

Although women were drawn to him he did not realize it and would not believe it if he was told. In fact, the suggestion would both astonish and amuse him.

FRONTIER WAYS: The skills Tell acquired were simply those of many such men who lived his kind of life. They learned to do by doing, repairing wagons, splicing rope, shoeing horses, building cabins or fence lines, repairing or altering their own firearms, treating minor cuts or abrasions on themselves or their stock. More serious wounds they would treat if there was no doctor near, and the nearest was apt to be a hundred or more miles away.

The frontier world was a do-it-yourself world, and if anything needed doing you simply did it. If you didn't know how, you sat down and tried to figure it out. If there was not a woman around, men mended their own clothes, often made their own shoes, and most could make moccasins. Nobody ever bought an axe handle in a store until around the 1880s. A man simply chose the right wood and whittled one himself. He sharpened his own axes, saws, and knives.

To Tell Sackett all this was not new. He had grown up in the Smoky Mountain country, where everybody did for themselves. Folks got together for barn-raisings, quiltings, corn-husking, and the like, but those were social occasions. If there wasn't a fiddler around, or a banjo or dulcimer, they could always sing their own accompaniment and dance to "play-party" songs like *Green Coffee Grows on High Oak Trees, Skip to My Lou*, or *Hello, Susan Brown!*

Aside from the goods peddled by occasional pack peddlers, everything was homemade.

LAURA PRITTS SACKETT: An almost beautiful girl, until you looked again. She idolized her father but the Sacketts helped to defeat his plans to seize land from the Mexican owners. To Orrin Sackett she had symbolized everything he wanted in a woman. He saw her beauty, and read into her what he wanted to find in a woman, never guessing it was not there.

They separated and her hatred grew until she was utterly possessed by it—a hatred not only for Orrin but for Tyrel as well, he who had always known her for what she was. Her hatred grew like a festering wound and when she saw Tell Sackett and realized he knew nothing of what had taken place she saw her chance. Jonathan Pritts had known how to handle rough men and she had some of the same facility, and with it the courage to face them.

How did others see her? Lieutenant Jack Davis was a very young officer and there were few women on the frontier. To him, Laura Pritts Sackett seemed the embodiment of grace, culture, and all a young woman could be. Captain Lewiston reserved his opinions and was a bit more skeptical. Mrs. Wallen had no doubts but she was also puzzled. What was such a woman doing in this Arizona town in the heat of summer when she might be elsewhere? Tucson in the early 1870s was a town where people came for a reason or passed on quickly, going either east or west. Mrs. Wallen found herself liking that tall, easy-moving young man called Tell Sackett. He did handle himself well but gave the impression of being awkward, and he was obviously shy. And Mrs. Wallen was worried. There was something about that Laura that bothered her.

TAMPICO ROCCA: Part Spanish, part Apache; a tough, hard-working man who had never known anything but the rough side of things. A top-hand on any man's outfit, scout for the army, shotgun messenger, cowhand, sheepherder, a good friend, a dangerous enemy, but a man without malice.

You never looked to see where he was because he was always where he was supposed to be, right where he could do the most good.

SPANISH MURPHY: Spanish was not a nickname; his mother named him that because it sounded right. He was Black Irish, and none of that nonsense about the Black Irish having Spanish blood. The number of Spaniards who got ashore after their Armada ships were wrecked on the Irish coast was never enough to make a difference. There were Black Irish in Ireland a thousand years before the Armada, maybe two thousand. The Armada story was a quick explanation for those who did not look any further. Some of those who settled Ireland were from Miletus in the eastern Mediterranean, and some of them had stopped in Spain but that was before there was such a thing as the Spanish people we now know. There were Iberians there, and some Phoenicians, but even the Visigoths had not arrived yet, and the Moors, who contributed their blood for seven hundred years, had not yet moved out of Arabia into North Africa en route to Spain.

Spanish Murphy was a good hand in any kind of a fight, a top-hand when he worked but he worked only when he needed the money. He liked women and he liked cards, although he drank sparingly and never smoked at all. Once in a while he lit a cigarette, but when he did you knew he was stalling for time or thinking about something. He was a man with quick hands and a natural skill with a rope, cards, or a gun.

JOHN J. BATTLES: From New England, a young business-man on his way up—until he killed a man over a girl. It had been self-defense, but when the trial was over and he was acquitted, he was no longer welcome in town, nor at his girl's house. He sold his business and rode west. He had driven stage, ridden with a cattle drive, and had been a deputy marshal in a wild cow town. One brother was a banker, another a teacher, and that was what Battles had really wanted, to teach. It was a case of being shot down by a drunken man or shooting in self-defense. He won the gun battle but lost everything else.

Like many another who came west he found himself liking the rough, hard life and the wild frontier towns. Men like Spanish Murphy, Tampico Rocca, and Tell Sackett were his kind of people, and when his girl wrote to him and wanted to join him he could no longer even remember exactly what she looked like, nor could he imagine himself returning to the easier life in Vermont. He remembered the leaves turning and the crunch of snow underfoot, and sometimes he thought of returning, just to visit.

Yet he found himself liking far horizons and a good horse between his knees. He knew riding into the Sierra Madres was taking a chance, but who lived forever? And if Tell Sackett was going down there, why, he'd just ride along to be sure he got out alive.

PETE KITCHEN: The consummate Arizona pioneer; there are a hundred stories about Pete, most of them true, and all of them might be. He was one of the men who built the state into what it has become.

The Apaches used to raid Pete's place quite often, but he kept a few expert riflemen behind a parapet on his roof, and after they buried a couple of dozen Apaches, the rest just rode by and saluted him. He had proved himself as a warrior and enough was enough.

He raised melons, fruit, cabbages, potatoes, grain, and such, and his home was a noted stopping place along the trail from Tucson to Nogales. For those unwise enough to attempt stealing his horses or cattle, he maintained his own boot hill graveyard.

He was a man possessed of all the virtues and vices of the frontier, noted for his honesty as well as his courage.

Every state has its pioneers about whom there are stories no fiction writer can surpass, and Pete was one of them.

THE SHOO-FLY RESTAURANT: Operated by Mrs. Wallen, the Shoo-Fly was patronized by everybody who came and went in Tucson around 1869 and for some years after. The menu was limited in scope but answered to healthy appetites and was remembered fondly years after by many a hungry traveler. It was a low-ceilinged room of adobe, and the ceiling was of stretched muslin. It served beef, beans, and chili, fruit occasionally and eggs most of the time. The floor was of hard-packed earth, the tables of pine. The seats were benches or hide-bottomed chairs, the latter usually reserved for the "regulars." Common talk over the eight or nine tables covered range conditions, Army affairs, the state of the nation, the latest gun battles, or what the Apaches were up to. It was not only a place to eat but a place to pick up information on just what was actually happening in Arizona and along the trails in or out.

WILLIAM S. OURY: Former Texas Ranger, first mayor of Tucson, pioneer rancher. As in the case of Pete Kitchen, books might be written about his life and adventures.

DORSET BINNY: In my story she rode into Mexico to find her sister, and found help in Tell Sackett and his friends, who were on the same sort of mission.

KAHTENNY AND TOCLANI: Both are actual characters, Apache Indians known in their time. Toclani served as a scout with Emmet Crawford, one of the most noted Army officers in the wars against the Apaches.

ARCH AND WOLF HADDEN: Two very tough men on the outlaw side who were considered bad men where they came from. The trouble was, they traveled too far and got into a country where people took nothing for granted. They had to be shown.

HARRY BROOK: A child prisoner of the Apaches; when they grew up on the frontier they learned to survive, and Harry was a survivor.

SIERRA MADRES: The Mother of Mountains. A range that lies along the border of Chihuahua and Sonora. Very rugged country, and the last refuge of the Apaches.

RANCHERIA: The name given to an Apache village, often temporary.

DESERTED RANCHOS: In northern Sonora and Chihuahua there were, at the time, a number of deserted ranches that had formerly been occupied by Mexican ranchers. The Spanish and the Mexicans had been fighting the Apaches long before the Americans came on the scene. A few of the officers leading the fight were very efficient and skillful fighting men who understood such fighting. Unhappily, much the same situation existed in Mexico City as existed in Washington, D.C. The national government simply did not understand conditions on the frontier and often the best efforts of Mexican officers were defeated by rulings made from desks far from the Apache country.

GALLOWAY

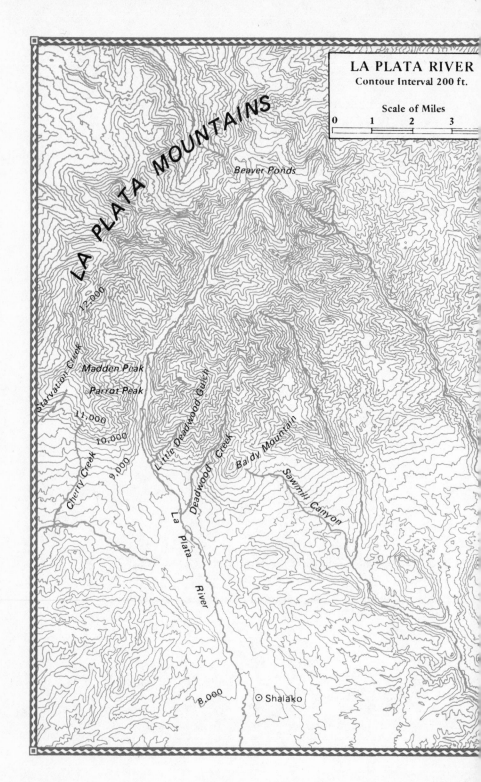

LA PLATA MOUNTAINS

LA PLATA RIVER
Contour Interval 200 ft.

Scale of Miles
0   1   2   3

Beaver Ponds

12,000

Starvation Creek

Madden Peak

Parrot Peak

11,000

10,000

9,000

Cherry Creek

Little Deadwood Gulch

Deadwood Creek

Baldy Mountain

Sawmill Canyon

La Plata

River

8,000

⊙ Shalako

170

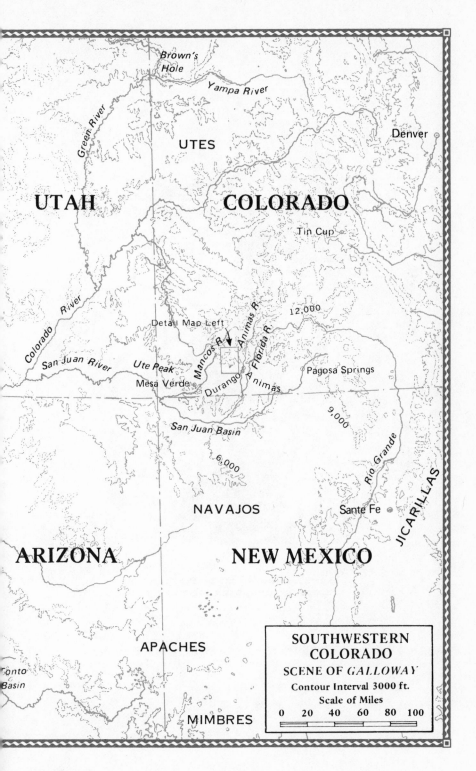

Brown's
Hole
Yampa River

UTES

Denver

UTAH   COLORADO

Tin Cup

12,000

Detail Map Left

San Juan River   Ute Peak
Mesa Verde   Durango   Ánimas   Pagosa Springs

San Juan Basin

9,000

6,000

NAVAJOS   Sante Fe

ARIZONA   NEW MEXICO   JICARILLAS

onto
Basin

APACHES

SOUTHWESTERN COLORADO
SCENE OF *GALLOWAY*
Contour Interval 3000 ft.
Scale of Miles
0   20   40   60   80   100

MIMBRES

GALLOWAY

First publication: Bantam Books paperback, July 1970
Narrator: Flagan Sackett
Time Period: c. 1875–1879

Flagan and Galloway Sackett were just looking for a place to start ranching. It was a big, wide, lovely country and lovely country and there seemed to be room enough, unless, of course, one was greedy—and the Dunns were. Flagan and Galloway were brothers from Tennessee, descendants through Kin-Ring Sackett from old Barnabas, the first one of the family in America. They were cousins of Tell, Orrin, and Tyrel Sackett.

First off, Flagan was taken by Apaches, and by the time he escaped he was in pretty rough shape. Just surviving left him in even worse condition and unready for any kind of trouble, and Curly Dunn was determined to make the trouble.

WILD COUNTRY: The La Plata River runs down a canyon of the same name, gathering its waters as it travels away from its beginning up in the Cumberland Basin. Here and there other small streams join it, a couple of them making miniature waterfalls as they tumble down the slopes through the pines.

Nowhere are the wild flowers more beautiful, and there's good grass for grazing. Deer and elk haunt the forests, and there are beaver in the streams again. It's high up country, over ten thousand feet when you get to the Basin, and the rim of the Basin is up to over eleven thousand. The La Platas were named for the silver found there, and they were named by the Spanish even before Rivera rode north in 1765.

The true limits of exploration by the Spanish and French are unknown, and we must remember that all history of the time is based upon reports, many of them official, made by those who returned safely. As far as the Spanish are concerned, I am quite sure that in the years to come reports will be discovered in Spanish archives of travels yet unknown. But we also know that much travel was clandestine, carried out by fur traders or prospectors who did not want to share their discoveries. Any gold they found was theoretically the property of the King, and all travels were supposed to be with permission from the governor or someone in official capacity. Men being what they were, many evaded that permission, knowing it was rarely granted. Hence, many rivers and mountains were named before the official discoverers arrived.

French officials were more lenient than the Spanish, and much exploration was carried out by fur traders or trappers who left few if any records behind. Elsewhere I have mentioned the colony of Frenchmen who left Illinois for the Pacific Northwest several years before Lewis and Clark. The only report of them I have so far seen was that by David Thompson, the Canadian explorer who met some of them in the Northwest in 1797.

Flagan's survival in this instance was not unusual for the time. Of one thing I am sure: if one is determined to survive, no matter what, a human being is almost impossible to destroy. I have read every story of survival I can find, and many of them surpass belief, but survival is more a matter of the mind and of character than it is of the physique. Certainly health and strength are important, but the sheer will to live is most important. The well-known stories of Hugh Glass and John Coulter are cases in point, but one can list hundreds of others, many of them in our own time.

JOHN COULTER: Also, Colter. (1774–1813) Member of the Lewis & Clark Expedition. On the return, he left them at the Mandan villages and returned to the Rockies with two trappers, where he spent four years, including two dramatic escapes from the Blackfeet Indians. On one of these he was scheduled to run the gauntlet, running between two lines of Blackfeet, each striking him with whatever weapon they wished until he was beaten or cut to death.

Coulter spotted a weak spot in the line and broke through, taking off, stark naked, across the plains. They pursued him for nearly one hundred miles but he escaped, his feet horribly torn. (I drew upon this episode for my escape of Flagan Sackett in GALLOWAY.)

Coulter discovered the geysers of Yellowstone, and they were first named Coulter's Hell.

He later assisted Meriwether Lewis in making maps of the area.

HUGH GLASS: (died in 1833, birthdate unknown) It was said by one who knew him that Glass had been a pirate with Jean LaFitte, and had lived for a time with Pawnee Indians. He is best known for encountering a female grizzly and her cubs. Although he killed the grizzly he was horribly chewed and clawed. From what they could see he was good as dead, and they were in the heart of Indian country and wanted to get out, so they took up a collection and paid two men to stay behind until he died.

He did not die. Their party was getting further and further away and Indians were all about them. Glass was obviously dying, so when he passed out they left, taking his rifle, knife, and tomahawk with them so the Indians would not get them.

After they had gone, Glass became conscious and, furious that they had not only deserted him but taken his weapons, he crawled down to the stream for a drink, rolled in the mud to stop his wounds from bleeding (some such mud has curative properties), ate some berries, and started out across the plains, crawling.

Driven by a furious hate for those who deserted him, Glass kept going. He was found by some other trappers who took him downstream in their boat. When they camped at night he was in such bad shape they left him near the canoe. During the early morning hours Indians attacked and wiped out the camp, but did not find Glass, who was some distance from the others.

Glass survived and reached Fort Atkinson, where almost the first person he saw as he came through the gate was Fitzgerald, one of those who had deserted him and taken his rifle. Glass had intended to kill him on sight, but changed his mind. He had many further adventures and was finally killed by the Arikara.

One thing it is well to remember: that sea, that desert, that arctic cold can kill just as easily today as a hundred or a thousand years ago. One should always go prepared for the worst, in a mental way always, in a material sense if possible.

NICK SHADOW: He felt it was as good a name as any. His father had left him without a name but with a good education. He put in some time as a school teacher and was a good one, but things happened when a man had a view of things he liked to preserve. He became involved in a corpse and cartridge occasion and moved west where the climate was more favorable for survival.

BULL DUNN: A family man, whose family were renegades, outlaws, and whatever it took to gather another man's cattle or horses. They had been a traveling family until they found the La Plata country, and there they decided to stay. They had a way of riding roughshod over opposition but this time it did not seem likely there would be any. Flagan and Galloway were just two men, and even Nick Shadow didn't add up to much, or so they believed. The trouble was that nothing worked out like they planned.

ROCKER DUNN: The best of the Dunns with a gun, a quiet, reasonable young man who had begun to grow up mentally and to see that the country was changing. The old, wild riding days that followed the War Between the States was coming to an end, and he was bright enough to realize that a bullet looking for a home didn't care where it landed. But the rest of the Dunns didn't want to listen. He was telling them the only life they could understand was coming to an end.

LOGAN SACKETT: A Clinch Mountain Sackett, descended from Yance and a lot of others, tough men all. He had grown up fighting bears in the rhododendron jungles in Tennessee, places where spruce trees were fifteen feet through and so tall you had to look twice to see to their tops. There'd been times when he'd left the Clinch Mountains and gone on along the ridges to Clingman's Dome and then down into the deep, deep forest to places where the sun never shone. He trailed the bears right back to their dens in the rhododendrons where they thought they were safe. Then he rode off to fight for the

Confederacy in the Civil War, even though most of the Sacketts had gone the other way.

PARMALEE SACKETT: The Flatland Sacketts had money and Parmalee came from Grassy Cove. One of his ancestors had found Grassy Cove back in the middle 1600s and was nearly done in by a mountain lion there. Jubal Sackett had holed up there until his broken leg mended but he left a Sackett sign for those who came later. It was a good place to live, and Jubal had left his cave with regret to push on west.

Parmalee's ancestors had settled there but they held land elsewhere, too, and they did well with raising stock and breeding horses. Parmalee went west, and for a time he worked as an actor in a traveling show. Here and there he had his share of difficulties. He always enjoyed the cornhuskings, sorghum-making, and bean-stringings back in the high-up hills. He was a handsome man with a good voice for singing and he could play a fiddle more than somewhat when the mood was on him. Back in the mountains at the cornhuskings a man who found a red ear of corn could kiss the girl of his choice, and they do say Parmalee was right handy at finding the red ears—and when he found one the girls all started edging closer. Here and there folks said Parmalee knew where the red ears were before the husking started, but that was mostly jealousy, others thought. Parmalee was a man of the cities as well as the mountains and the plains and might have done well as an actor had he chosen to remain with the company.

SHALAKO: The village of Shalako in this story does not exist, though I had hoped to build it. At the time the story was written only one log house was on the site but others were planned. Plans do not always come to fruition, however, and these plans were dependent upon others than myself. Hence, for the time being, the deer, elk, and beaver are left undisturbed, and the mountain lion who followed me over a saddle in the hills one day is probably still roaming the area.

No doubt that mountain lion had followed hunters and

feasted off what they had left behind, or he may simply have been curious, as animals are inclined to be. I never saw him (one sees them but rarely, even when many are about, for they do not wish to be seen) and would not have realized his presence except that after pausing at the far side of the saddle, looking over the country beyond, I returned to find his tracks over mine. My tracks were plain in the sandy trail left by cattle, and his large paw prints blotted the edges of my tracks.

I was armed, a simple matter of insurance against what could happen, but I had no wish to disturb him (or her), and went back down the mountain to more frequented areas.

It is amusing to me that travelers frequently go to the Himalayas looking for the yeti, the so-called "abominable snowman" and return after a few weeks, saying there is no such thing. In all my years in the mountains I have seen many tracks and droppings as well, but the only mountain lions I have seen were two, treed by dogs. Wild animals are not standing around waiting to be photographed or to be seen by intruders.

CURLY DUNN: Another of the renegade Dunns, not the man his brother Rocker was, but determined to be considered so. Big, strong, handsome but with a streak of meanness in him, he invited trouble, which he could usually handle. If not, there was the threat of his father and Rocker to warn off the opposition. He courted Meg Rossiter.

MEG ROSSITER: A young girl, romantic, but in a place where there were few young men to be romantic about. She was determined to find romance, anyway. Curly had the appearance and she read into him what she wished to see, as many a girl has done (and many a man) in other times and places. Yet underneath the romantic notions there was a grain of good common sense and she began to see in Flagan Sackett what she had been hoping to find in Curly.

FATHER ESCALANTE: He left Santa Fe to find a route to Monterey, California in 1776. He was one of a group of ten men led by Father Dominguez, who left Santa Fe in August of that year. As Escalante kept the diary of the expedition it is generally named for him.

Poorly armed (they seem to have had but one musket and a lance as weapons) and equipped, they traveled for five months over some very, very rough country. Although they did not reach their objective, turning back just short of Salt Lake City, they did discover a route and a way in which it could be done. Miera, the soldier and mapmaker, wanted to continue on but the fathers decided against him, and the party turned back.

The Escalante expedition passed through the area of this story on August 10, 1776. They camped the previous night near the site of present-day Hesperus, and the following night on the Mancos River, to the west.

The expedition explored much of what is now Utah, had many peaceful contacts with various tribes of Utes, although their preaching was not always welcomed. In spite of the difficulties encountered on the expedition, the Miera maps were the best of the region for many years.

PAT BERGLUND: A saloon-keeper, solid citizen, and friendly man.

VERN HUDDY: Killing was his business, and usually business was good. One of Bull Dunn's followers.

OLLIE HAMMER AND TIN-CUP HONE: Followers of Bull Dunn, professional pistolfighters. Their trouble was they suddenly found themselves in faster company than they had been dealing with. You couldn't scare such men as the Sacketts and Nick Shadow; they had to be shown. Tin-Cup proved the wiser man.

POWDER-FACE: Also, POWDER FACE. A wise old Indian trying to do the best for his people.

TREASURE
MOUNTAIN

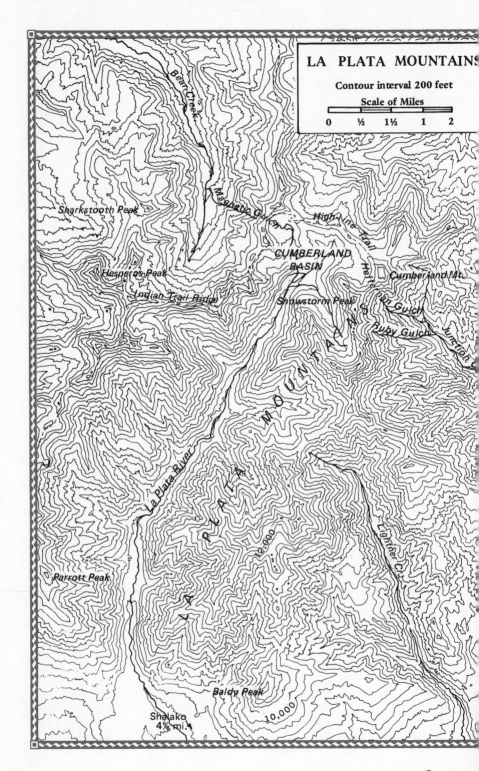

LA PLATA MOUNTAINS

Contour interval 200 feet

Scale of Miles

0   ½   1½   1   2

Bear Creek

Sharkstooth Peak

Magnetic Gulch

High Line Trail

CUMBERLAND BASIN

Hesperus Peak

Cumberland Mt.

Indian Trail Ridge

Snowstorm Peak

So. Madden Gulch

Ruby Gulch

Junction

M O U N T A I N S

La Plata River

L A   P L A T A

9,000

Lightner Cr.

Parrott Peak

10,000

Baldy Peak

Shalako
4½ mi.

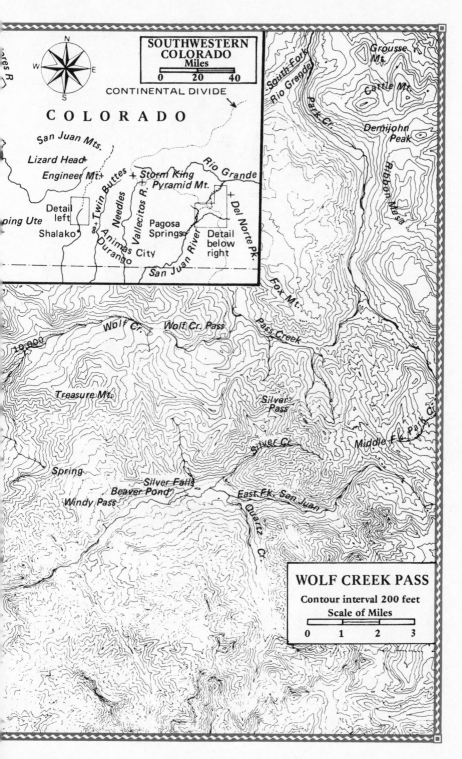

SOUTHWESTERN
COLORADO
Miles
0   20   40
CONTINENTAL DIVIDE

COLORADO

San Juan Mts.
Lizard Head
Engineer Mt.
Twin Buttes
Storm King
Pyramid Mt.
Rio Grande
Del Norte Pk.
Detail
left
Shalako
Needles
Vallecitos R.
Pagosa
Springs
Detail
below
right
Animas City
Durango
San Juan River

Grousse
Mt.
South Fork
Rio Grande
Park Cr.
Cattle Mt.
Demijohn
Peak
Ribbon Mesa

Fox Mt.

Wolf Cr.   Wolf Cr. Pass
Pass Creek

10,000

Treasure Mt.
Silver
Pass
Middle Fk. Park Cr.

Silver Cr.

Spring
Silver Falls
Beaver Pond
Windy Pass
East Fk. San Juan
Quartz Cr.

WOLF CREEK PASS
Contour interval 200 feet
Scale of Miles
0   1   2   3

183

TREASURE MOUNTAIN

First publication: Bantam Books paperback, October
    1972
Narrator: William Tell Sackett
Time Period: c. 1875–1879

The story of Treasure Mountain is well known in Colorado, and the location of the mountain itself is certainly no secret. Wolf Creek Pass, famous in song and story, curves around one side of the mountain, and it is there for anybody to see. As it is 13,442 feet in altitude, Treasure Mountain is hard to miss. According to the story the treasure was buried there about 1790, although some say it was earlier. The Spanish were bringing gold home from Mexico and Peru and the French did not understand why Louisiana was not producing as much. They did not grasp the idea that the terrain was completely different and that Louisiana was not gold country. They demanded gold, or else.

The governor outfitted a detachment of soldiers and sent them west to find gold, but at the time no line had been surveyed between territory that belonged to Spain and that which was claimed by France. When the French soldiers moved into Colorado the Spanish believed they were trespassing, but the French kept their presence as secret as possible. Nonetheless the Spanish became aware of it and, unwilling to start a war with a then-stronger country, they prevailed upon the Ute Indians to attack the French.

It was hit-and-run warfare. French soldiers were hunting for meat and did not return. Others traveled from one place to another and disappeared. There were sporadic attacks until the numbers of French soldiers were whittled down to a point where their numbers were no longer sufficient to carry the gold away.

The gold miners were soldiers and one of their officers was an engineer. The origin of the gold they mined has not been located but it was not on Treasure Mountain itself. Under directions from the engineer a shaft, or, some say, two shafts, were sunk into the ground, and the gold was carefully buried with every intention of returning with a stronger force to remove it.

In the meantime the Napoleonic wars had begun and France had much else to consider. Years passed, Louisiana was sold to Jefferson and the United States and a map of the gold came into the possession of a Frenchman who led his own expedition to recover it. They, too, fell to the guns and arrows of the Utes. So the gold remains where it was left.

However, the original commandant had permitted each of the soldiers to dig a little gold for himself, and some of this gold was brought away. At least one cache of such gold has reportedly been found in the area.

This story, with varying details, has been told and retold and various people have turned up with maps, most of them spurious. At least one map seems to have been accurate and its owners located the spot, but they came upon it late in the season. Unable to remain at that altitude but fearing that somebody else might come with an equally good map, they destroyed the landmarks. After all, they knew where the place was.

The winter brought deep snow, several avalanches, and storms, and when spring came they could no longer find the place. To those unfamiliar with mountains this may seem strange, but locating one spot on a vast sweep of mountainside can be next to impossible. The landmarks that seem so obvious can look very different when you return after a few months, especially when lightning may have struck a tree or if a boulder has been displaced by frost or heavy snow.

The trail Tell Sackett was riding when shot from ambush is easily recognized. It is now a road leading to the Bessie G Mine. The road passes through a notch not there in Tell's time. He followed an old Indian trail that came over the ridge from the Junction Creek side. This is four-wheel-drive country.

The bench where Colborn Sackett hid his daybook is hidden behind trees and on the very rim of the dropoff into the basin of Bear Creek.

It is difficult to say at just what moment a story comes into being, or what it is that triggers the imagination. Often it can be a place or a situation, perhaps a bit of history that needs to be enlarged upon. The story of Treasure Mountain was a natural, but every time I walked into Cumberland Basin it demanded a story. A rider coming down the trail from the Notch was vulnerable, and the bench where Pa Sackett was killed was secluded and lovely.

All that high country fascinates me, and the High-Line Trail that is often called the Ute Trail I believe to be much, much older. In each area of the Rockies such trails are found, and always with simply local names, but I believe it is all one trail, perhaps a migration route, or more likely an ancient trade route for Indians.

When you are above where the canyons begin, the traveling is much easier. No climbing in and out of canyons or continually crossing streams is required. Also, you can see for greater distances. Of course, the route could only be traveled in the warm months, but Indians never traveled in the snow if it could be avoided. Winter was a time for staying in the lodge, and it was storytelling time, too.

Actually, if one wished he could travel from Alaska to Mexico following high-line trails, dipping down only between mountain ranges.

I feel those trails are thousands of years old. A government man was making a survey of the population of elk and found a Folsom point on the Ute Trail, and another found a broken Folsom point. And that takes us back a few thousand years, perhaps eight to ten thousand.

CUMBERLAND BASIN: It's where the La Plata River begins, high up in the mountains, most of it around 10,500 feet, in a waving sea of wildflowers most times of the year. In the winter, early spring, and late fall it is many feet deep in snow. As it is right about timberline, there are patches of trees here and there, but the higher peaks are all smooth and green except for outcroppings of rock or old mines. The sky is usually a deep blue tufted with white clouds, but in the afternoon the clouds turn dark and there are rain showers, sometimes serious thunder storms. There's a lake up there, some marshy spots, a few beginning springs, and a trail leading to the high-line trail along the ridges.

Don't look for the crack from which Tell Sackett took Pa's daybook. It's gone. Souvenir hunters have carried rocks away until the place can no longer be recognized. Most of the old four-wheel-drive roads have been closed and if you want to go anywhere you walk. You walk slowly. At that altitude heart attacks come quickly if you hurry. Anyway, who wants to hurry when there's so much beauty just to stand and see?

There are scattered clumps of spruce trees. The aspen don't grow quite that high. The earth you walk on is tundra because at that altitude you are in an arctic region. The flowers you see will be those found in the Arctic Circle, in northernmost Siberia, Alaska, or Canada. It is not generally understood that as you climb a mountain the growth changes as if you were going north.

Be careful of the turf underfoot. Because of the short growing season, it takes the land a long time to recover from injury. Those riding motorcycles or jeeps should remember this.

COLBORN (PA) SACKETT: Father of William Tell, Orrin, Jim, Bob, and Tyrel Sackett, a mountain man, trapper, and hunter who had several times gone to the western mountains as a free trapper. And then he went once again and did not return. Ma wished to be sure he lay in a proper grave, if dead, and in any event wished to know what became of him. Traveling at the time was dangerous. Many men disappeared traveling eastern highways and byways, for there were long stretches of lonely road where anything might happen, but the sons of Ma Sackett also wished to know. Orrin Sackett traveled to New Orleans to make inquiries, to be followed shortly by William Tell Sackett.

New Orleans is not a strange city. Men from the mountains of Tennessee often rafted their goods down the river to sell or trade at the port. They had friends there and a few enemies.

The arrival of the Sacketts would bring them new enemies, people who had no wish to have old mysteries examined nor questions asked that might arouse further questions.

188

ANDRE BASTON: One of those men who for personal reasons preferred to let sleeping dogs lie. He was a skilled swordsman, and an excellent shot, and his skills had resulted in the deaths of a dozen men. Never simply content to draw blood or for simple victory, he preferred to kill, and did so.

PAUL AND FANNY BASTON: They were cut from the same pattern, and all three hoped to inherit from Uncle Philip, as all three presently lived on what he provided.

PIERRE BONTEMPS: Brother-in-law to Andre, liked by Uncle Philip. He recruited Colborn Sackett and led the expedition west to find the French gold. Murdered by Andre and Pettigrew in the western mountains, he was a good man, daring and adventurous but not as careful of his company as he should have been. Yet, when dealing with relatives, what can you do?

HIPPO SWAN: A waterfront thug in New Orleans, recruited by Andre Baston. A big man, a very tough man, a man known around the riverfront dives in New Orleans and Mobile.

BRICK-TOP JACKSON: A notorious New Orleans character well known to the police of the time. The account of her life as told in my story is true. Her criminal record would cover a dozen pages of such a book.

THE CANTON HOUSE, MOTHER BURKE'S DEN, THE AMSTERDAM, THE BLUE ANCHOR AND THE BALTIMORE: All were infamous places at the time, as was **MURPHY'S DANCE HOUSE.** Whenever I mention such a place by name in any of my books you may be sure it is not a made-up or imagined place, but the genuine article.

SAINT CHARLES HOTEL: A famous place then and now. In those days it served the most fashionable clientele.

THE OLD ABSINTHE HOUSE: In New Orleans, a place visited by most tourists and famous for many years. The pirate Jean LaFitte used to spend time there, and it is home to a thousand stories.

THE TINKER: He reappears in this story. A pack peddler in the mountains, he has been a seaman, a trader, and many other things. A gypsy, he seems to have been everywhere, moves like a young man and might be young, but who knows his age or his background?

DIXIE LAND: As explained in TREASURE MOUNTAIN, the name is purported to have come from some ten-dollar notes issued at the time which had a ten on one side, a *dix*—French for ten—on the other side. People called them Dixies so the term came to mean the area where the notes came from: Dixie Land.

There are other explanations for the term. This, I believe, makes the most sense.

DOC HALLORAN: Who bought and sold cattle and horses, often racing the latter. He also appeared in the story of LANDO in that capacity.

WEBBER'S FALLS: In what is now Oklahoma, on the Arkansas River. There was once a nice little fall here, several feet high. Named for Walter Webber, a Cherokee of mixed blood, and a wealthy man for his time, it was a well-known stopping place on the river, visited by Washington Irving, among others. Webber was an important man, well-known on the plains. When Arrow-Going-Home, the Osage chief, wished to bring a halt to hit-and-run warfare and horse stealing with the Cherokees, it was to Webber he sent his messenger. During the Civil War, Colonel Stand Watie, a Cherokee chief, captured a Yankee wagon train at the Falls, and later Watie called a meeting of the Cherokee Legislature there.

FORT GIBSON: A military post in eastern Oklahoma, situated on the left bank of the Neosho above its meeting with the Arkansas. Built to bring an end to the fighting between the Osage and the Cherokee, the log-palisaded fort was finished in 1824 and became a famous place on the frontier. During a part of his western period Sam Houston lived here with Tiana. It was here also that Hatrack, a lady given to entertaining her passing lovers in the local cemetery, plied her trade. According to Herbert Asbury, who wrote an account of her, she is reported to have replied to one of her visitors, who offered her a dollar: "You know darned well I ain't got any change!"

JUDAS PRIEST: A black man of some education and considerable skill with weapons who had more than one reason for befriending the Sacketts, and who went west with them. His brother Angus had been a slave to Pierre Bontemps, but more than a slave, he had been a friend as well.

McCLELLAN CREEK: Named for the Civil War general. Many of the officers who later became famed for their operations in the Civil War had previously served on the Indian-fighting frontier, and McClellan had been a part of the small force with Marcy when he was exploring in the western states.

VALLECITOS: Mentioned in TREASURE MOUNTAIN and featured in SACKETT. This was where Tell Sackett and Cap Rountree located some mining claims, and up on the ridge beyond was where Tell found Ange. If you've a notion for some hiking in the high country, and are prepared to camp out, you can get off the Durango to Silverton Narrow Gauge Railroad at Needleton and follow Needle Creek up to Chicago Basin. You will be hiking up where the eagles soar and where a trail dips down into Vallecitos. Don't try it unless you're used to hiking and like high altitude, but it's beautiful country and you'll see some of the finest mountains in creation. When I first hiked up through Chicago Basin and over the pass into Vallecitos, Pearl Harbor was something off in a future nobody would have believed. We topped out in a thick cloud and when we came out of it the Vallecitos Basin lay before us. We'd seen a few men working claims back in Chicago Basin but there were no hikers in those days, and we were alone on top of the world. A half mile away as the eagle flies we could see a bear digging into the slide rock after a marmot. Across the Basin we could see the mountains where, in a story that would be written twenty years or so later, Tell Sackett would find Ange.

In those years I was just somebody who wanted to be a writer but the extent of my writing had been a few items in newspapers for which I did not get paid. Still, I was gathering impressions, absorbing information and preparing for what was to come. Nothing one learns is ever discarded.

During those early years I taught myself to observe and remember, and from where I stood that day I had before me an unbelievable panorama of mountains, of sharp peaks, jagged ridges, and the impossible green of meadow grass and forest. Here and there were spots of snow, some of which would last the summer through. We went on down the trail into the Vallecitos, but I did not forget, could not forget what I had seen and was seeing.

One does not need to see mountains to observe. Having traveled much, I am often asked if such travel is essential for a writer. My answer would be no. A writer must learn to see and to understand, and some of the greatest writers have restricted themselves to an area or a period and have done well. Stories are about people and how they live their lives. Each generation is inclined to believe theirs is the worst, and we Americans like to view things with alarm. We like to tell ourselves how bad things are, but no people on earth ever had it so good.

BRANDS: A good rewrite man working with a running iron, some wire or a cinch-ring could alter any brand into the one he wished, and here and there it was done often, as in the case where Charley McCaire altered Tyrel Sackett's brand. It was a hanging offense, if a man was caught, and ranchers in the earliest days seldom waited for a trial. The rustler received a suspended sentence—at the end of a rope from a branch of the nearest tree. The nearest court house and jail might be a hundred miles away and a busy rancher had little time for traipsing back and forth to deliver a prisoner and then testifying in court. If a man was caught with a tied-down calf and an iron in the fire, that was enough. In fact, one rustler was found hanging from a tree with a sign on his chest: *Too many irons in the fire.*

TRELAWNEYS: In the Sackett stories they were people who lived in the mountains nearby. They seem to have run as long on girls as the Sacketts did on boys, which seems to present a most pleasant situation. The Trelawney girls were as strongly individual as the Sacketts, however, and they might show up anywhere. Whenever they did, they knew how to take care of themselves.

JACK BEN TRELAWNEY: A good man with a gun, especially a shotgun loaded with rock salt and bacon rinds. It wouldn't kill a man but could leave him with some anguished days and nights. Jack Ben was a man with several courtin'-age daughters, so he didn't get much sleep, which no doubt had much to do with the shortness of his temper.

TALLY-BOOK: Also, DAYBOOK. You will see them referred to in several of my stories and elsewhere in western literature. A rancher usually kept, and a cowboy often did, a small notebook in his pocket for keeping a count of cattle on the range, brands he saw, or anything he might need to remember. Often these books were used beside a branding fire to keep a count of the brands on cattle. When a tally-book wasn't available, many methods were used, such as tying knots in string, cutting notches, and anything else an inventive mind could think of.

Fur trappers and traders often used them to keep track of the numbers of skins of various kinds. It was about the only system of bookkeeping known to most of the early westerners.

INDIANS: Contrary to what many might believe, the relationship between whites and Indians was often friendly. Troublemakers were often new men out from the East with preconceived notions about Indians. Some tribes were always friendly, others were friendly only at times, and certain ranchers and western men won friends from among the Indians that lasted down the years. Very few Indians fought for their land. The idea that they might lose it was beyond their conception, until it was much too late. Indians fought for scalps, for loot, for any one of a dozen reasons, just as white men did. A wagon train or ranch house represented a treasure trove to an Indian, just as Sir Francis Drake looked to the Spanish galleons he attacked for profit. Personally, I resent the impression that the Indian was a poor creature of whom the white man took advantage. The American Indian was a fine, fierce fighting man of great personal pride and reasons for it. His trouble was that while he had to breed his future generations of warriors, which took time, there seemed to be, for some distant source of which he knew nothing, an endless supply of white men.

From my personal study, reading of reports, diaries, and early newspapers, my impression is that for every Indian who died in the settling of the West at least ten white people died. Not necessarily in fighting, though by one means or another.

But I object to the picture of the Indian as portrayed by some of those who profess to love him. No finer figure of a man ever lived than an Indian mounted and ready for battle. Among the Indians, also, were some of the finest orators, men whose speeches stand comparison with the best of Demosthenes or Winston Churchill, orators with a gift for picturesque language. The Indian was a Stone Age man, yet in his speeches and stories he often revealed a sensitivity, and sense of beauty and judgment far beyond what has usually been accorded such people. If the American Indian was an example of what Stone Age man could be, I believe that all our ideas on such peoples are subject to drastic revision.

NATIVITY PETTIGREW: A man who wanted it all; a deceptive, conniving man who seemed bland and simple, an appearance that served to conceal what he really was, a man ready for murder if it served his purposes. His first name is not unusual for that time. Many names were taken from the Bible, not only because most people were closer to religion than now but because the Bible was often the only source of names available. Birth control was rarely a factor in the thinking of early Americans, and large families were the norm. Moreover, on a farm or ranch, children, particularly boys, could be an economic asset. If family names were used, the parents soon ran out of Johns, Henrys, and so on, and sought recourse in the Bible, if they had not begun that way.

The gold on Treasure Mountain is probably still there, but as I've said, it's a big mountain and whoever finds it will probably do so by accident. You can be sure it was buried deep and well because it was an engineer who did it, and he and his men expected to return for it with a larger force. Anybody who buries gold does not expect to leave it in the ground for long, but the French army officer who is said to have supervised the burying also expected to have a good-sized force with him, and he didn't plan on doing any of the digging.

There is gold in the San Juans, and silver also, but the real treasure is in the air, the trees, the wildflowers, and the big, wide, open wonderful country. If you don't have it, all the money in the world won't buy it. And it is there for anybody who will use it kindly.

LONELY
ON THE
MOUNTAIN

WESTERN CANADA

Scale of Miles

0   50   100   150

Ft. Pitt

Jackfish Lake

Ft. Carlton

CRE[E]

Bear Hills

Eagle Cr.

Bad Hills

South Saskatchewan River

SAND HILLS

Cassiar

Dease Lake

Dease

Dease Mountains

Dease Lake

Stikine R.

Wrangell

COAST MOUNTAINS

ROCKY MOUNTAINS

MONTAN[A] TERR.

Bear Lake

Fraser River

Barkerville

Cariboo Mts.

BRITISH

COLUMBIA

North Saskatchewan

Clinton

C A N A D[A]

PACIFIC OCEAN

Columbia River

Victoria

UNITED ST[ATES]

LONELY ON THE MOUNTAIN

First publication: Bantam Books paperback,
    November 1980
Narrator: William Tell Sackett
Time Period: c. 1875–1879

Whatever Logan sent word that he was in trouble in the far north and needed a herd of cattle to get him out of it, the other Sacketts never gave it a second thought. They would find the cattle, and drive them north even if there were Higginses involved.

The Sackett-Higgins feud now seemed to have played itself out, but for years the name Higgins had meant trouble for a Sackett. Hence, when the Sacketts needed a code word for trouble they used the Higgins name.

The Dakota country in those days was Sioux country, as the name itself implies. The Sioux were a proud, often arrogant people who, starting from the Wisconsin-Minnesota border country had, after acquiring horses, become a conquering people. Sweeping westward they conquered much of Minnesota, all of the Dakotas, and well into Wyoming and Montana as well as southward into Nebraska, before conflict with the white man brought their conquests to a halt.

The Sacketts had to make their drive through the heart of Sioux country, and the valley referred to where the James River and the Pipestem meet is the valley where I was born. It was a green and lovely place then and as good a place to hold cattle as any I know, with plenty of grass, water, and shade.

There were rarely any Indians around when I was growing up except a few who occasionally dropped by to talk to my grandfather. They would sit cross-legged on the lawn and drink coffee heavily laced with sugar and talk over old battles as those who came later would talk of football games.

There were also a few who occasionally camped down near the tracks where some old stumps with huge masses of spiderlike roots were lying.

These were, I understood, trees ripped up from miles away by a tornado and dropped here. The tops had long been cut away for firewood but the stumps remained. They had been giant trees, larger than any around in my time with a few possible exceptions.

In the days when the Sacketts rested their herd near the rivers it was all Indian country. Soon settlers would be coming in, many of them former soldiers such as my grandfather who had first seen the country when pursuing the Sioux into Dakota after the Little Crow Massacre in Minnesota.

The troubles in Canada were drawing adventurers, land speculators, and others all out to pick up a little quick money if opportunity allowed. Pembina was a gathering point for those traveling north, as it had been for fur trappers and traders at a still earlier time, and Fort Garry was usually the immediate destination. Louis Riel had returned from Montreal in an attempt to forestall these would-be landgrabbers. It was unfortunate that his actions were misunderstood by many of the eastern Canadians.

FORT CARLTON: A fairly large palisaded enclosure with bastions at each corner. It stood back about a quarter of a mile from the North Saskatchewan in an almost parklike setting of green hills and clumps of forest. It was a regular stopping place for parties going west and often a dropoff for furs whose owners wished to approach no nearer to civilization.

The fort was established about 1795, and the first steamer to come that far up the river arrived in 1877, the *Northcote*. Shortly after, a regular service was established on the river and maintained for some time.

Carlton House was also a headquarters for the Mounted Police, and witnessed a confrontation there with Big Bear, a Cree. Later, Poundmaker, one of the most noted chiefs, spent time in the area. At the time of this story there were only traders and trappers at Fort Carlton.

TURTLE MOUNTAINS: A gathering of hills, lakes, and rolling plateau some three hundred-odd feet above the surrounding country. The borderline runs through the mountains, leaving a part of them in Canada. A favored hunting ground of the Indians in bygone years.

PEMBINA: Named for the colorful highbush cranberries growing in the area, a Chippewa name. Charles Chabboillez established a fur trading post there in 1797, and it soon became a
gathering point for the *métis,* the French-Indian buffalo hunters
who formed their expeditions there for buffalo hunts. These
were highly organized, sometimes accompanied by more than a
thousand Red River carts, and more than that number of
people. They were disciplined, carefully coordinated hunts by
skilled hunters. Pembina was to remain an important port in
the Red River for many years.

HAWK'S NEST: A flat-topped hill rising some four hundred
feet above the plains, with a spring near its top. This was long
a camping place for Indians moving across the country, and a
well-known landmark for travelers. The hill was well-forested.
Sibley camped near here before the Battle of Big Mound. My
great-grandfather, Lieutenant Ambrose Freeman, had been slain
by the Sioux about a week earlier, at a point further east.

FORT GARRY: Later, it became Winnipeg. At the junction
of the Assiniboine and Red Rivers. The Fort was originally
built in 1806, and destroyed in 1816, known then as Fort
Gibraltar. In 1822, when the Hudson's Bay Company and the
Northwest Companies became one, the Fort was rebuilt and
christened Fort Garry. In 1835 it was rebuilt in stone with
round bastions at each corner with embrasures for guns and
frequent loopholes for muskets. The walls were about twelve
feet high with a wooden walk near the top from which to fire in
defense. The residence of the Hudson's Bay Company governor
faced the north gate. Four other buildings were barracks
for soldiers, each fitted to accommodate one hundred men.
There were other buildings, including a store and an officers'
quarters.

The village that was the beginning of Winnipeg lay about
a half mile from the Fort. The road was lined with houses, forty
or fifty in number; a chemist's shop, several saloons, an hotel
and a saddle shop were among other places of business. In the

village of St. Boniface there was a cathedral, and several other churches, including an Anglican cathedral and a Presbyterian church.

McCAULEYVILLE, MINNESOTA: Riverboat town; white frame hotel owned and operated by Nolan. A clean, well-kept place. There were a number of houses in the village, which lies across the river from Fort Abercrombie.

DEASE LAKE AND RIVER: Relatively easy of access today, but in the 1870s it was back of beyond, one of those places often heard about but rarely visited. Chief Trader McLeod discovered Dease Lake in 1833, and some three years later a man named Hutchinson was sent with a party to open a trading post there. Word got out they were to be attacked by Russians and they fled. Irritated, Sir George Simpson commissioned Robert Campbell to explore the area of the upper Stikine and Pelly Rivers. A post was established and held briefly, then abandoned for some thirty-five years.

BARKERVILLE AND THE CARIBOO: Billy Barker is credited with the first rich strike in the vicinity of the town named for him. He was a tough little man who had been a potter and then went to sea. He was forty feet down and about to give up when he hit pay dirt, and took out better than six hundred thousand in gold if sold at 1860s values. Like so many of his kind, Billy met a lady, who was less than a lady, and Billy Barker wound up broke. He died in Victoria in 1894, and no doubt the lady met a gentleman who was less than a gentleman who no doubt spent her money and abandoned her.

The Cariboo was the name given to a district between Quesnel and Barkerville, and gold was found over the whole area in greater or lesser quantities. Later the name came to be extended to cover more country and was a symbol for riches, if you could get them. There was Cache Creek in that same area, and stories of buried gold and of a running horse with blood on his saddle, and a ghost who watched over the cache, wherever it was.

Laketon, near the mouth of Dease Creek, was for a time the metropolis of the Cassiar district and, as with all such places, the town bred its collection of characters and inherited a few from the surrounding country. They were men of grand deeds and fearsome appetites and there was little they would not do in their quest for gold. They included Cariboo Cameron, Dutch Bill, Nellie Cashman, and many others.

MARY McCANN: A much-traveled lady who could ride anything that wore hair and do a man's work as well as her own; an attractive lady who added poundage without losing shape. In E-Town she ran a saloon-restaurant, and in Bodie she washed clothes for the miners and panned out the mud she washed from them and made four times as much as she charged for the washing. She and Cap Rountree had crossed trails before and the results had been mutually agreeable.

SHANTY GAVIN: A handy man with a gun who believed he was big time until he met a big timer. It was a mistake that could only be made once.

COUGAR: No excuses for him; he recognized the situation and did not make the mistake the first time. But there was a second time.

DEVNET MOLRONE: Her last relative but one had died, and there was but little money, with employment for women almost nonexistent. Fortunately, she had a brother. She trusted he would care for her, until. . . .

She did not guess how wild Prince Rupert's Land was but was sure she could find her brother. Yet she did not know how wide the land nor that her brother had changed.

THE OX: He was large, strong, and sure of himself. His sheer size and presence usually got him what he wanted—until he suddenly got more than he wanted.

GILCRIST: A sandlot winner about to face big league pitching; how good you look depends on how tough the competition.

You win a few and get to believing you're good, and then you try to prove it against somebody who is really good. The next morning they are patting you in the face with a shovel, and somebody is writing an epitaph: *He was good, but not good enough.*

THE CENTURY AND THE ATLANTIC: Magazines referred to in the story. Such magazines were widely circulated on the frontier, and as with all other reading material passed from hand to hand until worn out. **SCRIBNER'S** was another magazine frequently found at trading posts, forts, and other frontier establishments.

HIGHPOCKETS HANEY: Any tall, lean man of six feet four inches or more was apt to be nicknamed "Highpockets." This one was a top-hand in any company.

DOUG MOLRONE: A young man of education and intelligence who simply took the wrong route. A brother to Devnet, he lacked her strength of character and left town running. Such characters have a way of turning up again. Did he learn his lesson or not?

ORRIN SACKETT: Self-educated lawyer, peace officer, and congressman, a man of engaging personality with a fine speaking or singing voice and only a shade less good with a gun than Tyrel or Tell.

Growing up where hunting was a daily occupation, all the Sacketts could handle guns. Growing up with an already existing feud going on, all lived with the awareness of danger.

Orrin began his study of law as did many frontier lawyers, by carrying a copy of Blackstone wherever he went and reading whenever opportunity allowed. He had also studied Greenleaf on Evidence and then for two years worked with a country lawyer. His first marriage to Laura Pritts ended in divorce.

He was the best educated of the postwar generation of Sacketts.

LOGAN SACKETT: One of the Clinch Mountain Sacketts, descended from Yance. They were generally a wild, rough lot, the Clinch Mountain Sacketts, considered outlaws by some, and when they went west they were always riding on the fringe of the wild bunch. A twin brother to Nolan Sackett, but they were rarely seen together, each preferring to go his own way, yet on occasion. . . .

Logan has also appeared in RIDE THE DARK TRAIL.

LAURIE GAVIN: A blood sister to Kyle, and Shanty Gavin was her stepbrother. She was in the Dease River country with no place to go but out, if she could get out. And then she met Logan.

ISOM BRAND: Called Brandy; a young cowboy hired en route. Like many others of his time and later, he had left home to find work wherever and however it could be had. Much of our country was built by such itinerant labor.

SHORTY: A man to ride the river with, and a man who rode for the brand. A man with a love for far horizons, and when he cashed in his chips they buried him where his grave overlooked a lot of beautiful country, with horizons wherever you turned. Shorty would have liked it that way.

BAPTISTE: An old man who wasn't that old and took to the trail again. Once they've traveled the trails of a far country, there is always the urge to go on to a still farther country.

KYLE GAVIN: From Toronto, and headed west, but for what? A full brother to Laurie, and a connection by name only to Shanty Gavin. He, too, wanted to stop the delivery of cattle and hoped to profit from the jumped mining claims, but he was prepared to go only so far, and as the situation developed he became uneasy. His moral judgment was possibly nudged into place by the possibility of decisions by Winchester.

THE MÉTIS: A French-Canadian-Indian mix; hunters and trappers, famed for their well-organized buffalo hunts and their rebellion. The latter began as an effort to protect their rights in land long occupied by them when surveyors appeared and began surveying right across what the métis considered their property lines. Louis Riel, whose father had been a spokesman in the past, was sent for by his mother to return from Montreal. He endeavored to set up a provisional government that would keep things under control until the eastern Canadians decided whether they wanted to be bothered with Prince Rupert's land or not.

The *métis* were a colorful lot in costume, song, and language. Some of their boating songs, sung to accompany their paddling of canoes or larger boats, are favorites of mine. My father often sang them and since then I've heard them sung by Canadian lumberjacks with whom I've worked.

As for the mix mentioned above there might also be added a touch of Scotch here and there. Many of the early Bay Company factors were Scots, and others came west and fell into the fur trade as if born for it.

Western Canada was a country of rare beauty, of vast distances, and forests that seemingly went on forever, with some fine rivers and along the coast many islands and coves that permitted easy access to the country. There was gold and there was fur, but most of all was the country itself.

There was plenty of wild game, and a man with a rifle could live mighty well without even half trying. The *métis* were great hunters and had some of the finest horseflesh you'd be likely to see.

They also had the Red River carts, often to be seen in long caravans stretched across the country, carrying buffalo hides to market or bringing back the goods they'd bought in St. Paul or Minneapolis.

It was a wild and beautiful land to which the Sacketts rode, and they were the men to understand and appreciate it.

RIDE THE
DARK TRAIL

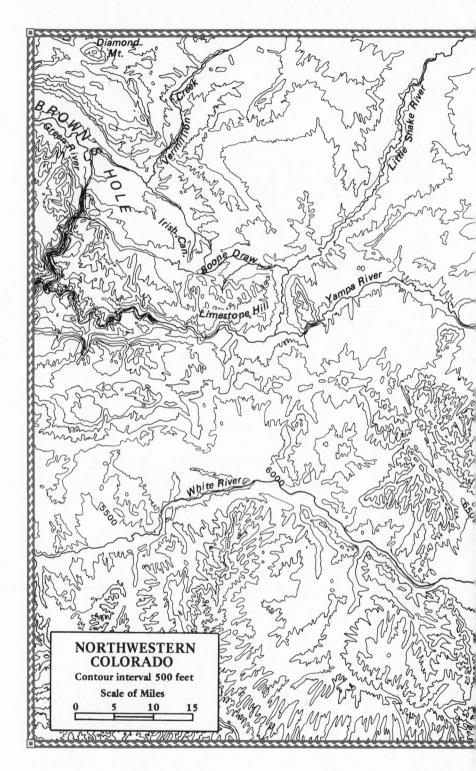

Diamond
Mt.

BROWN'S HOLE

Green River

Vermillion Creek

Little Snake River

Irish Can.

Boone Draw

Limestone Hill

Yampa River

White River

6000

5500

6500

**NORTHWESTERN
COLORADO**

Contour interval 500 feet

Scale of Miles

0   5   10   15

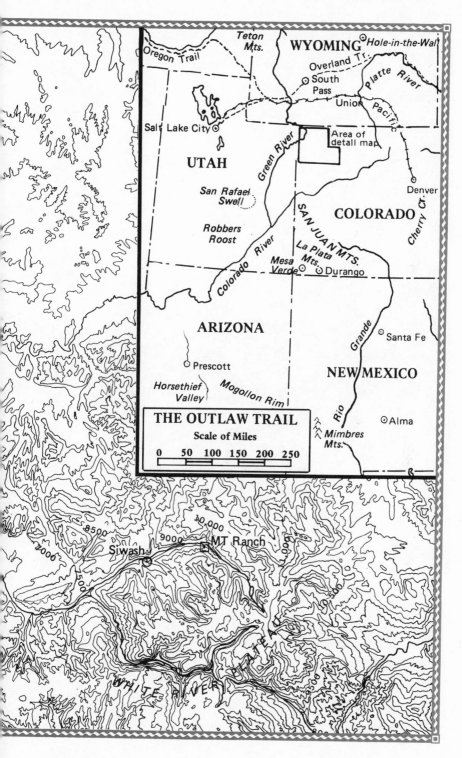

THE OUTLAW TRAIL

Scale of Miles

0   50   100   150   200   250

RIDE THE DARK TRAIL

First publication: Bantam Books paperback, June 1972
Narrator: Logan Sackett
Time Period: c. 1875–1879

Reed Talon knew good land when he saw it and this place had prairie, mountain meadow, timber, and water. Reed Talon was a builder and it was to the timber he looked first because he planned to build not a house but a *home*.

This was to be the place where he took off his boots and hung up his hat, and riding over the land he looked at it with pleasure. This place had everything. Most important, the mountain meadows were bordered by cliffs and protected from invasion, and the open prairie below was useless without water.

Reed did not have a woman but he had one in mind. She lived away back in Tennessee and he had never so much as glimpsed her but he had a working partner who was forever talking about this tall mountain girl who could shoot better than any man he knew, but who could also bake a cake and sew a fine seam. The more his partner talked, the more Reed knew she was the girl for him.

He had worked with heavy timber most of his life, joining and fitting and working with broadaxe and adze. He had built bridges, barns, churches, school buildings, and silos, so when he built for himself he built carefully and well.

When he told Colly Sackett he was going east to propose to that mountain girl he'd been talking about Colly looked him over afresh. "I've had it in mind. She's some kind of cousin to me but a Clinch Mountain Sackett and I don't hold with their ways, although they be kin.

"A year or so back I come through her country and stopped a night thereabouts, and thinks I, there's a woman who needs a man, but an almighty good man. We'd trapped a spell in the Wind Rivers, you an' me, and thinks I, 'that's the man for her.' "

Colly paused, then added, "She's a mite taller than you, but don't you ever let her know it. She's all woman. Not beautiful, but a fine-lookin' girl, an' she could take her pick of the mountain boys, but she's held off. I don't know what she wants but she surely does, and I've a hunch it might be you."

Colly stayed on at the ranch so Reed could go a-courtin', and he took off for the eastern lands. When Reed rode up to Emily Sackett's door he didn't waste around. He told her what he had come for and she told him to get down and come in, that he couldn't do much courtin' settin' upon a horse, thataway.

He was shorter than Em but broad in the shoulders and strong from a lifetime of lifting heavy timbers. He bedded himself down under a big oak tree and helped with the chores. That night they went to a church social and a few days later to a barn-raisin', then a box supper. The womenfolks talked him over at a quiltin' bee and on the third Sunday they stood up before the gospel-shouter and were married. Trulove came down from the high-up hills to give the bride away and Macon stood in for best man. The church was crowded because everybody liked Em and most of the womenfolks had 'lowed she'd probably never marry. There was nigh onto a hundred folks there and thirty-two of them were Sacketts. On the other side of the church, the bridegroom having no family present, there were twenty or so of the Higginses.

The Sacketts and the Higginses had a feud going but it was considered right sinful to shoot a man on a Sunday, all forms of entertainment being left for weekdays except for funerals or weddings.

Reed Talon had brought a black broadcloth suit with him and Em had hand-stitched her own wedding gown, having it laid away and ready. They made a handsome couple, folks said. Even a couple of Higginses said it.

After the ceremony one of them said, "Mr. Talon, you all are a Sackett now, so come daylight when you take out of here you be sure you will be follered and shot."

Reed Talon just looked him over and said, "Boy, if you foller us you be durned sure you can't catch up."

Colly Sackett had furs to trap and wanted no part of ranching so he left them to handle it and went off to meet Jim Bridger or Kit Carson or some such person, and Reed went to cutting poles for corrals, cleaning out waterholes and fixing up the barn to handle hay cut for winter days.

When spring came, Reed Talon hired hands. He bought cattle to stock the range, and a milk cow for the house. He built an icehouse near the spring and when winter came next he cut ice from a nearby river and bedded it down with sawdust to keep meat and vegetables fresh.

Reed Talon was a knowing man and a careful man and he killed only what wild meat he needed and put out hay and salt for game as well as for his cattle. There were always elk and deer around and he made it comfortable for them to stay.

By the time he passed on, there was money in the bank and cattle on the range, and Barnabas Talon went to school in England. Milo, who took after the Sacketts, rode the wild country, working here and there, breaking broncs and cutting a wide swath wherever the girls were.

Reed Talon died under strange circumstances, and Em Sackett had her own idea how.

JAKE FLANNER: A man who wanted wealth and power. The trouble was that the best ranch was owned by the Talons, who wouldn't sell and wouldn't scare. He arranged the murder of Reed Talon but Em Talon broke both his knees and left him a cripple, and all his efforts to dislodge her failed. The country was changing and Jake Flanner could see the handwriting on the wall clearly enough. When the change took place he wanted to be sitting on the Empty, the Talon ranch, in complete command. How he acquired the property was his business, and afterward he would be a smiling, affable rancher and businessman, such a one as might be considered for governor or the senate. The only trouble was, he could not move Em Talon.

One by one he eliminated her hands and restricted her movements. He controlled the town but he could not reach Em. It was frustrating, irritating, and a challenge.

At first sight his conclusion was that the man who called himself Logan was a trouble-hunting drifter, a man both useful and expendable. Undoubtedly if he approached the Empty he would be shot at and he would return the fire, hopefully with effect. In any event, nothing would be lost and much might be gained.

EMILY TALON: A Clinch Mountain Sackett, and none of her life had been easy until she married Reed Talon. After that it was hard, hard work but she knew what she was working for and for whom. She and Reed had settled the land when the West was young and she had seen her boys grow tall and strong and each take to his own particular trail. The ranch was theirs, and she would hold it for them until they came to claim it, as someday they would.

The West was built by the strong, men and women, each with a role to play. Often a man was gone on a trail drive or working away from home and his wife ran the ranch or the homestead. It was not only the men who knew how and when to use a gun. Annie Oakley did not become one of best rifle shots who ever lived by doing the dishes, and she was only one of many such.

Em Talon also appears, briefly, in THE MAN FROM THE BROKEN HILLS.

BARNABAS TALON: Named for Barnabas Sackett, the first of the Sackett clan to come to America. Barnabas studied in France and England and fought as an officer in the Franco-Prussian War in 1870. Excellent rifle shot, middling good with a pistol. A young man with a future.

MILO TALON: Brother to Barnabas, some years younger. Takes after the Clinch Mountain Sacketts, a bit on the wild side but a rover and a gunfighter. Also appears in THE MAN FROM THE BROKEN HILLS and MILO TALON. A man who knows his way around wild country but who knows the cities, too. Well-educated for his time although not a college man like his brother.

LEN SPIVEY: He walked a very wide path in a very small town until he met Logan Sackett. The meeting could have been educational for Spivey but he was a slow learner. He flunked the six-shooter course and wound up in a shallow grave, wrapped in his own blanket.

ISOM DART: An historical character, known in Brown's Hole. A black man, an outlaw, but well-liked along the trail.

Isom Dart was murdered by Tom Horn, who shot him down from ambush. Tom Horn, using the name Tom Hicks, had been stopping over with Matt Rash, according to the Brown's Hole stories, and it was Matt whom he killed first.

SPUD TAVIS: When he asked Pennywell Farman to care for his children, he had more than that in mind. But Pennywell was a girl who knew her own mind and she took the buckboard and ran away. He had no idea anybody would take up for a no-account nester's kid, but the big, rough-looking stranger did, and after a brief discussion of the situation Spud Tavis decided to take his buckboard and go home.

PENNYWELL FARMAN: Not quite sixteen, thin but growing up to be pretty, she had small chance in life with a no-account father and no home to speak of. But she had her own standards of behavior and was prepared to fight for them.

DEKE FARMAN: A natural-born loser who accepted his role too willingly. His daughter had all the backbone he lacked.

CON WELLINGTON: A gambler with rheumatic hands; he could no longer deal them from the bottom so he opened a store, and when a stronger, more desperate man came along he drew in his horns and took to playing soft music until the situation changed. Con Wellington had lived long enough on the frontier to know that nothing was forever.

DUTCH BRANNENBERG: Success had given him confidence and the name of being a tough, dangerous man. The trouble with having such a name is that the time always comes when you have to live up to it, and Dutch didn't choose the time or the man, they chose him.

JOHANNES DUCKETT: A young man who was good with a rifle and had no hesitation about shooting from ambush when the price was right, and Jake Flanner had the price. Flanner trusted in what he believed was Duckett's loyalty and Duckett trusted in what was left of Flanner's bankroll. Johannes Duckett had saved more than a thousand dollars, more money than he could imagine, so when the odds mounted his supposed loyalty disappeared with the morning mist.

JOE HERRARA: Known as Mexican Joe Herrara. A dangerous man, but he left Chihuahua because some quiet but honest men thought he was too much trouble and suggested travel might be softening to his nature. The people at South Pass City thought the same but Brown's Hole was tolerant, up to a point. But they all knew that when Joe Herrara started sharpening his knife it meant trouble. He had a very cutting way about him.

THE OUTLAW TRAIL: Led down the backbone of the Rockies from Canada to Mexico with hide-outs along the way, either on the trail or close to it—the Crazy Mountains in Montana; Jackson's Hole and the Hole-in-the-Wall country in Wyoming; Brown's Hole, largely in Colorado but edging over into Wyoming and Utah; Robbers' Roost on the San Rafael Swell in Utah; a ranch near Alma, New Mexico; and Horse-Thief Valley in Arizona. All of these were spots where an outlaw could find a place to stop, no questions asked, and none answered if he was followed. There were towns a bit off the route, too, such as Baggs, Wyoming, where Butch Cassidy once owned a house (it is still there, owned by one of the family who bought it from Butch on condition they keep a room where he might sleep), as well as a half dozen other such towns.

BROWN'S HOLE: An area in northwestern Colorado and bordering sections of Utah and Wyoming that was a main stop on the Outlaw Trail. Also a rendezvous for trappers in earlier days, it was home to a number of colorful, exciting characters. Tom Horn pulled off at least one of his killings here, that of Matt Rash.

The Hole was well-sheltered from the worst winds, and had water, fuel, and good range.

BENTON HAYES: A man who found hunting wanted men paid better than hunting buffalo or bear. Only trouble was, sometimes you believed you were trailing a small black bear but at the end of the trail you discovered you had cornered a grizzly. Up to this point Benton Hayes had tracked down a number of small black bears. He wasn't prepared for what he found in his trap this time.

ALBANI FULBRIC: A man with a sense of history, and a memory of his own family's story. Like many of his generation he had grown up reading Sir Walter Scott.

DOLORES ARRIBAS: A lady of Spanish-Indian ancestry, a lady who was quite a woman and she had it where it could be seen. Wherever she went she turned heads. She took in washing and it was said she entertained a little on the side, but it was very selective entertainment and she did the selecting. A woman of independence and courage, as well as beauty.

CHOWSE DILLON: An occasional outlaw of small calibre; a good hand with stock, not so good at choosing the right companions.

WILL SCANLAN: He had a sister named Zelda and a house by the side of the road where travelers sometimes stopped. He ran a few head of cattle, owned a few moth-eaten broncs, and Zelda could cook, so he made out.

JERK-LINE MILLER: A teamster, a passerby, a man not unwilling to pick up a few dollars of blood money as long as he was out of shooting range.

SIWASH: A crossroads with a store, a saloon, and a half dozen houses, a place born to die, and like many another it did.

The new highway passed it by and when I last saw the place there was nothing left but a stretch of concrete floor and a rusted gas-pump, a few charred timbers and a stone foundation.

Dolores Arribas? One of the gentlemen she entertained passed on, leaving her a house in the city and considerable wealth. When we last talked she was a quiet, elderly lady with gray hair who sponsored the ballet, the opera, and a few aspiring young people who never knew their fairy godmother.

THE
SACKETT
BRAND

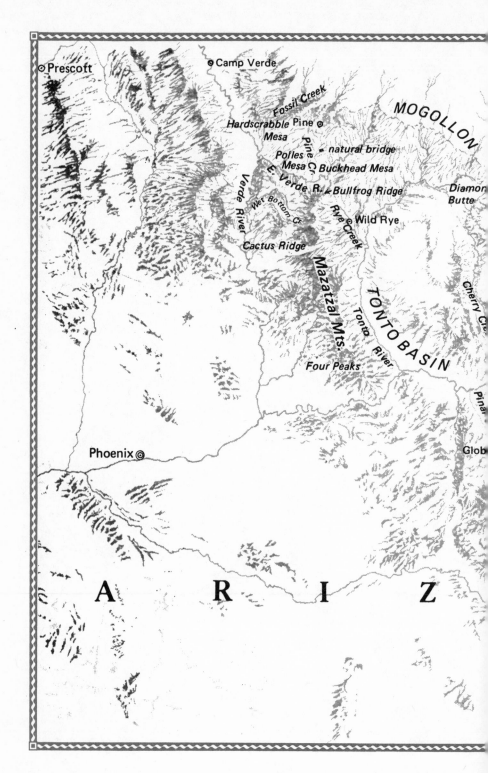

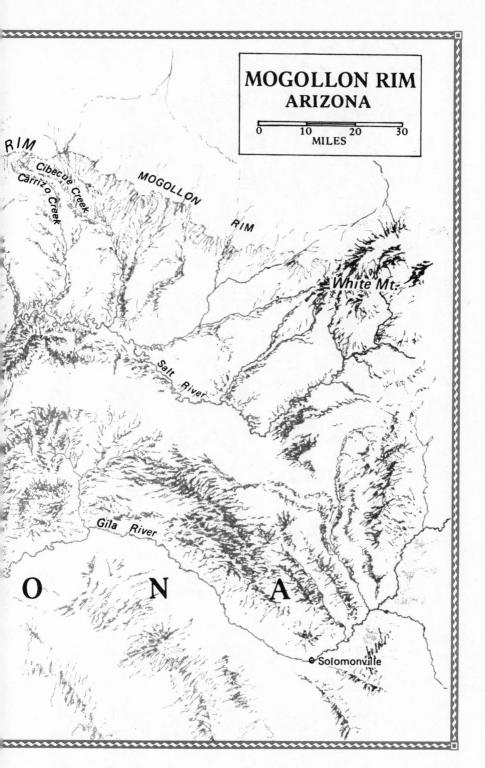

MOGOLLON RIM
ARIZONA

0   10   20   30
MILES

RIM

Cibecue Creek

Carrizo Creek

MOGOLLON

RIM

White Mt.

Salt River

Gila River

O   N   A

Solomonville

THE SACKETT BRAND

First publication: Bantam Books paperback, June 1965
Narrator: William Tell Sackett
Time Period: c. 1875–1879

News had a way of traveling in western country. Somebody told a stage driver and he told a bartender and the bartender passed the news to some friend over the bar, and the story was on the grapevine.

When the Lazy A riders started hunting Tell Sackett in the Mogollon Rim country the story started from Camp Verde and Globe, but within the week they were talking about it in Fort Worth and Ogalalla, in Dodge and Tombstone. And wherever the story reached a Sackett, that Sackett headed for the Mogollon on the run.

When Tell found Ange in the mountains of Colorado he found a girl as lonely as he himself. Long ago, back during the Civil War, there had been another girl, but that had come to nothing, and when he found Ange they knew it was forever. With gold from their mining claim they bought cattle and headed for the Tonto Basin. Trails were few and they were finding their way, with Tell scouting ahead, and then he was attacked without warning and Ange murdered.

It was a wild and broken country known only to the Apache, miles and miles of forest and running streams bordering on the half-desert lying to the west and south, a country in which a man could both run and hide.

What chance did one man have against forty? One man, already badly hurt and without weapons?

Then the Sacketts began to come from wherever they heard the news. Some were near, some far, but a Sackett was in trouble so they asked no questions. They came running: Nolan, Orlando, Flagan, Galloway, Tyrel, Orrin, and Falcon. Even Parmalee, the Flatland Sackett. Riding for the Mogollon from wherever the news found them, and as has been said, even one Sackett was quite a few.

Van Allen treated all women with contempt but this time he had gone too far. His own men deserted him, and what he hired to replace them was, by and large, the riffraff of western saloons. Even some of those refused to follow when they discovered the truth, that he had attacked and murdered a decent woman.

SWANDLE: A cattleman whose investment entangled him in a web in which he had no part. All he wanted was out, hopefully without losing his shirt.

ANGE SACKETT: Born Ange Kerry. Her story is told in SACKETT, of how Tell Sackett followed a strange trail to a hanging valley in the Colorado mountains and found not only a lost mine of the Spaniards but a lovely girl, left alone after her grandfather died, a girl he subsequently married.

BOB O'LEARY: A bartender who found himself in the middle. He had seen it all in bars from Dodge to Deadwood and wanted no part of a fight in which he had no stake.

There were many such bartenders. Like the gamblers and the gunfighting marshals, they followed the boom camps, drawn not only by the ready money but by the flavor and color of the camps themselves. You found them in the end-of-track towns, places that were born and died within weeks or months as the railroad moved on. You found them in the sudden cattle and mining towns until half the faces in any boom camp were faces you remembered even if you did not know the people.

New ones appeared, lasted a camp or two, and disappeared, but by and large they knew each other, talked over the other camps, and went their ways.

Not only the gamblers, saloon-keepers, bartenders, and gunfighting marshals but the women as well followed the excitement and the promise of easy money from El Paso to the Yukon. Bat Masterson, for example, who ended his days as a sportswriter for a New York newspaper, was at the Battle of Adobe Walls; he was sheriff of Ford County where Dodge City was; and he showed up in Denver, Leadville, Tombstone, and Trinidad. And they included Luke Short, Wyatt Earp and his brothers, Doc Holliday, Dave Rudabaugh, Mysterious Dave Mathers, Rowdy Joe Lowe, John Wesley Hardin, Silver Heels, Poker Alice, Calamity Jane, and dozens of others, names forgotten now but known to all that crowd in the rough old days before the country began to settle down.

DANCER: A good man riding for the wrong brand.

AL SEIBER: 1844–1907. A German who scouted Apache country for the army. A Union soldier, he fought at Gettysburg, among other battles, and was wounded twice. That was only the beginning, as he was wounded many times by bullet, arrow, and knife in his fights with the Apache.

The scouts he led were also Apache, and he was respected both by the Indians he led and those with whom he fought as a decent, honorable man whose word was good.

He was one of the many men, referred to in my stories, that the gunfighters left alone, if they were smart. As I have written elsewhere, for every gunfighter of whom one heard there were a dozen just as capable of whom you heard little or nothing at all. Al Seiber and Major Frank North were two such.

AL ZABRISKY: A gunman for hire; a warrior to handle gun trouble who did not ask too many questions.

SONORA MACON: Another such, and the man who shot Tell Sackett off the cliff, a man with a gun for hire, but one who had his own standards. He was a fighting man who fought for fighting men, not for the killers of women. Badly shot up, he survived.

LORNA: A lady of uneasy virtue who was sent to lure a man to his death for money. Her first thought was for what the money would buy in San Francisco, but she had second thoughts.

BRISCOE: A young man who was suddenly scared, suddenly realized he could *die*, so he got on his horse and rode away into many sunsets and sunrises, and with every one of them he remembered how easy it would have been to lose them all in exchange for a little piece of lead near his heart.

WILLIAM TELL SACKETT: A tall mountain boy who lived out the Civil War fighting for the Union; who found the great love of his life during that war and lost her almost as soon as he found her. Who rode away to the West when the war ended and drove cattle over the Bozeman Trail to Montana, a lonely man with a lost dream who found a girl alone in a cave and married her. Part of it was love and part of it was because she was lost and alone and needed taking care of, just as he was lost and alone and needed someone to watch over and care for.

All he had was a horse, a saddle, and a gun and with it all a wistful longing for something more, something he had known briefly, then lost forever.

NOLAN SACKETT: One of the so-called outlaw Sacketts from the Clinch Mountains. It was said those Clinch Mountain Sacketts were so rough they wore their clothes out from the inside first and Nolan was one of the roughest. When he heard a Sackett was up against long odds he got up in the middle of a horse and started west.

FALCON SACKETT: One-time sea captain, adventurer, father of Orlando, and married to Gin, formerly Virginia Locklear. He was traveling by stage when he heard the news. Somebody had a Sackett treed up in the Tonto Basin country so he didn't waste around.

ORRIN SACKETT: Politician, singer of Welsh songs, peace officer, cattleman. A handsome, smooth-talking man who was good with a gun when the situation demanded.

FLAGAN AND GALLOWAY: Brothers, cousins to Orrin, Tyrel, and Tell, cowhands, cattlemen. Two long-tall mountain boys who come when needed.

PARMALEE SACKETT: A Flatland Sackett whose home was in Grassy Cove; a Sackett with money, a sometime actor, cattleman, gambler, a man good with a gun but who preferred other methods when possible. Has property near the Highland Rim, as well.

VANCOUTER ALLEN: Forty years old, a strong, arrogant man who rode roughshod over anything that got in his way. Brutal and uncaring with women, he suddenly found himself guilty of an ugly murder and in a panic tried to cover it up and destroy the evidence. Tell Sackett was a part of that evidence and he wasn't easy to get rid of.

CAP ROUNTREE: A salty old customer, a mountain man, trapper, cowboy, all-around western man. Dry as alkali dust and twice as bitter. A tough old mountain man who had hunted gold and fought Indians and had the scars to prove it. You will find him in THE DAYBREAKERS, SACKETT, LONELY ON THE MOUNTAIN, and others. A man to ride any river with.

DODIE ALLEN: Cut from the same pattern as Vancouter, only younger. The pattern was wrong and the time was wrong so Dodie would never get any older.

CAMP VERDE: The post was established under the name of Fort Lincoln in 1861 to protect travelers from the raids of the Apache. Under the command of Captain C. Porter of the Eighth Infantry, the fort had a force including two companies, A and D of the Eighth Infantry and one company, A, of the Sixth Cavalry. First occupied by volunteers, the post was taken over by regulars in 1866, when Porter took command.

MOGOLLON RIM: Although the name is Spanish, the pronunciation is not. Usually known in the area as the Muggyown. A bold escarpment marking the edge of the plateau, the Rim runs from a spot near Ash Fork through the Blue Range and joins the Mogollon Mountains of New Mexico. It is approximately two hundred miles long, but the heart of the Rim country lies from Strawberry across the Tonto Basin and Pleasant Valley. The canyons, mesas, and such mentioned in this story can all be found there. The Natural Bridge is a tourist attraction and the cave in which Tell Sackett took shelter is there.

It is without doubt one of the most beautiful areas in the West, with fine forests of pine, fir, and aspen and many running streams.

It is an interesting thing that the highways through the West seem always to miss the most delightful places, and those most worth seeing. One can travel through Arizona or Nevada on the highways and never realize there are such places as the White Mountain country of Arizona or many of the finest sights in Nevada. The same is true of a half dozen other western states. Highways are built where it is easiest, and such routes do not take one into the forests and the canyons except where they cannot be avoided.

GLOBE: A mining town, first settled in 1876 as a result of a silver strike, beginning as a few tents and buildings on the banks of Pinal Creek. Its most famous mine was probably the Old Dominion.

TONTO NATURAL BRIDGE: An arch of travertine some 180 feet above Pine Creek. The caves beneath are extensive and supposedly were discovered by Dave Gowan when he was trying to hide from Apaches.

PLEASANT VALLEY WAR: This area was the site of the famous Tonto Basin War, the feud between the Grahams and the Tewksburys. The fight lasted for several years and the last survivor was Jim Roberts, later marshal of Jerome and at one time of Clarkdale.

KNIGHT'S RANCH: A famous stopping place in traveling from Arizona into New Mexico. Billy the Kid was well known there.

WILD RYE: In the time of this story, a scattered settlement centering around the tiny village of Rye.

FOUR PEAKS: A wild region just south of Rye where several lost mine stories have their focal points. It was well known in the years of the Apache wars, and a number of battles were fought within a few miles.

THE
SKY-LINERS

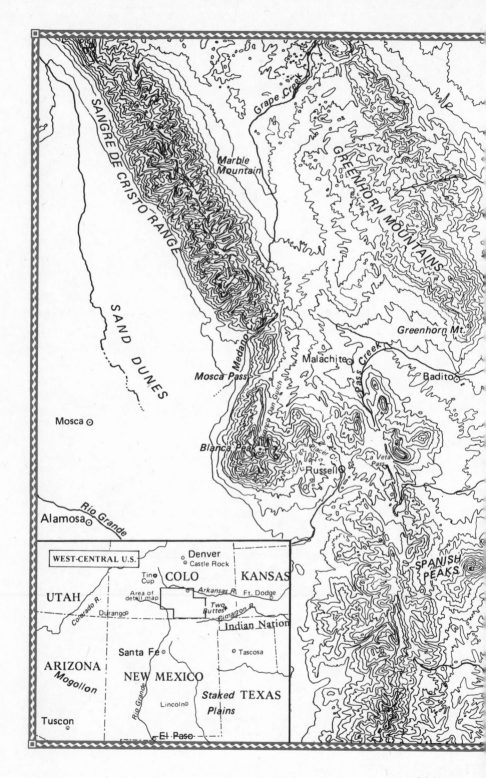

Grape Creek

SANGRE DE CRISTO RANGE

Marble
Mountain

GREENHORN MOUNTAINS

SAND DUNES

Greenhorn Mt.

Medano

Malachite

Baditoo

Mosca Pass

Pass Creek

Mosca ⊙

Placer Dan Gulch

Blanca Peak

Placer Cr

La Veta
Pass

Russell⊙

Rio Grande

Alamosa⊙

SPANISH
PEAKS

Denver ⊙
Castle Rock ⊙

Tin ⊙
Cup   COLO   KANSAS

UTAH   Area of
detail map   Arkansas R.   Ft. Dodge

Colorado R.   Durango⊙   Two
Buttes   Cimarron R.

Indian Nation

ARIZONA   Santa Fe ⊙   ⊙ Tascosa

Mogollon   NEW MEXICO

Rio Grande   Lincoln⊙   Staked   TEXAS
Plains

Tuscon ⊙   El Paso⊙

232

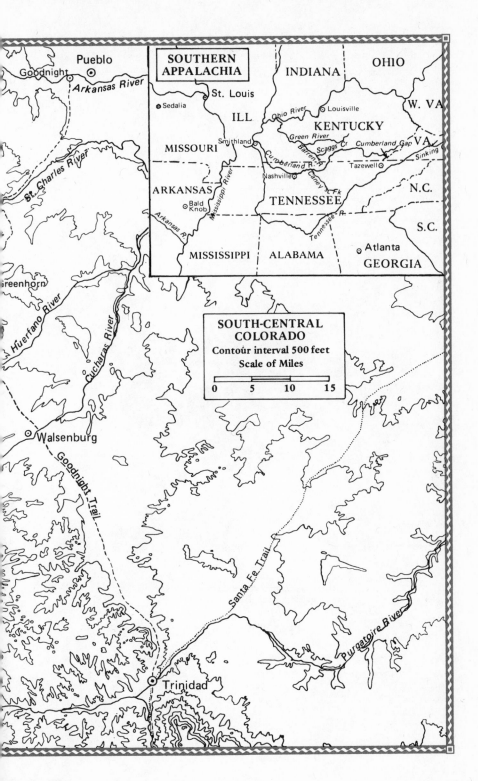

THE SKY-LINERS

First publication: Bantam Books paperback, April 1967
Narrator: Flagan Sackett
Time Period: c. 1875–1879

When Flagan and Galloway went to Tazewell to pay off a debt their father had incurred they were not looking for trouble. They hoped to simply pay the debt and return to the West where their future seemed to lie.

They had heard stories about Black Fetchen but did not expect to meet him and were not eager for the opportunity. Neither did they like being almost run down in the street, but one thing led to another and Black Fetchen and his crowd found themselves dropping their weapons into the street and then at the behest of two strangers, singing *Rock of Ages*, and demonstrating to all who watched that they were not as tough as they had assumed.

Flagan and Galloway had no idea of taking any freckle-face girl west with them, not until they heard the arguments Laban Costello offered and saw the horses he was giving them, along with money enough for a roadstake.

All they wanted was to get back to the buffalo range but they did need horses. What they did not need was to ride herd on a girl who had it in mind to marry Black Fetchen.

Flagan knew very well that a freckled-face girl with romantic notions could get a man into more trouble than three lawyers could get him out of, but there was no help for it. Galloway had already made up his mind.

What Flagan and Galloway were never to realize was that when they rode into the Greenhorn country they were riding a trail blazed three hundred years before by another Sackett.

Our history as a nation and as a country is largely a family history, but succeeding generations often have little knowledge of the previous generations or their activities. Even when a genealogist has traced a family history, it still deals largely with the high spots, and few such stories recount the day-to-day lives of those involved.

Jubal Sackett went west in the 1600s and was lost to his family. Occasionally there was a rumor, but it was like a leaf blown on the wind. Jubal was gone west, and as in many such cases, after his own generation has passed on, the others occasionally wondered, but nobody thought to discover his trail.

Jubal had, they believed, found his way to the Shining Mountains, and had married an Indian girl he met en route. That much they believed, but beyond that, nothing. Each generation had its own troubles, with wars, migrations, local politics, and illness.

GREENHORN INN: A place frequented by Kit Carson, among others, and named as was the nearby mountain for Cuerno Verde, or Greenhorn, a Comanche chief. The Inn still stands.

There are legends that fabulously rich gold mines once existed near the Spanish Peaks, near here. If such was the case, the mines and their workings have long since disappeared, and the gold was taken away to Mexico as an offering to the ancient gods of the Aztecs. Certainly the Aztecs possessed gold in great quantities and much was offered to Cortes when he first came to Mexico. No doubt little of that gold came from so far away, for there was, and is, plenty of gold in old Mexico itself. Carrying gold over such immense distances without pack animals other than man seems impossible, yet who can say?

BUZZARD ROOST RANCH: Tom Sharp settled there, building his trading post in 1870. An old Ute trail led through his ranch to the Sangre de Cristos by way of Badito and the Greenhorn country. As in my story, Sharp was one of the first to bring thoroughbred horses into the West, occasionally crossing them with wild mustangs for stamina.

BADITO: Near the opening into Huerfano Valley.

SPANISH FORT: Near Oak Creek are the ruins of an old Spanish fort built around 1820.

REYNOLDS GANG: A band of outlaws led by Jim Reynolds, who claimed they were robbing others to raise money for the Confederacy, but there is no evidence that any of the money went any further than the gang itself. There are stories that they hid most of the gold that came from the Kenosha stage holdup. Supposedly the thieves buried the gold, intending to come back after they had eluded their pursuers. (The heavy gold would of course have been a handicap in their escape.)

However, such stories probably originated in the hopeful imaginations of those who wanted to believe. Outlaws rarely let go of any gold they acquired until reaching the nearest saloon or bordello. Nor did they trust one another, and with good reason. They were all thieves.

The Reynolds gang was estimated to have included twenty-two men, any one of whom might have returned to take the buried gold for himself, as the others realized. Despite many such stories, few outlaws ever buried any loot. Indeed, when one checks the records few had much to bury. Reynolds and several of his men were captured, and en route to Fort Lyons they suddenly departed this life. There is no record of any tears being shed.

TAZEWELL: Rugged country; the area was settled about 1800, and named for Senator Henry Tazewell. The county seat of Claiborne County, Tennessee.

JUDITH COSTELLO: A daughter of the Irish Nomads, horse traders known throughout the southeastern part of the country. She was sixteen at this time and cute as a button. When Flagan and Galloway took on the job of escorting her west they got more than they expected, but Flagan had his doubts from the beginning. It did him no good, no good at all to doubt. Even though he dodged and sidestepped, he couldn't get away, and maybe her grandfather knew it all the time.

BLACK FETCHEN: Came from somewhere up near Sinking Creek but the family had moved in from elsewhere. A handsome scoundrel with brothers and cousins who rode together for all the wrong reasons, but a daring, dangerous man, just the sort who might catch the eye of an impressionable young girl.

EVAN HAWKES: A cattle drover, a tall, spare-built man with reddish gray hair, who bore some resemblance to Andrew Jackson.

BAT MASTERSON: He was born William Barclay Masterson in Iroquois County, Illinois. He moved further west as a teenager, grading for the railroad, then hunting buffalo. He was involved in the Battle of Adobe Walls, when several hundred Kiowa and Comanche Indians attacked that trading post, was briefly a deputy marshal, and later was elected sheriff of Ford County, Kansas.

His first gun battle was with Sergeant King, who objected when Molly, whom King considered his girlfriend, paid attention to Bat Masterson. King opened fire on Bat and Molly threw herself in front of Bat, taking the bullet meant for him. Molly was killed, but Bat killed King.

Later when two troublemakers killed his brother Ed, who was deputy marshal, Masterson killed both men in the gun battle that followed.

Masterson was to engage in one more gun battle when he went to the aid of his brother Jim back in Dodge. As he left the train, he was attacked, and he shot and wounded Al Undegraf. His other activities in Colorado and Tombstone have no place here. As a peace officer or gambler he visited Trinidad, Creede, Silverton, and Denver, to name but a few. At times he served as referee for prizefights and eventually lived the last twenty-five of his years as a sportswriter in New York for the old *Morning Telegraph*. He died at the typewriter there. Some years ago I interviewed Louella Parsons, the Hollywood columnist, on Bat. She had worked for the *Telegraph,* and Bat had often advised and guided her in her first months on the paper. He had also been a friend of Teddy Roosevelt, who knew many of the old-time frontiersmen and enjoyed their company.

WYATT EARP: A deputy marshal in Dodge City, an officer in various other places, a buffalo hunter, occasional gambler. A man well-known on the frontier, Wyatt Earp was a controversial figure. When years have passed and the evidence is conflicting I have established my own rules for judging men: I judge them by who their friends were. By and large Wyatt's friends were on the side of the angels. His enemies usually ended up in jail or were killed by peace officers. Pony Deal and Ike Clanton, for example, were killed resisting arrest in eastern Arizona.

All men and women, no matter what their time, have their enemies and detractors. Wyatt has been overpraised by some, viciously attacked by others. In Tombstone the opinions one got depended very much on the political stance of those involved. The Earps were Republican, and Johnny Behan was a Democrat. That Johnny was friendly to the outlaw faction has never been denied. Another element was that Wyatt won the affections of the lady in whom Johnny Behan was interested.

Despite what the movies say, the only shooting in which Wyatt was involved in Dodge was when a drunken cowboy rode down the street shooting wildly. A couple of his bullets came through the walls where Eddie Foy was on stage performing, Foy dropped to the stage. Wyatt and another officer yelled at the man to halt, and when he did not, they both fired. One of them killed him.

THE LADY GAY: A saloon, dance hall, and gambling house operated in Dodge City at the time of my story and for several years before and after.

In writing my stories I try to present as accurate a background as possible. The stories may be fiction, the settings are not. In such situations as are presented in this story, Earp and Masterson would undoubtedly have appeared in their actual capacity, as I have had them do. Masterson's as well as Earp's reactions are typical both of their characters and the times.

BOB WRIGHT: Mayor of Dodge City, trader in buffalo hides. Prominent local businessman.

CHALK BEESON: Part-owner of one of Dodge City's first saloons, occasionally a city official, a man with many friends, few enemies.

LARNIE CAGLE: A young man who thought he was good with a gun. He didn't live long enough to find out he wasn't.

TORY FETCHEN: One of the clan from the mountains. He went into a dark barn with the notion of killing a Sackett. It was a darkness from which he never emerged.

COLBY RAFIN: A cousin of the Fetchens who rode with them, rode from Tennessee to a pass in the Colorado mountains. He reached the pass with James Black Fetchen but he did not leave it. Neither did Fetchen.

KYLE SHORE: A good cowboy turned into an occasional gun-for-hire fighter in cattle wars. A tough but loyal man.

BURR FETCHEN: One of the Tennessee Fetchens who rode west with his brother James Black Fetchen. Involved in the killing of Laban Costello.

RUSS MENARD: A gunman-outlaw working with the Fetchens. He bought a lead ticket to wherever he was going that night on the Muleshoe. He died game, but he died.

MOSS REARDON: A tough old survivor, who survived once again.

LADDER WALKER: A top-hand in any outfit.

TIREY FETCHEN: He had been one of the Reynolds gang, or so it was believed. Killed in Colorado, fighting with the Sacketts.

Three of the Fetchen outfit pulled out for Tennessee, deciding that following James Black Fetchen was leading them into trouble.

Many of the old trading posts are gone. Several of these survived briefly, then vanished, leaving nothing behind. Towns began and were abandoned. Indian attacks, local disagreements and the changing fortunes of those living there led to some sites being abandoned. Some left to prosper in other areas, some simply drifted away to be lost in gold and silver camps that sprang up overnight and vanished when the rich ore played out.

The story told in THE SKY-LINERS is simple enough. Two young men agree to escort a young lady to the home of her father in Colorado. What happens after develops as a result of the personalities involved, the country itself, and the circumstances that attended their travel through it.

The period of exploration was past, and so was most of the Indian fighting. The country was beginning to settle down into communities that would become towns, and towns that were on the verge of becoming cities.

The law had arrived but was mostly occupied in keeping the peace in towns. What happened outside the populated areas was something else, and a man was expected to take care of himself.

Feuds or fighting such as I've described in this story actually happened. The best known are probably the Lincoln County War in New Mexico in which Billy the Kid was involved, the Tonto Basin War in Arizona, and the Johnson County War in Wyoming. There were dozens of others. These included the fighting between the Regulators and the Moderators in Texas, as well as the Sutton-Taylor feud, the sheep and cattle wars, and fights over land, mining claims, and rights-of-way for roads or railroads.

Such fights continue to this day, only they have moved from the gun battle to the court room, but are no less viciously fought. Yet as recently as when I was sixteen, a neighbor was killed in a fight over a waterhole in Arizona, and another, somewhat later, was killed over another waterhole in Oregon.

The men who settled the West were a hardy lot, as were their women, and they did not accept being pushed around either by people, events, or even the elements.

Once, on a television show, I was asked what particular quality western men and women possessed. I probably said something about courage, but on the way home (when one always thinks of what should have been said) I knew my reply should have been "Character, character and dignity."

It is true. Wherever you see them, the men and women who went west, old now and often poor, they carry themselves with pride and they possess a quiet dignity that comes from having met the worst that life can offer, and survived.

THE MAN
FROM THE
BROKEN HILLS

A word of explanation seems appropriate about THE MAN FROM THE BROKEN HILLS. This story has been included among the Sackett stories since its publication, but it is actually a Talon story, as are RIVERS WEST and MILO TALON. At the time the book appeared the decision was made to call it a new Sackett story because Milo's mother was a Sackett. Now, with the publication of THE SACKETT COMPANION, I've decided to no longer list THE MAN FROM THE BROKEN HILLS as one of the Sackett stories.

As many of my readers are aware, I started writing this series with the intention of showing how the United States and Canada were opened to settlement, as seen through the eyes of three families: the Sacketts, the Chantrys, and the Talons.

The first book of the Talon series remains to be written, though it has been started, and put aside for the time. The first of the Chantry series was FAIR BLOWS THE WIND, in which the vessel abandoned with much of its cargo of silver still aboard is the same hulk in which Barnabas Sackett takes shelter on a sandy island in the river.

When and how that silver will be discovered again remains to be told in a future story, but at least now you know the connection. It is not often I share such secrets beforehand.

A few words about THE MAN FROM THE BROKEN HILLS. It is rare in a western story to find cowboys actually working. They are in town, in a saloon, on a trail, but rarely involved in doing what a cowboy does. I have tried here and there to show him at work, and some of this is in BROKEN HILLS.

Some of the best riders and ropers were Hispanic, but in the early days they were only found in Texas, New Mexico, Arizona, and California. Without a doubt, the riatas used by California ropers were the longest used anywhere, except in Mexico itself. A California rope, of plaited rawhide, might measure eighty-five feet, although sixty-five was more common. The average Texas cowboy used a rope of about thirty-five feet.

In my story RIDE THE DARK TRAIL, which is a Sackett story, I introduce Barnabas and Milo Talon for the first time, and one gets the family connection. But THE MAN FROM THE BROKEN HILLS is definitely a Talon story, and so it shall be listed from now on.

A SACKETT
GENEALOGY
AND FAMILY TREE

The Sackett family genealogy presented here has nothing to do with any Sackett family except the one created in my stories.

In creating the characters in my stories it has also been necessary to create a family tree. Not, I might add, the easiest thing to do.

Names present a problem for the simple reason that a name once used in a story cannot be used again without the possibility of confusion. In family histories sons and daughters were often named for their parents, uncles, aunts, or in-laws, with the same name often repeated many times. This can present a problem for those researching family history, as the duplication of names presents difficulties and strict attention must be paid to dates, marriages, and such.

Several of my readers have attempted, for their own satisfaction, to put together a genealogy of the Sacketts, but unfortunately for their efforts, all the names were not available to them, as many generations had been skipped over to be left for future stories. Naturally, I sympathize with their frustration in trying to grasp the relationships, hence this book.

One of the ideas attending a SACKETT COMPANION was to offer enough of a family tree so the relationships could be understood and to provide a bit more history than accompanies the stories, which are all basically historical.

For the benefit of the curious I might add that none of the characters in the Sackett-Chantry-Talon series is based upon members of my own family or of anyone else whom I know or know of. Having lived with history most of my life, and having worked and traveled in many parts of the country, I have tried to create characters who, if they did not live as I have written, very well could have. The events in which they took part were actually happening, and happening to people like those of whom I write.

It is often overlooked that white men had been on this continent for some 250 years before the United States became a nation, and many of the patterns of behavior had been established by the ruling powers of Spain, France, and England or by their subjects. Relationships with many Indian tribes had been developed long before there was a United States, and when we became a nation we inherited both the good and bad feeling that resulted from previous dealings.

Often, in considering our history, it has been assumed we were always the powerful nation we eventually became, but this was far from the truth. At the time of our war with Mexico, for example, our standing army was less than one-third the size of theirs, comprising some twenty-five thousand men scattered in garrisons in outposts mostly in Indian country.

In 1803 we acquired the Louisiana Purchase from France, a vast stretch of territory which more than doubled the size of the country but which was virtually uninhabited except by nomadic and warlike Indians. The few scattered settlements were largely located along the Mississippi or its tributary rivers.

Texas became an independent nation in 1836, and some nine years later joined us as a state. Mexico had threatened that if such became the case, it meant war. Shortly after that, war began with the annihilation of an American patrol by a much larger force near the border between Texas and Mexico. This precipitated the war with Mexico. Neither in a military or a financial sense were we prepared for such a conflict.

When Barnabas Sackett landed in Carolina, the land was in theory a possession of the King of England. Spain possessed Florida where the French had also made attempts to establish themselves. In Nova Scotia, far to the north, the French were already settled, as well as along the St. Lawrence River.

Barnabas had no grant from the King, nor had he any official right to be where he was beyond the right of possession. Hence his desire to avoid the colony that was later established at Jamestown, in Virginia. It was also the motive behind his desire for further exploration westward, as he could foresee a time when their location at Shooting Creek might be usurped by the King or some colonial official.

It is always interesting to speculate on how much exploration was done by Long Hunters and others before there was any recorded movement west. The few reports we have are those official explorations or those by men who could write, and who took the time to write.

In the East a man's family name could open doors for him, but in the West it meant nothing. A man was known by his deeds, and whether his word was good or bad. Names meant nothing and often a man lived out his western years known only as Slim or Shorty or some other such name without anybody knowing or caring what his real name was. That was still true during my knockabout years.

There is an amusing poem entitled *What Was Your Name In The States?* that makes the point very well. The fact was that nobody cared. Often a man went to his grave with only a nickname on his tombstone because he was unknown by any other.

The movement of the Sacketts toward the West was part of what was happening at the time. Aside from mountain men, trappers, and fur traders, the first movement west was that of the Mormons to Utah, followed and accompanied by the Gold Rush to California and the Land Rush to Oregon. With the Civil War's end many young men returned to plantations devastated by war or to cities already crowded with men seeking jobs.

Tell Sackett had joined a cattle drive through Indian country to the ranges of Montana, and unaware of what had happened to him, Tyrel and Orrin started west to find a home for their mother. Lando, gathering his few belongings, had started south and west to find a better life for himself as did Flagan and Galloway. None of these Sacketts knew any others of the name outside their immediate family, but all had heard of the Clinch Mountains Sacketts of whom everyone in the mountains knew.

Colborn or Colly Sackett, as he was known, had disappeared into the western mountains some years before. He was the father of Tell, Tyrel, Orrin, etc. His brother Ethan, after much trapping in the mountains, had gone west guiding a wagon train (BENDIGO SHAFTER) and their sister Echo had remained, so far as they knew, at Tuckalucky Cove.

Many stories of the Sacketts remain to be told, and some may, for various reasons, remain untold. The ramifications of any family can stretch out in every direction and eventually grow so tangled and complicated that following every line is virtually impossible.

In this COMPANION to the Sackett stories I have chosen to follow only a few branches of the family, those immediately concerned with the published stories, and in the main lines of descent. In some cases—for example, Macon, Mordecai, and Trulove Sackett—I have included their stories in THE SACKETT COMPANION but have not included them on the family tree. Their exact connection to the rest of the Sacketts is information that is yet to be revealed. Occasionally I have used only the first names of wives leaving their stories to be told at some later date. Nor shall I, at this time, provide the full line of descent for the sons and daughters of Barnabas.

In drawing up the family tree of the Sacketts I have arranged a number of marriages for better or worse, and these couples have given birth to a colorful assortment of children, all of whom I have named. Even writing their names is a challenge: what is *their* story? How did they get together? Yet I have other stories to write first and these must simmer on the back burner for the time being. One morning I will awaken and know that is the day for that and I shall write it. By that time my subconscious will have put together many of the ingredients and it will also have directed my reading, somewhat, so the necessary material is there.

One thing I have discovered. For each story there is a time in which it must be written, and it is often fatal to begin too soon.

Nobody can suggest a story to me. At least, not one that I will write. My stories must come from within me and from what I have learned or am learning. If someone else has a story that is their story, not mine.

My characters are very real to me. They are created from the materials my life has given me or which history has provided. Once created the characters often take on a life of their own, and often I find that I cannot leave them alone, and must return and offer a further glimpse of their lives and fortunes.

When the idea occurs to me I get a few lines on paper, sometimes about the story, more often the beginning. Once that is done the story remains mine forever and I can return to it at any time. Some stories come to mind on the spur of the moment; others, such as THE LONESOME GODS, THE WALKING DRUM, and LAST OF THE BREED were years in the developing. There is no set rule for me, at least.

Barnabas Sackett had four sons and a daughter. Brian and Noelle returned to England with their mother, he to read for the law at the Inns of Court, she to become a lady in surroundings more suited to that development.

Jubal went west to disappear into the mountains. That he met and married a Natchez Indian girl they knew, but beyond that, nothing.

So the Sacketts with whom my present stories deal are largely descendants of Kin-Ring and Yance.

Kin married Diana Macklin, and in due time they had three sons and a daughter who lived. These were Philip, Malaby, Anne, and Bretton.

Philip married a Ruth Bernard and seven generations later Parmalee was born.

Malaby married a girl whose only name was Vanora, and in the fourth generation Daubeny was born.

Daubeny fought in the American Revolution and married a girl named Nata under strange circumstances and they were to have four sons, Mawney, Pym, Regal, and John. Mawney was to marry Fiora Clyde. From them came two sons, Ethan and Colborn, and a daughter, Echo.

> "Not all of the Sacketts I have introduced to date appear on this family tree. For example, Mordecai, Macon, and Trulove Sackett, as well as Emily Sackett, her husband Reed Talon, and her children Barnabas, Milo, and four unnamed others are not included. Their exact connection to the rest of the Sacketts remains to be revealed."
>
> —Louis L'Amour

SPECIAL REFERENCES:

*1. Robert Macklin's wife is mentioned, but not named in THE WARRIOR'S PATH.

*2. Yance and Temperance had other children besides Boyne.

*3. Jubal and Itchakomi's unborn child, referred to in JUBAL SACKETT.

*4. Pym Sackett and Cindy Larraway had other children in addition to Falcon.

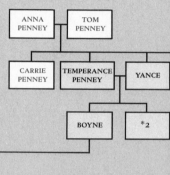

—— 3 GENERATIONS ——

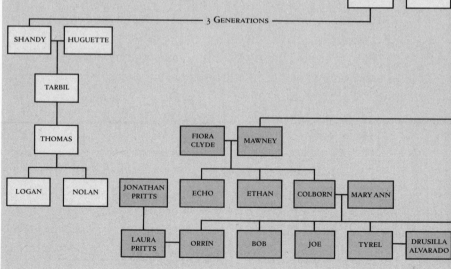

FAMILY TREE

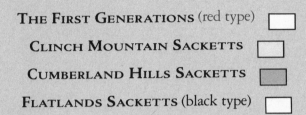

THE FIRST GENERATIONS (red type) ▢

CLINCH MOUNTAIN SACKETTS ▢

CUMBERLAND HILLS SACKETTS ▢

FLATLANDS SACKETTS (black type) ▢

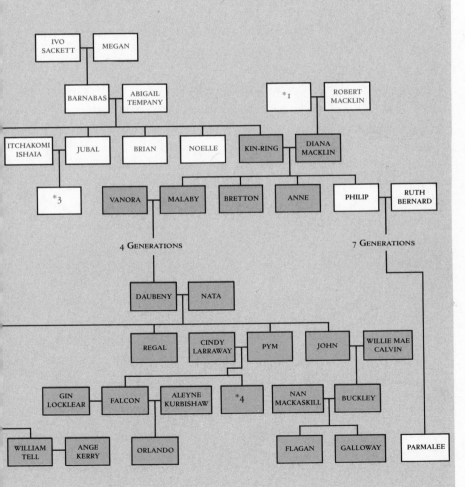

And from Colborn and his wife Mary Ann were five sons, William Tell, Orrin, Tyrel, Bob, and Joe.

Pym, Daubeny's second son, married Cindy Larraway, who among others had a son named Falcon.

Falcon married Aleyne Kurbishaw by whom he had a son, Orlando.

Falcon married a second time, to Gin Locklear.

Daubeny's third son John married Willie Mae Calvin, by whom there was a son named Buckley who married Nan MacKaskill.

They had two sons, Flagan and Galloway.

Yance Sackett married Temperance Penney, and his youngest son was Boyne, and in the third generation thereafter was born Shandy Sackett, who married Huguette and fought in the War of the Revolution.

They returned to the Clinch Mountains and after a few years was born Tarbil, who fathered Thomas who sired twin sons, Logan and Nolan.

There is no need now to list the names of the intervening generations, which will be done in due time. These are sufficient for the curious to grasp the relationships of the Sacketts of whom they have read. I have discovered that no sooner do I mention a Sackett than a story is expected, and each must await its time.

Several of those who have attempted, for their own pleasure, to shape family trees of the Sacketts have listed a Seth.

In my story there is no such character although I have mentioned in other places a Seth Sackett who was a real man. Apparently he came west originally with the Baker party, which named the Silverton area Baker's Park, and he returned to establish himself in the Durango area. At this point I know nothing about his life.

It was an interesting coincidence that I decided to move my Sackett family west from Mora, New Mexico and have them settle in the Durango vicinity only to find a real Sackett had preceded them.

As anyone can see, reading these pages, the story of the Sackett family has only begun, and there are many stories yet to be told of the Chantry and Talon families as well.

The people who created what we know as the West almost always came from elsewhere. By the time anyone could grow up in the West the wild old days were coming to an end. Wild Bill Hickok, Long-Haired Jim Courtright, and Bat Masterson were all born in Illinois; Clay Allison and Cullen Baker, among dozens of others, were from Tennessee; Heck Thomas and Doc Holliday were from Georgia, and so it was.

Those who came west brought their songs, their stories, and their memories from Europe or the East. It took time for the West to generate its own stories and to alter the customs of those who chose to live there.

In two of the Sackett stories and at least one of the Chantry stories I have touched on the life of William Shakespeare. At the time of which I was writing he was not a famous writer. In fact he was not known as a writer at all.

He was one of a company of actors, and in that company at least two actors were much better known than he: Richard Burbage and Will Kempe. Shakespeare was only known as a writer by people of the theatre itself, and perhaps a few patrons who patronized the theatre as a hobby and who sponsored various companies of actors so they could exist at all. Early in his London years Shakespeare had published two long poems and perhaps some minor work, but the sales of such items were never enough to cover the cost of publication. For that the printer, not the writer, usually found some wealthy man to defray the costs, and as a result books were often dedicated to these men. In most cases they had no contact with the actual author at all.

It is always necessary when writing of times gone by, whether in the early west or in Shakespeare's England, to judge them by their standards and not ours. Supposedly we speak the same language but actually it is much different and many words have taken on meanings other than those intended by the author. For example there are the stories of Robin Hood and his Merry Men. The word "merry" in their time did not mean somebody who was happy or amused. Merry Men in those days meant Bawdy Men, a rather different thing. I surmise that Robin Hood's men were not unlike a bunch of cowboys or mountain men in manners, actions, and language.

Another example might be the word "haberdasher," which in our time means a purveyor of men's furnishings but in Shakespeare's time it meant a school teacher or an usher.

The English language has gone through many changes and when speaking or writing of a period one had best understand the usages of the time.

For some reason the writings of William Shakespeare have been considered by many as something reserved for an intellectual elite, but as a matter of fact he wrote his plays for the common man of which most of his audience was composed. Studies of his audience shows that most of them were artisans and apprentices, not unlike the average movie-going audience of today.

Interestingly enough, his plays were popular in the early west, and at one time in Virginia City, Nevada, several companies were playing Shakespeare at the same time.

Theatre was of great importance in the West and usually there were a dozen companies touring the western cattle towns or mining camps. Theatre then, as now, tends to go where the money is, and the West not only had money to spend but a desperate need for entertainment.

My next story of the Sacketts will probably be one concerning the American Revolution, but who knows what other whim may take me? I can always be led astray by a good story.

IN THE BEGINNING,
THERE WAS
THE STORY. . . .

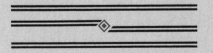

Undoubtedly demonstration was the first means to education. The primitive child learned to do things by observing his parents or other nearby adults. He or she learned how to build a fire, choose a spear shaft, chip out an arrowhead or prepare a hide by seeing it done. And then came the story. . . .

The story was man's first and best means of transmitting knowledge or information, of preparing the child as well as the adult for what might come. All the sciences had their birth in tales told over a campfire or in some moment of leisure.

The returning hunter or warrior was expected to tell what he had done and how it was done. In so doing he taught others not only how to hunt and trap but how to conduct a war party. No doubt the tales of returning hunters and warriors were not thought of as educational. They were entertainment, theatre, and news.

He may have drawn a map in the dust. "We started from camp when the sun was over our left shoulders, and we entered the forest near the big hollow tree. We walked to the water that falls over rocks into the deep pool, and then we went down the hill to the swamp where we drive the mammoth to kill them."

Here could have been the beginning of geography. It may also have been the beginning of navigation.

The hunter may have told of a hot spring he found, and of a hill where there were chips of flint, and this could have been the beginning of geology.

No doubt at first the accounts were told in the stark details, brief and to the point, while the hunter took great bites from the fresh meat, but such storytelling would not satisfy. Then as now people love drama, excitement, and interesting detail.

The bears or lions he killed would soon become larger and fiercer, the enemies stronger and better armed. To simply win a battle was not enough, there must be detail. "My spear went deep into the flesh near the left shoulder, and it died." Here, perhaps, the beginning of anatomy.

To embellish his stories the hunter and the warrior learned to add details, to describe the setting, to identify it by references to where certain edible plants have been found or where a kill was made, all of which made the stories more interesting to the listener.

The children, as well as others, listening to the stories, learned not only how to hunt and fight but where water might be found, salt and wild rice or nuts might be. So was knowledge passed on to the children, and so was the story begun.

We still, today, learn from stories, and the apt story of anecdote remains in the mind when details are forgotten.

It has often been said that we have but one life to live; that is nonsense. If one reads fiction he or she can live a thousand lives, in many parts of the world or in outer space. One can cross a desert, climb the Himalayas, or experience the agony of defeat, the triumph of victory, the pangs of starvation, or the choking thirst of the desert, all while safely at home.

The book has been man's greatest triumph, his most profound success. Seated in my library I live in a Time Machine. In an instant I can be transmitted to any era of history, any part of the world, even to outer space. Often I am asked in what period of history I would have preferred to live, and I wonder that they do not see, for I have lived in them all. I have listened to Buddha speak, I have marched with Alexander, sailed with the Vikings, or in their double canoes with the Polynesians. I have been at the courts of Queen Elizabeth and Louis the XIV; I have explored the West with Jedediah Smith and Jim Bridger; I have been a friend to Captain Nemo and have sailed with Captain Bligh on the *Bounty*. I have walked in the agora with Socrates and Plato, and listened to Jesus deliver the Sermon on the Mount.

Above all, and the most remarkable thing, I can do it all again, at any moment. The books are there. I have only to reach up on the shelves and take them down and live over again the moments I have loved. Surely, we live today in the greatest moment of history, for at no other time have books been so readily available, in the book stores, in the public libraries, and in the home.

GLOSSARIES
FOR THE
SACKETT NOVELS

FICTIONAL AND HISTORICAL CHARACTERS IN THE SACKETT NOVELS

A

Abel, RIDE THE DARK TRAIL
Abreu, Martin, THE DAYBREAKERS
Achilles, TO THE FAR BLUE MOUNTAINS
Acho Apache (people), JUBAL SACKETT
Adams, John, RIDE THE RIVER
Adapa, TO THE FAR BLUE MOUNTAINS
Africans (people), THE WARRIOR'S PATH
Aiken, THE DAYBREAKERS
Akicheeta, JUBAL SACKETT
Alexander the Great, SACKETT'S LAND
Ali Baba, TO THE FAR BLUE MOUNTAINS
Alicia, RIDE THE RIVER
Allah, TO THE FAR BLUE MOUNTAINS
Allen, Dodie, THE SACKETT BRAND
Allen, Gabriel, MOJAVE CROSSING
Allen, Skeeter, THE SACKETT BRAND
Allen, Vancouter, THE SACKETT BRAND
Alleyn, SACKETT'S LAND
Allison, SACKETT
Allison, Clay, THE DAYBREAKERS
Alvarado, Drusilla, THE DAYBREAKERS; SACKETT; TREASURE MOUNTAIN;
    THE SACKETT BRAND
Alvarado, Luis, THE DAYBREAKERS
Alvarado (family), THE LONELY MEN
Americans (people), JUBAL SACKETT; THE DAYBREAKERS; THE LONELY
    MEN; LONELY ON THE MOUNTAIN
Ananta (king of Kashmir), TO THE FAR BLUE MOUNTAINS
Anderson, Bloody Bill, MOJAVE CROSSING
Anderson, Curly, THE SACKETT BRAND
Andrew, THE WARRIOR'S PATH

Angles (people), TO THE FAR BLUE MOUNTAINS; JUBAL SACKETT
Anglos (people), THE DAYBREAKERS
Antoninus Pius, JUBAL SACKETT
Apaches (people), JUBAL SACKETT; THE DAYBREAKERS; SACKETT; LANDO;
    MOJAVE CROSSING; MUSTANG MAN; THE LONELY MEN; GALLOWAY;
    TREASURE MOUNTAIN; RIDE THE DARK TRAIL; THE SACKETT BRAND
Appleton (family), LANDO
Ar the Silent, TO THE FAR BLUE MOUNTAINS
Arabs (people), TO THE FAR BLUE MOUNTAINS; THE WARRIOR'S PATH;
    JUBAL SACKETT
Arapahoes (people), THE DAYBREAKERS; SACKETT; MUSTANG MAN;
    GALLOWAY
Archie, RIDE THE RIVER
Aristotle, THE WARRIOR'S PATH
Arnaud, GALLOWAY
Arribas, Dolores, RIDE THE DARK TRAIL
Arthur (King of England), SACKETT'S LAND
Asatiki, JUBAL SACKETT
Ashanti (people) THE WARRIOR'S PATH
Ashbrandson, Bjorn, TO THE FAR BLUE MOUNTAINS
Asiatics (people), JUBAL SACKETT
Atasha, JUBAL SACKETT
Avicenna, TO THE FAR BLUE MOUNTAINS
Ayllon, Lucas Vazquez, TO THE FAR BLUE MOUNTAINS
Aztecs (people), TO THE FAR BLUE MOUNTAINS

B

Babcock, THE DAYBREAKERS
Baca, MUSTANG MAN
Baca, Antonio, THE DAYBREAKERS
Bacon, Francis, THE WARRIOR'S PATH
Bainbridge, William, SACKETT
Baker, RIDE THE RIVER
Baker, TREASURE MOUNTAIN
Baker, Bully Ben, THE DAYBREAKERS
Baker, Cullen, LANDO; MUSTANG MAN
Baker, Jim, THE DAYBREAKERS
Bald Knobbers, LANDO; THE SKY-LINERS
Baldwin, THE SKY-LINERS
Baltimore (Lord), THE WARRIOR'S PATH
Baptiste, LONELY ON THE MOUNTAIN

Bardle, Nick, SACKETT'S LAND; TO THE FAR BLUE MOUNTAINS; THE
    WARRIOR'S PATH
Barres, TREASURE MOUNTAIN
Barthram, Doll, SACKETT'S LAND
Bashford, THE LONELY MEN
Basques (people), TO THE FAR BLUE MOUNTAINS; THE DAYBREAKERS
Baston, Andre, TREASURE MOUNTAIN
Baston, Fanny, TREASURE MOUNTAIN
Baston, Paul, TREASURE MOUNTAIN
Baston, Philip, TREASURE MOUNTAIN
Battles, John J., THE LONELY MEN
Bauer, Max, THE WARRIOR'S PATH
Beale, THE DAYBREAKERS; MOJAVE CROSSING
Beeson, Chalk, THE SKY-LINERS
Belden, THE DAYBREAKERS
Belisarius, SACKETT'S LAND
Benito, THE LONELY MEN
Benson, Bully, RIDE THE RIVER
Benton, Thomas Hart, THE SACKETT BRAND
Benton (family), MUSTANG MAN
Bents, THE DAYBREAKERS
Berglund, Pat ("Swede"), GALLOWAY; TREASURE MOUNTAIN
Berkeley, John, TO THE FAR BLUE MOUNTAINS
Bermudez, Juan de, TO THE FAR BLUE MOUNTAINS
Berryman, SACKETT'S LAND
Bett, THE WARRIOR'S PATH
Bianco, Andrea, TO THE FAR BLUE MOUNTAINS
Bienville, TREASURE MOUNTAIN
Bigelow, Benson, SACKETT
Bigelow, Ira, SACKETT
Bigelow, Tom, SACKETT
Bigelow, Wes, SACKETT
Bigelow (family), SACKETT
Binny, Dorset, THE LONELY MEN; TREASURE MOUNTAIN
Birkbeck, RIDE THE RIVER
Bishop, Noble, MUSTANG MAN
Bishop, the, LANDO
Black Knight, the, THE SKY-LINERS
Blackfeet (people), THE DAYBREAKERS; LONELY ON THE MOUNTAIN; THE
    SKY-LINERS
Blackstone, William, THE DAYBREAKERS; SACKETT; TREASURE MOUNTAIN
Bland, Jeannie, THE LONELY MEN

Blaxton, William, THE WARRIOR'S PATH
Blount, LANDO
Blue, TO THE FAR BLUE MOUNTAINS
Bob, LONELY ON THE MOUNTAIN
Bogardus, Rafe, THE WARRIOR'S PATH
Boleyn, Anne, TO THE FAR BLUE MOUNTAINS
Bonaparte (mule), LANDO
Bontemps, Pierre, TREASURE MOUNTAIN
Boone, Daniel, RIDE THE RIVER
Boone, James, RIDE THE RIVER
Boudicca, TO THE FAR BLUE MOUNTAINS
Boyd, Will, SACKETT
Brady, Martin, THE DAYBREAKERS
Brand, Isom, LONELY ON THE MOUNTAIN
Brannenberg, Dutch, RIDE THE DARK TRAIL
Breedlove, THE SKY-LINERS
Brennan, Mary, RIDE THE RIVER
Bretons (people), SACKETT'S LAND
Bretons (people), SACKETT
Brewer, Jim, RIDE THE DARK TRAIL
Bridger, Jim, THE DAYBREAKERS; TREASURE MOUNTAIN; THE SACKETT
    BRAND; THE SKY-LINERS
Briggs, SACKETT
Briggs, Harry, THE SKY-LINERS
Briscoe, THE SACKETT BRAND
British (people), THE WARRIOR'S PATH; RIDE THE RIVER
Brock, Bill, RIDE THE DARK TRAIL
Brook, Harry, THE LONELY MEN
Brooks, Al, THE DAYBREAKERS
Brown, Caribou, THE DAYBREAKERS
Brown, Kootenai, LONELY ON THE MOUNTAIN
Browne, TO THE FAR BLUE MOUNTAINS
Brunn, Adam, RIDE THE RIVER
Brunn (Adam's widow), RIDE THE RIVER
Bruno (dog), SACKETT'S LAND
Brus, Robert de, RIDE THE DARK TRAIL
Bryan, THE SKY-LINERS
Buchanan, Essie, RIDE THE RIVER
Buck (horse), THE DAYBREAKERS
Burbage, Cuthbert, SACKETT'S LAND
Burbage, James, SACKETT'S LAND
Burbage, Richard, SACKETT'S LAND

Burke, Pimmerton, TO THE FAR BLUE MOUNTAINS
Burns, THE SACKETT BRAND
Burrough, THE WARRIOR'S PATH
Burshill, Trent, THE SKY-LINERS
Button, Charlie, MOJAVE CROSSING
Button, Willie, MOJAVE CROSSING
Butts, Ephraim, RIDE THE RIVER

C

Cabot, John, TO THE FAR BLUE MOUNTAINS
Caddoans (people), JUBAL SACKETT
Caffrey, Duncan, LANDO; TREASURE MOUNTAIN
Caffrey, Will, LANDO
Caffrey (Mrs.), LANDO
Cagle, Larnie, THE SKY-LINERS
Cain, RIDE THE DARK TRAIL
Cajuns (people), TREASURE MOUNTAIN
Californians (people), MOJAVE CROSSING
Campbell, LONELY ON THE MOUNTAIN
Canadians (people), LONELY ON THE MOUNTAIN
Canton, TREASURE MOUNTAIN
Carboy, Tom, THE WARRIOR'S PATH
Caribs (people), THE WARRIOR'S PATH
Carlisle, Bob, MOJAVE CROSSING
Carney, Reed, THE DAYBREAKERS; MUSTANG MAN
Carpenter, Jim, THE DAYBREAKERS
Carson, Kit, THE DAYBREAKERS; SACKETT; TREASURE MOUNTAIN; THE
    SACKETT BRAND; THE SKY-LINERS
Carthaginians (people), TO THE FAR BLUE MOUNTAINS; JUBAL SACKETT
Cartwright, LANDO
Case, THE LONELY MEN
Catawbas (people), TO THE FAR BLUE MOUNTAINS; THE WARRIOR'S PATH;
    JUBAL SACKETT
Cator, Jim, MUSTANG MAN
Causie, Nathaniel, TO THE FAR BLUE MOUNTAINS
Celts (people), SACKETT'S LAND; TO THE FAR BLUE MOUNTAINS; JUBAL
    SACKETT; TREASURE MOUNTAIN; RIDE THE DARK TRAIL
Chantry, TO THE FAR BLUE MOUNTAINS
Chantry, Dorian, RIDE THE RIVER
Chantry, Finian, RIDE THE RIVER
Chapman, Joseph, MOJAVE CROSSING

Conchita, THE LONELY MEN
Conejeros (people), JUBAL SACKETT
Conn of the Hundred Battles, TO THE FAR BLUE MOUNTAINS
Cook, Dave, THE SKY-LINERS
Cookie, SACKETT
Cookie, GALLOWAY
Cornwallis, Charles, RIDE THE RIVER
Corte-Real, Gaspar, TO THE FAR BLUE MOUNTAINS
Cortes, Hernando, TO THE FAR BLUE MOUNTAINS
Cortina, Juan Nepomuceno, LANDO
Corvino, SACKETT'S LAND
Costello, THE SKY-LINERS
Costello, Judith, THE SKY-LINERS
Costello, Laban, THE SKY-LINERS
Cougar, LONELY ON THE MOUNTAIN
Coulter, John, LONELY ON THE MOUNTAIN; THE SACKETT BRAND
Courtney, SACKETT'S LAND
Crawford, Emmet, THE LONELY MEN
Creed, Dan, THE LONELY MEN
Creeks (people), TO THE FAR BLUE MOUNTAINS; JUBAL SACKETT; RIDE
      THE RIVER; TREASURE MOUNTAIN; RIDE THE DARK TRAIL
Crees (people), LONELY ON THE MOUNTAIN
Crocker, Barnabas, TO THE FAR BLUE MOUNTAINS
Crockett, Davy, THE DAYBREAKERS; THE LONELY MEN
Crook, George, THE SACKETT BRAND
Croppie, Henry, TO THE FAR BLUE MOUNTAINS
Cruz, Chico, THE DAYBREAKERS
Cuchulainn, TO THE FAR BLUE MOUNTAINS

D

Dalton, Michael, THE WARRIOR'S PATH
Dammerill, THE WARRIOR'S PATH
Dancer, THE SACKETT BRAND
Danes (people), SACKETT'S LAND; TO THE FAR BLUE MOUNTAINS; JUBAL
      SACKETT
Danny, LONELY ON THE MOUNTAIN
Dapple (horse), THE DAYBREAKERS
D'Aquila, Juan, TO THE FAR BLUE MOUNTAIN
Darby, TO THE FAR BLUE MOUNTAINS
Darkling, SACKETT'S LAND
Dart, Isom, RIDE THE DARK TRAIL
   see also Huddleston, Ned

Davis, Edmund Jackson, LANDO; MUSTANG MAN
Davis, Jack, THE LONELY MEN
Dawes, Ephraim, TO THE FAR BLUE MOUNTAINS
Dayton, MOJAVE CROSSING
de Bermudes, Juan, TO THE FAR BLUE MOUNTAINS
de Guzman, Diego, TO THE FAR BLUE MOUNTAINS
de Malebisse, Hugh, TO THE FAR BLUE MOUNTAINS; RIDE THE DARK
    TRAIL
De Pineda, Alvarez, JUBAL SACKETT
De Soto, Hernando, SACKETT'S LAND; TO THE FAR BLUE MOUNTAINS;
    JUBAL SACKETT
de Valdez, Alonzo, TO THE FAR BLUE MOUNTAINS
Dearborn, Henry, SACKETT; THE LONELY MEN
Decatur, Stephen, SACKETT
Deckrow, Franklyn, LANDO
Deckrow, Lily Anne, LANDO
Deckrow, Marsha, LANDO
Delve, Jonathan, TO THE FAR BLUE MOUNTAINS; THE WARRIOR'S PATH
Dickens, Charles, RIDE THE RIVER; THE DAYBREAKERS
Dickey, THE DAYBREAKERS
Dickinson, Charles, MUSTANG MAN
Diego, JUBAL SACKETT
Dillon, Chowse, RIDE THE DARK TRAIL
Doubleout Sam, THE DAYBREAKERS
Dowell, Uncle Ben, THE SACKETT BRAND
Drake, Francis, SACKETT'S LAND; TO THE FAR BLUE MOUNTAINS
Drennan, Emily, RIDE THE RIVER
Drennan, Jimmy, RIDE THE RIVER
Drennan, Laura, RIDE THE RIVER
Drennan, Ralph, RIDE THE RIVER
Druids (people), TO THE FAR BLUE MOUNTAINS
Duckett, Johannes, RIDE THE DARK TRAIL
Dumont, Gabriel, LONELY ON THE MOUNTAIN
Dunkirkers (people), SACKETT'S LAND
Dunn, Abel, GALLOWAY
Dunn, Alf, GALLOWAY
Dunn, Bull, GALLOWAY
Dunn, Curly, GALLOWAY
Dunn, Jobe, GALLOWAY
Dunn, Pete, GALLOWAY
Dunn, Rocker, GALLOWAY
Dunn (family), GALLOWAY

Durango Kid, THE DAYBREAKERS
Dutch (people), TO THE FAR BLUE MOUNTAINS; JUBAL SACKETT
Duval, TO THE FAR BLUE MOUNTAINS; THE WARRIOR'S PATH; LANDO
Dwyer, Jim, THE DAYBREAKERS
Dyer, Sandeman, MOJAVE CROSSING

E

Earl, *see* Robert (Sir)
Earl of Southesk, LONELY ON THE MOUNTAIN
Earp, Wyatt, MOJAVE CROSSING; THE SKY-LINERS
Egyptians (people), THE WARRIOR'S PATH
Elder, THE LONELY MEN
Elizabeth I (queen of England), SACKETT'S LAND; TO THE FAR BLUE
    MOUNTAINS; THE WARRIOR'S PATH; JUBAL SACKETT
Elmer, RIDE THE RIVER
Emmden, TO THE FAR BLUE MOUNTAINS
English, Charlie, THE DAYBREAKERS
English (people), SACKETT'S LAND; TO THE FAR BLUE MOUNTAINS; THE
    WARRIOR'S PATH; JUBAL SACKETT; RIDE THE RIVER; SACKETT;
    LANDO; TREASURE MOUNTAIN; RIDE THE DARK TRAIL
Eno (people), SACKETT'S LAND; TO THE FAR BLUE MOUNTAINS; THE
    WARRIOR'S PATH
Enriquez, Roderigo, MOJAVE CROSSING
Escalante, Francisco Silvestre Velez de (Father), SACKETT; GALLOWAY;
    TREASURE MOUNTAIN
Essex, SACKETT'S LAND; TO THE FAR BLUE MOUNTAINS
Europeans (people), SACKETT'S LAND; TO THE FAR BLUE MOUNTAINS;
    THE WARRIOR'S PATH; JUBAL SACKETT

F

Farley, Eb, TREASURE MOUNTAIN
Farman, Deke, RIDE THE DARK TRAIL
Farman, Pennywell, RIDE THE DARK TRAIL
Farnum, Charlie, GALLOWAY
Feebro, THE WARRIOR'S PATH
Feghany, TO THE FAR BLUE MOUNTAINS
Fentrell, John, LONELY ON THE MOUNTAIN
Fernandez, Tina, THE DAYBREAKERS
    see also Mendoza, Tina
Fernando, JUBAL SACKETT

Fetchen, Burr, THE SKY-LINERS
Fetchen, Clyde, THE SKY-LINERS
Fetchen, James Black, THE SKY-LINERS
Fetchen, Len, THE SKY-LINERS
Fetchen, Tirey, THE SKY-LINERS
Fetchen, Tory, THE SKY-LINERS
Fetterson, THE DAYBREAKERS
Fiddletown Jack, RIDE THE DARK TRAIL
Fields, MOJAVE CROSSING
Fink, Mike, THE LONELY MEN
Fitch, Peter, TO THE FAR BLUE MOUNTAINS
Fitch, Tom, THE SACKETT BRAND
Fitzpatrick, SACKETT'S LAND
Flanner, Jake, RIDE THE DARK TRAIL
Fleming, Charlie, LONELY ON THE MOUNTAIN
Flemish (people), TO THE FAR BLUE MOUNTAINS
Fletcher, John, SACKETT'S LAND
Flinch, MUSTANG MAN
Flores, LANDO
Foster, THE LONELY MEN
Fothergill, RIDE THE RIVER
Frances, RIDE THE RIVER
French (people), TO THE FAR BLUE MOUNTAINS; THE WARRIOR'S PATH;
    JUBAL SACKETT; LANDO; GALLOWAY; TREASURE MOUNTAIN
Frobisher, Martin, TO THE FAR BLUE MOUNTAINS
Fry, Ed, THE DAYBREAKERS
Fryer, Tom, MUSTANG MAN
Fuentes, Tony, THE MAN FROM THE BROKEN HILLS
Fulbric, Albani, RIDE THE DARK TRAIL

G

Gallegos (family), SACKETT
Gama, Vasco da, TO THE FAR BLUE MOUNTAINS
Gardner, THE WARRIOR'S PATH
Gault, Tip, RIDE THE DARK TRAIL
Gavin, Kyle, LONELY ON THE MOUNTAIN
Gavin, Laurie, LONELY ON THE MOUNTAIN
Gavin, Shanty, LONELY ON THE MOUNTAIN
Genester, Rupert, SACKETT'S LAND; TO THE FAR BLUE MOUNTAINS
Genghis Khan, TO THE FAR BLUE MOUNTAINS
Gibbons, Johnny, RIDE THE RIVER

Gilcrist, LONELY ON THE MOUNTAIN
Glasco, Tim, TO THE FAR BLUE MOUNTAINS
Gomez, JUBAL SACKETT
Gomez, Estevan, TO THE FAR BLUE MOUNTAINS
Gordillo, TO THE FAR BLUE MOUNTAINS
Gosnold, Bartholomew, SACKETT'S LAND; TO THE FAR BLUE MOUNTAINS
Grant, Ulysses S., SACKETT
Gray, Thomas, LONELY ON THE MOUNTAIN
Greek George, MOJAVE CROSSING
Greeks (people), TO THE FAR BLUE MOUNTAINS; THE WARRIOR'S PATH;
    JUBAL SACKETT; GALLOWAY; TREASURE MOUNTAIN; RIDE THE
    DARK TRAIL
Gregg, THE DAYBREAKERS
Grenville, Richard, SACKETT'S LAND; TO THE FAR BLUE MOUNTAINS
Griffin, Reed, THE SKY-LINERS
Gudlaugson, Gudlief, TO THE FAR BLUE MOUNTAINS

H

Hadden, Arch, THE LONELY MEN
Hadden, Wolf, THE LONELY MEN
Hakluyt, Richard, SACKETT'S LAND
Haliday, George, RIDE THE RIVER
Halliday, Doc, TREASURE MOUNTAIN; THE SKY-LINERS
Halloran, Doc, LANDO; TREASURE MOUNTAIN
Hamilton, Alexander, THE DAYBREAKERS
Hammer, Ollie, GALLOWAY
Hanberry, James, TO THE FAR BLUE MOUNTAINS
Handsel, Peter, TO THE FAR BLUE MOUNTAINS
Haney, Highpockets, LONELY ON THE MOUNTAIN
Hannibal, SACKETT'S LAND
Hanno, TO THE FAR BLUE MOUNTAINS; JUBAL SACKETT
Hans, THE WARRIOR'S PATH; RIDE THE RIVER
Hardin, John Wesley, SACKETT; MUSTANG MAN
Hardy, William, MOJAVE CROSSING
Harpes, RIDE THE RIVER
Harry, RIDE THE RIVER
Hasling, Coveney, SACKETT'S LAND; TO THE FAR BLUE MOUNTAINS
Hawkes, Evan, THE SKY-LINERS
Hawkins, John, JUBAL SACKETT
Hawkins, Richard, TO THE FAR BLUE MOUNTAINS
Hayes, Benton, RIDE THE DARK TRAIL

Hebrews (people), THE WARRIOR'S PATH
Henry, Alexander, LONELY ON THE MOUNTAIN
Henry, Patrick, RIDE THE RIVER
Henry VII (king of England), TO THE FAR BLUE MOUNTAINS
Henry VIII (king of England), TO THE FAR BLUE MOUNTAINS
Henry (Sir), TO THE FAR BLUE MOUNTAINS
Henry, TO THE FAR BLUE MOUNTAINS
Henry, THE WARRIOR'S PATH
Hera (goddess), RIDE THE RIVER
Hereward the Wake, TO THE FAR BLUE MOUNTAINS
Herrara, Antonio, LANDO
Herrara, Mexican Joe, RIDE THE DARK TRAIL
Heywood, LANDO
Hickok, Wild Bill, SACKETT; MOJAVE CROSSING; THE LONELY MEN
Higgins, Billy, THE LONELY MEN
Higgins, Long, THE DAYBREAKERS; SACKETT; MUSTANG MAN
Higgins, Rose Marie, MOJAVE CROSSING
Higgins (family), RIDE THE RIVER; THE DAYBREAKERS; SACKETT; LANDO; MOJAVE CROSSING; MUSTANG MAN; THE LONELY MEN; TREASURE MOUNTAIN; LONELY ON THE MOUNTAIN; THE SACKETT BRAND
High-Backed Bull, LONELY ON THE MOUNTAIN
Highland Bay (horse), LANDO
Hobes, Ben, SACKETT
Homer, THE DAYBREAKERS
Hone, Tin-Cup, GALLOWAY
Hooker, Steve, MUSTANG MAN
Horst, Felix, RIDE THE RIVER
Houston, Sam, TREASURE MOUNTAIN
Houston, Temple, TREASURE MOUNTAIN
Hoy, RIDE THE DARK TRAIL
Hualapais (people), MOJAVE CROSSING
Huddleston, Ned, RIDE THE DARK TRAIL
    see also Dart, Isom
Huddy, Vern, GALLOWAY
Huerta, TREASURE MOUNTAIN
Huguenots (people), JUBAL SACKETT
Hume, David, THE DAYBREAKERS
Hume, Nathan, MUSTANG MAN
Hume, Penelope, MUSTANG MAN
Hurons (people), THE WARRIOR'S PATH
Hurst, Charlie, MUSTANG MAN

Hutton, Luke, SACKETT'S LAND
Hyatt, TO THE FAR BLUE MOUNTAINS

I

Ibn Khaldoun, TO THE FAR BLUE MOUNTAINS
Icelandics (people), TO THE FAR BLUE MOUNTAINS
Iceni (people), SACKETT'S LAND; TO THE FAR BLUE MOUNTAINS
Incas (people), TO THE FAR BLUE MOUNTAINS; THE WARRIOR'S PATH;
    JUBAL SACKETT
Indians (people), SACKETT'S LAND; TO THE FAR BLUE MOUNTAINS;
    THE WARRIOR'S PATH; JUBAL SACKETT; RIDE THE RIVER; THE
    DAYBREAKERS; SACKETT; LANDO; MOJAVE CROSSING; MUSTANG MAN;
    THE LONELY MEN; GALLOWAY; TREASURE MOUNTAIN; LONELY ON
    THE MOUNTAIN; RIDE THE DARK TRAIL; THE SACKETT BRAND; THE
    SKY-LINERS
    see also names of individual tribes, e.g., Apaches; Utes
Indios (people), THE LONELY MEN
Ingram, David, TO THE FAR BLUE MOUNTAINS
Irish (people), SACKETT'S LAND; TO THE FAR BLUE MOUNTAINS; THE WAR-
    RIOR'S PATH; RIDE THE RIVER; THE DAYBREAKERS; SACKETT;
    LANDO; GALLOWAY; LONELY ON THE MOUNTAIN; RIDE THE DARK
    TRAIL; THE SACKETT BRAND; THE SKY-LINERS
Iroquois (people), TO THE FAR BLUE MOUNTAINS; THE WARRIOR'S PATH;
    JUBAL SACKETT; SACKETT; THE LONELY MEN
Irving, Washington, THE DAYBREAKERS
Irwin, John, RIDE THE RIVER
Italians (people), THE WARRIOR'S PATH; JUBAL SACKETT
Itchakomi Ishaia, JUBAL SACKETT
Ivanhoe, MUSTANG MAN; THE SKY-LINERS

J

Jack, SACKETT'S LAND; TO THE FAR BLUE MOUNTAINS
Jack-of-the-Feather, see Nemattanow
Jacks, THE DAYBREAKERS
Jackson, Andrew, MUSTANG MAN; THE SACKETT BRAND; THE SKY-LINERS
Jackson, Brick-Top, TREASURE MOUNTAIN
Jacob, RIDE THE RIVER
Jacob (mule), TREASURE MOUNTAIN
Jago, TO THE FAR BLUE MOUNTAINS
James I (king of England), TO THE FAR BLUE MOUNTAINS; JUBAL SACKETT

Jason, TO THE FAR BLUE MOUNTAINS
Jayne, Augustus, THE WARRIOR'S PATH
Jefferson, Thomas, RIDE THE RIVER; LANDO
Jennie, MUSTANG MAN
Jenny, LONELY ON THE MOUNTAIN
Jesus, SACKETT'S LAND; TO THE FAR BLUE MOUNTAINS
Jicarilla Apaches (people), GALLOWAY
Jim, THE LONELY MEN; GALLOWAY
Joe (Uncle), LONELY ON THE MOUNTAIN
Joe, RIDE THE RIVER
Joe, LONELY ON THE MOUNTAIN
Joel, THE WARRIOR'S PATH
John (King of England), SACKETT'S LAND; TO THE FAR BLUE MOUN-
    TAINS; JUBAL SACKETT
Johnson, MOJAVE CROSSING
Johnson, Andrew, THE DAYBREAKERS
Jomini, THE DAYBREAKERS
Jonah, RIDE THE RIVER
Jones, THE DAYBREAKERS
Jonson, Ben, SACKETT'S LAND
Joshua, TO THE FAR BLUE MOUNTAINS
Juan, MOJAVE CROSSING
Juana, SACKETT; LANDO
Jublain, SACKETT'S LAND; TO THE FAR BLUE MOUNTAINS; THE WAR-
    RIOR'S PATH
Julius Caesar, SACKETT'S LAND

K

Kachinas (spirits), GALLOWAY
Kahtenny, THE LONELY MEN
Kapata, JUBAL SACKETT
Karankawas (people), JUBAL SACKETT; LANDO
Karnes, Andrew, MUSTANG MAN
Karnes, Ralph, MUSTANG MAN
Karnes, Sylvie, MUSTANG MAN
Kelly (horse), THE DAYBREAKERS
Kemp, Will, SACKETT'S LAND; JUBAL SACKETT
Keokotah, JUBAL SACKETT
Kerry, Ange, SACKETT; MOJAVE CROSSING; THE LONELY MEN; TREASURE
    MOUNTAIN; THE SACKETT BRAND
Kickapoos (people), JUBAL SACKETT

Killigrew, Peter, TO THE FAR BLUE MOUNTAINS
Killigrew (family), TO THE FAR BLUE MOUNTAINS
King, Henrietta, LANDO
King, Richard, LANDO
King brothers, MOJAVE CROSSING
Kiowas (people), TO THE FAR BLUE MOUNTAINS; THE DAYBREAKERS;
    SACKETT; MUSTANG MAN; TREASURE MOUNTAIN; LONELY ON THE
    MOUNTAIN; RIDE THE DARK TRAIL
Kitch, SACKETT
Kitchen, Pete, THE LONELY MEN
Komantsi (people), JUBAL SACKETT
    see also Comanches
Kurbishaw, Aleyne, LANDO
Kurbishaw, Elam, LANDO
Kurbishaw, Eli, LANDO
Kurbishaw, Gideon, LANDO
Kurbishaw (family), LANDO
Kyme, Johnny, GALLOWAY; TREASURE MOUNTAIN

L

LaCroix, Charles, TREASURE MOUNTAIN
LaCroix (Mrs.) TREASURE MOUNTAIN
LaFitte, Jean, LANDO; TREASURE MOUNTAIN
Lancelot, GALLOWAY
Landon, Ira, THE SKY-LINERS
Lane, Ralph, TO THE FAR BLUE MOUNTAINS
L'Archeveque, Sostenes, MUSTANG MAN
Lashan, THE WARRIOR'S PATH
Law, John, TREASURE MOUNTAIN
Lee, Bob, LANDO
Lee, Robert E., SACKETT
Legare, THE WARRIOR'S PATH
Legare, Adele, THE WARRIOR'S PATH
Leland, John, SACKETT'S LAND; TO THE FAR BLUE MOUNTAINS
Lepine, LONELY ON THE MOUNTAIN
Lewis, Davy, RIDE THE RIVER
Lewis, Meriwether, THE DAYBREAKERS
Lewiston, THE LONELY MEN
Liggitt, GALLOWAY
Lila, SACKETT'S LAND; TO THE FAR BLUE MOUNTAINS; THE WARRIOR'S
    PATH; JUBAL SACKETT
Lila's brother, TO THE FAR BLUE MOUNTAINS

Lila's mother, TO THE FAR BLUE MOUNTAINS
Lin, LONELY ON THE MOUNTAIN
Lincoln, Abraham, TREASURE MOUNTAIN
Lindsay (family), LANDO
Little Bear, LONELY ON THE MOUNTAIN
Locke, John, THE DAYBREAKERS
Locklear, Jonas, LANDO
Locklear, Virginia ("Gin"), LANDO; THE SACKETT BRAND
Longley, Bill, MUSTANG MAN
Loomis, Jacob, MUSTANG MAN
Lorenzoni (family), JUBAL SACKETT
Lorna, THE SACKETT BRAND
Luke, TO THE FAR BLUE MOUNTAINS

M

Mace, Jem, LANDO
Machiavelli, Niccolo, TREASURE MOUNTAIN
Mackaskill, Nan, GALLOWAY; THE SKY-LINERS
Macklin, Diana, THE WARRIOR'S PATH
Macklin, Robert, THE WARRIOR'S PATH
Macock, Samuel, TO THE FAR BLUE MOUNTAINS
Macon, Sonora, THE SACKETT BRAND
Madison, James, THE DAYBREAKERS
Madoc, Prince, TO THE FAR BLUE MOUNTAINS; JUBAL SACKETT
Mag, SACKETT'S LAND; TO THE FAR BLUE MOUNTAINS
Magellan, Ferdinand, SACKETT'S LAND; TO THE FAR BLUE MOUNTAINS
Magill, Barry, TO THE FAR BLUE MOUNTAINS
Maimonides, Moses, TO THE FAR BLUE MOUNTAINS
Malatesta, Sigismondo, TREASURE MOUNTAIN
Malays (people), TO THE FAR BLUE MOUNTAINS
Malmayne, Robert, TO THE FAR BLUE MOUNTAINS
Mandrin, Ben, MOJAVE CROSSING
Manuel, LANDO
Marco Polo, TO THE FAR BLUE MOUNTAINS
Marcy, Randolph, THE DAYBREAKERS; TREASURE MOUNTAIN
Margarita, TO THE FAR BLUE MOUNTAINS
Marlowe, Christopher, SACKETT'S LAND
Maroons (people), THE WARRIOR'S PATH
Mary (Virgin), TO THE FAR BLUE MOUNTAINS
Mason, George, RIDE THE RIVER
Massachusetts (people), THE WARRIOR'S PATH
Masters, Andy, TREASURE MOUNTAIN

Masters, Burt, TREASURE MOUNTAIN
Masterson, Bat, MOJAVE CROSSING; THE SKY-LINERS
Mathers, MOJAVE CROSSING
Motoaka, *see* Pocahontas
Matthews, RIDE THE DARK TRAIL
Maverick, Samuel, THE WARRIOR'S PATH
McCaire, Boley, TREASURE MOUNTAIN
McCaire, Charley, TREASURE MOUNTAIN
McCann, Mary, LONELY ON THE MOUNTAIN
McCluer, Tim, GALLOWAY
McDonald, GALLOWAY
McHenry, John, RIDE THE RIVER
McKirdy, Dan, THE SKY-LINERS
McNary, RIDE THE DARK TRAIL
McNelly, L. H., LANDO; THE SKY-LINERS
Meek, Joe, THE SACKETT BRAND; THE SKY-LINERS
Menard, Russ, THE SKY-LINERS
Mendoza, Esteban, SACKETT; TREASURE MOUNTAIN
Mendoza, Tina, SACKETT; TREASURE MOUNTAIN
   see also Fernandez, Tina
Mescaleros (people), MOJAVE CROSSING
Métis (people), LONELY ON THE MOUNTAIN
Mexicans (people), THE DAYBREAKERS; SACKETT; MOJAVE CROSSING;
     MUSTANG MAN; THE LONELY MEN; TREASURE MOUNTAIN, RIDE THE
     DARK TRAIL; THE SACKETT BRAND; THE SKY-LINERS
Mifflin, Barney, THE SACKETT BRAND
Miguel, THE DAYBREAKERS; LANDO
Miles, Nelson Appleton, LANDO
Miller, TREASURE MOUNTAIN
Miller, Jerk-Line, RIDE THE DARK TRAIL
Mims, Harry, MUSTANG MAN
Mohammed, TO THE FAR BLUE MOUNTAINS
Mohler, GALLOWAY
Mojaves (people), MOJAVE CROSSING
Molrone, Devnet, LONELY ON THE MOUNTAIN
Molrone, Doug, LONELY ON THE MOUNTAIN
Montaigne, Michel, TO THE FAR BLUE MOUNTAINS; THE DAYBREAKERS
Moors (people), SACKETT'S LAND; TO THE FAR BLUE MOUNTAINS
Morales, Juan, SACKETT
Morgan, Henry, TO THE FAR BLUE MOUNTAINS
Mountjoy (Baron), TO THE FAR BLUE MOUNTAINS
Mullin, Billy, THE DAYBREAKERS
Munson, GALLOWAY

Murchison, SACKETT
Murdoch, John, RIDE THE RIVER
Murphy, TREASURE MOUNTAIN
Murphy, Spanish, THE LONELY MEN
Murrell, RIDE THE RIVER
Myrick, THE DAYBREAKERS

N

Naegelin brothers, TREASURE MOUNTAIN
Naguska, TO THE FAR BLUE MOUNTAINS
Napoleon, THE DAYBREAKERS
Narcissus, RIDE THE RIVER
Narragansetts (people), THE WARRIOR'S PATH
Natchees (people), JUBAL SACKETT
Navajos (people), THE DAYBREAKERS; THE LONELY MEN; GALLOWAY;
    RIDE THE DARK TRAIL
Neapolitans (people), SACKETT'S LAND
Neb (dog), TREASURE MOUNTAIN
Neiss, THE LONELY MEN
Nelson, LONELY ON THE MOUNTAIN
Nemattanow (Jack-of-the-Feather), TO THE FAR BLUE MOUNTAINS
Netdahee Apaches (people), THE LONELY MEN
Newfoundlanders (people), TO THE FAR BLUE MOUNTAINS
Newhall, MOJAVE CROSSING
Newport, Christopher, SACKETT'S LAND; TO THE FAR BLUE MOUNTAINS
Newton, Kid, SACKETT
Nez Perce (people), THE DAYBREAKERS
Nial, TO THE FAR BLUE MOUNTAINS; JUBAL SACKETT
Nikonha, SACKETT'S LAND
Ni'kwana, JUBAL SACKETT
Noble, RIDE THE RIVER
Nolan, LONELY ON THE MOUNTAIN
Normans (people), SACKETT'S LAND; TO THE FAR BLUE MOUNTAINS;
    JUBAL SACKETT; MUSTANG MAN; TREASURE MOUNTAIN
Norsemen (people), TO THE FAR BLUE MOUNTAINS
Nunnehi (immortals), THE WARRIOR'S PATH

O

Oats, Tim, RIDE THE RIVER
O'Brien (Mrs.), RIDE THE RIVER

Occaneechee (people), TO THE FAR BLUE MOUNTAINS; THE WARRIOR'S
    PATH
Ochoa, Manuel, THE SACKETT BRAND
O'Donnell, Red Hugh, TO THE FAR BLUE MOUNTAINS
O'Donovan (family), TO THE FAR BLUE MOUNTAINS
O'Flaherty, LANDO
Ogletree, THE SACKETT BRAND
O'Hara, Kane, TO THE FAR BLUE MOUNTAINS; THE WARRIOR'S PATH;
    JUBAL SACKETT; RIDE THE RIVER
O'Leary, Bob, THE SACKETT BRAND
Oliphant, MOJAVE CROSSING
Omahas (people), JUBAL SACKETT
O'Neill (Earl of Tyrone), TO THE FAR BLUE MOUNTAINS
Oppecancanough, TO THE FAR BLUE MOUNTAINS
Orsini, Flavio, TREASURE MOUNTAIN
Ortiz, Juan, JUBAL SACKETT
Osage (people), JUBAL SACKETT
Otoes (people), JUBAL SACKETT
Oury, William S., THE LONELY MEN
Overhill Cherokees (people), JUBAL SACKETT; THE SACKETT BRAND
Owain, TO THE FAR BLUE MOUNTAINS
Owanda, LONELY ON THE MOUNTAIN
Ox, the, LONELY ON THE MOUNTAIN

P

Pace, TO THE FAR BLUE MOUNTAINS
Packer, Al, SACKETT
Paddy, RIDE THE RIVER
Paisano, THE DAYBREAKERS
Paisano (buffalo), JUBAL SACKETT
Palliser, LONELY ON THE MOUNTAIN
Papagos (people), THE LONELY MEN
Pardo, Juan, TO THE FAR BLUE MOUNTAINS
Parker, THE SKY-LINERS
Parker, Tex, MUSTANG MAN
Pasten, GALLOWAY
Pawnees (people), JUBAL SACKETT
Peacham, THE WARRIOR'S PATH
Pearson, LONELY ON THE MOUNTAIN
Pendleton, George, RIDE THE RIVER
Penney, Anna, THE WARRIOR'S PATH

Penney, Carrie, THE WARRIOR'S PATH
Penney, Temperance, THE WARRIOR'S PATH
Penney, Tom, THE WARRIOR'S PATH
Pennsylvania Dutch (people), RIDE THE RIVER
Pequots (people), THE WARRIOR'S PATH
Peter, LANDO
Pettigrew, Juana, TREASURE MOUNTAIN
Pettigrew, Nativity, TREASURE MOUNTAIN
Philistines (people), TO THE FAR BLUE MOUNTAINS; THE LONELY MEN;
    RIDE THE DARK TRAIL
Phillip, Billy, TREASURE MOUNTAIN
Phoenicians (people), TO THE FAR BLUE MOUNTAINS; JUBAL SACKETT;
    RIDE THE DARK TRAIL
Pico, Pio, MOJAVE CROSSING
Picts (people), TO THE FAR BLUE MOUNTAINS; JUBAL SACKETT; TREA-
    SURE MOUNTAIN
Pierce, Shanghai, LANDO
Pike, John, TO THE FAR BLUE MOUNTAINS; THE WARRIOR'S PATH
Pilgrims (people), THE WARRIOR'S PATH; JUBAL SACKETT; SACKETT
Pimas (people), THE LONELY MEN
Pio, MUSTANG MAN
Pitcher, Lute, GALLOWAY
Pitt, William, THE DAYBREAKERS
Pittingel, Joseph, THE WARRIOR'S PATH
Pizarro, Francisco, SACKETT'S LAND; JUBAL SACKETT
Plato, TO THE FAR BLUE MOUNTAINS; THE WARRIOR'S PATH
Plummer, Henry, GALLOWAY
Plutarch, TO THE FAR BLUE MOUNTAINS; THE DAYBREAKERS
Pocahontas, TO THE FAR BLUE MOUNTAINS; JUBAL SACKETT
Poe, Edgar Allan, GALLOWAY
Pokey Joe, RIDE THE RIVER
Polo, Marco, see Marco Polo
Polon, Jack, LONELY ON THE MOUNTAIN
Polon, Pete, LONELY ON THE MOUNTAIN
Poltz, Conrad, TO THE FAR BLUE MOUNTAINS
Poncas (people), JUBAL SACKETT
Porney, THE WARRIOR'S PATH
Porter, THE SACKETT BRAND
Portuguese (people), SACKETT'S LAND; TO THE FAR BLUE MOUNTAINS;
    THE WARRIOR'S PATH
Potaka, SACKETT'S LAND; TO THE FAR BLUE MOUNTAINS
Pottawattomies (people), TREASURE MOUNTAIN

Powder Face, GALLOWAY; TREASURE MOUNTAIN
Powell, Nathaniel, TO THE FAR BLUE MOUNTAINS
Powell, William, TO THE FAR BLUE MOUNTAINS
Powhatan, TO THE FAR BLUE MOUNTAINS
Prager, Leo, THE SACKETT BRAND
Prescott, RIDE THE RIVER
Price, Edmund, TO THE FAR BLUE MOUNTAINS
Priest, Angus, TREASURE MOUNTAIN
Priest, Judas, TREASURE MOUNTAIN
Pritts, Jonathan, THE DAYBREAKERS; THE LONELY MEN
Pritts, Laura, THE DAYBREAKERS; THE LONELY MEN
Puritans (people), THE WARRIOR'S PATH

Q

Quantrill, William Clarke, MOJAVE CROSSING; GALLOWAY
Quapaws (people), JUBAL SACKETT
Quill, John, TO THE FAR BLUE MOUNTAINS

R

Rafin, Colby, THE SKY-LINERS
Raleigh, Walter, SACKETT'S LAND; TO THE FAR BLUE MOUNTAINS
Ram (horse), THE SKY-LINERS
Rand, Back, THE DAYBREAKERS
Raqsh (horse), TO THE FAR BLUE MOUNTAINS
Reardon, Martha, RIDE THE RIVER
Reardon, Moss, THE SKY-LINERS
Red, THE DAYBREAKERS; GALLOWAY
Red, MOJAVE CROSSING
Reinhardt, Oscar, MUSTANG MAN
Reynolds, Jim, THE SKY-LINERS
Ribaud, Jean, JUBAL SACKETT
Riel, Louis, LONELY ON THE MOUNTAIN
Riley, THE SACKETT BRAND
Ring, Jeremy, SACKETT'S LAND; TO THE FAR BLUE MOUNTAINS; THE
    WARRIOR'S PATH; JUBAL SACKETT
Ring, Lila, see Lila
Rivera, Juan Maria, SACKETT; GALLOWAY; TREASURE MOUNTAIN
Rob, TO THE FAR BLUE MOUNTAINS
Rob Roy, THE SKY-LINERS
Robert (Sir), SACKETT'S LAND; TO THE FAR BLUE MOUNTAINS
Robin Hood, RIDE THE RIVER; THE SKY-LINERS

Robinson, RIDE THE RIVER
Robiseau, Dorinda, MOJAVE CROSSING
 see also Trelawney, Abigail
Rocca, Tampico, THE LONELY MEN
Rockefellow, THE LONELY MEN
Rodriguez, THE SKY-LINERS
Rolfe, John, TO THE FAR BLUE MOUNTAINS
Romans (people), SACKETT'S LAND; TO THE FAR BLUE MOUNTAINS;
    THE WARRIOR'S PATH; JUBAL SACKETT; THE DAYBREAKERS;
    SACKETT
Romero, Pete, THE DAYBREAKERS
Romero, Rafe, THE SACKETT BRAND
Romero, Vincente, THE DAYBREAKERS
Rory, RIDE THE RIVER
Rose, Isaac, THE SACKETT BRAND
Rosenbaum, Rosie, THE DAYBREAKERS
Rossiter, John, GALLOWAY
Rossiter, Maighdlin ("Meg"), GALLOWAY
Rountree, Cap, THE DAYBREAKERS; SACKETT; GALLOWAY; TREASURE
    MOUNTAIN; LONELY ON THE MOUNTAIN; THE SACKETT BRAND;
    THE SKY-LINERS
Rufe, THE SKY-LINERS
Rufin, Guillaum, JUBAL SACKETT
Rufisco, SACKETT'S LAND
Rugger, Joe, SACKETT
Running Bear, JUBAL SACKETT
Rustum, TO THE FAR BLUE MOUNTAINS
Ryan, Big John, THE DAYBREAKERS
Ryland, Pete, THE SACKETT BRAND

S

Sackett, Abigail, *see* Tempany, Abigail
Sackett, Barnabas, SACKETT'S LAND; TO THE FAR BLUE MOUNTAINS; THE
    WARRIOR'S PATH; JUBAL SACKETT; RIDE THE RIVER; LONELY ON THE
    MOUNTAIN
Sackett, Bob, THE DAYBREAKERS
Sackett, Brian, TO THE FAR BLUE MOUNTAINS; THE WARRIOR'S PATH;
    JUBAL SACKETT
Sackett, Buckley, GALLOWAY; THE SKY-LINERS
Sackett, Colborn ("Colly"), THE DAYBREAKERS; SACKETT; MOJAVE CROSS-
    ING; THE LONELY MEN; GALLOWAY; TREASURE MOUNTAIN; LONELY
    ON THE MOUNTAIN; RIDE THE DARK TRAIL; THE SACKETT BRAND

Sackett, Daubeny, RIDE THE RIVER; THE LONELY MEN
Sackett, Drusilla, *see* Alvarado, Drusilla
Sackett, Echo, RIDE THE RIVER
Sackett, Emily, *see* Talon, Emily
Sackett, Ethan, RIDE THE RIVER
Sackett, Falcon, LANDO; THE SACKETT BRAND
Sackett, Flagan, GALLOWAY; TREASURE MOUNTAIN; THE SACKETT BRAND;
    THE SKY-LINERS
Sackett, Galloway, GALLOWAY; TREASURE MOUNTAIN; THE SACKETT
    BRAND; THE SKY-LINERS
Sackett, Ivo, SACKETT'S LAND; TO THE FAR BLUE MOUNTAINS
Sackett, Joe, THE DAYBREAKERS
Sackett, Jubal, TO THE FAR BLUE MOUNTAINS; THE WARRIOR'S PATH;
    JUBAL SACKETT; RIDE THE RIVER
Sackett, Kin-Ring, TO THE FAR BLUE MOUNTAINS; JUBAL SACKETT; RIDE
    THE RIVER
Sackett, Logan, GALLOWAY; TREASURE MOUNTAIN; LONELY ON THE MOUN-
    TAIN; RIDE THE DARK TRAIL
Sackett, Macon, RIDE THE RIVER
Sackett, Mary Ann, THE DAYBREAKERS; SACKETT; THE LONELY MEN;
    TREASURE MOUNTAIN; LONELY ON THE MOUNTAIN; THE SACKETT
    BRAND
Sackett, Mawney, RIDE THE RIVER; SACKETT; MOJAVE CROSSING
Sackett, Megan, TO THE FAR BLUE MOUNTAINS
Sackett, Mordecai, RIDE THE RIVER
Sackett, Nata, RIDE THE RIVER
Sackett, Noelle, TO THE FAR BLUE MOUNTAINS; THE WARRIOR'S PATH;
    JUBAL SACKETT
Sackett, Nolan, MOJAVE CROSSING; MUSTANG MAN; THE LONELY MEN;
    TREASURE MOUNTAIN; LONELY ON THE MOUNTAIN; RIDE THE DARK
    TRAIL; THE SACKETT BRAND
Sackett, Orlando, LANDO; GALLOWAY; TREASURE MOUNTAIN; LONELY
    ON THE MOUNTAIN; THE SACKETT BRAND; THE SKY-LINERS
Sackett, Orrin, THE DAYBREAKERS; SACKETT; LANDO; MOJAVE CROSSING;
    MUSTANG MAN; THE LONELY MEN; GALLOWAY; TREASURE MOUNTAIN;
    LONELY ON THE MOUNTAIN; THE SACKETT BRAND; THE SKY-LINERS
Sackett, Parmalee, GALLOWAY; THE SACKETT BRAND
Sackett, Regal, RIDE THE RIVER
Sackett, Seth, TREASURE MOUNTAIN
Sackett, Tarbil, RIDE THE DARK TRAIL
Sackett, Trulove, RIDE THE RIVER

Shaddock, Ollie, THE DAYBREAKERS; SACKETT; MUSTANG MAN; THE
    SACKETT BRAND
Shadow, Nick, GALLOWAY
Shakespeare, William, SACKETT'S LAND; TO THE FAR BLUE MOUNTAINS
Sharp, Tom, THE SKY-LINERS
Shawnees (people), TO THE FAR BLUE MOUNTAINS; THE WARRIOR'S
    PATH; JUBAL SACKETT; RIDE THE RIVER; TREASURE MOUNTAIN;
    RIDE THE DARK TRAIL
Shea, Bill, THE DAYBREAKERS
Sheldon of Warwick, SACKETT'S LAND
Shep (dog), RIDE THE RIVER
Sherman, William Tecumseh, GALLOWAY
Shore, Kyle, THE SKY-LINERS
Shorty, LONELY ON THE MOUNTAIN
Shoshones (people), SACKETT
Shreve, TREASURE MOUNTAIN
Sinbad, TO THE FAR BLUE MOUNTAINS
Singleton, Ed, LANDO
Sioux (people), THE DAYBREAKERS; SACKETT; MUSTANG MAN; LONELY
    ON THE MOUNTAIN
Skidis (people), JUBAL SACKETT
Slanting Annie, MUSTANG MAN
Slater, Matthew, TO THE FAR BLUE MOUNTAINS
Slim, GALLOWAY; RIDE THE DARK TRAIL
Smith, Charley, THE DAYBREAKERS
Smith, John, TO THE FAR BLUE MOUNTAINS; THE WARRIOR'S PATH;
    JUBAL SACKETT; SACKETT
Smith, Peg-Leg, MOJAVE CROSSING
Smyth, William, SACKETT'S LAND
Solomon (king of Israel), TO THE FAR BLUE MOUNTAINS
Somadeva, TO THE FAR BLUE MOUNTAINS
Spanish (people), SACKETT'S LAND; TO THE FAR BLUE MOUNTAINS; THE
    WARRIOR'S PATH; JUBAL SACKETT; THE DAYBREAKERS; SACKETT;
    LANDO; MOJAVE CROSSING; MUSTANG MAN; THE LONELY MEN;
    GALLOWAY; TREASURE MOUNTAIN; THE SKY-LINERS
Spivey, Len, RIDE THE DARK TRAIL
Springer, Ben, THE SKY-LINERS
St. Vrain, Ceran, THE DAYBREAKERS
Stamper, George, LONELY ON THE MOUNTAIN
Stamper, Perry, LONELY ON THE MOUNTAIN
Standish, Harry, RIDE THE RIVER
Stockton, Clint, SACKETT

Storey, Nelson, SACKETT; LONELY ON THE MOUNTAIN
Stott, THE DAYBREAKERS
Stouton, Eric, LANDO
Streat, SACKETT'S LAND
Sulky, Amy, RIDE THE RIVER
Sullivan, John, THE LONELY MEN
Sunday, Tom, THE DAYBREAKERS; SACKETT
Suryavati, TO THE FAR BLUE MOUNTAINS
Swalley, TO THE FAR BLUE MOUNTAINS
Swan, Hippo, TREASURE MOUNTAIN
Swandle, THE SACKETT BRAND
Swedes (people), SACKETT; GALLOWAY; TREASURE MOUNTAIN
Sweet Woman, TO THE FAR BLUE MOUNTAINS

T

Tabaguache Utes (people), GALLOWAY
Taliesin, TO THE FAR BLUE MOUNTAINS
Tallis, Peter, SACKETT'S LAND; TO THE FAR BLUE MOUNTAINS; THE
     WARRIOR'S PATH
Talon, *see* Claw
Talon, Barnabas, RIDE THE DARK TRAIL
Talon, Emily, RIDE THE DARK TRAIL
Talon, Milo, RIDE THE DARK TRAIL
Talon, Reed, RIDE THE DARK TRAIL
Tamerlane, *see* Timur
Tanner, Ned, TO THE FAR BLUE MOUNTAINS
Tao, MOJAVE CROSSING
Tatton, TO THE FAR BLUE MOUNTAINS
Tatum, Emmy, THE LONELY MEN
Tavis, Spud, RIDE THE DARK TRAIL
Taylor, Zachary, LANDO
Taylor, THE LONELY MEN
Taylor, LONELY ON THE MOUNTAIN
Tempany, Abigail, SACKETT'S LAND; TO THE FAR BLUE MOUNTAINS;
     THE WARRIOR'S PATH; JUBAL SACKETT
Tempany, Brian, SACKETT'S LAND; TO THE FAR BLUE MOUNTAINS
Tenaco, THE WARRIOR'S PATH
Tennyson, Alfred Lord, GALLOWAY
Tensas (people), JUBAL SACKETT
Texans (people), LANDO
Thackeray, William Makepeace, RIDE THE RIVER
Thompson, THE DAYBREAKERS

Thompson, Ben, THE LONELY MEN
Thomson, David, THE WARRIOR'S PATH
Thorpe, George, TO THE FAR BLUE MOUNTAINS
Thorpe (Master), TO THE FAR BLUE MOUNTAINS
Thorvald, TO THE FAR BLUE MOUNTAINS
Tilghman, Bill, MOJAVE CROSSING
Tilly, John, TO THE FAR BLUE MOUNTAINS; THE WARRIOR'S
    PATH
Tilson, LONELY ON THE MOUNTAIN
Timur, TO THE FAR BLUE MOUNTAINS
Tinker, the, RIDE THE RIVER; LANDO; MUSTANG MAN; GALLOWAY; TREA-
    SURE MOUNTAIN; RIDE THE DARK TRAIL; THE SACKETT BRAND
Titus, John, THE LONELY MEN
Toclani, THE LONELY MEN
Tom, THE WARRIOR'S PATH; TREASURE MOUNTAIN
Tomas, TREASURE MOUNTAIN
Tonto Apaches (people), THE SACKETT BRAND
Torres, Juan, THE DAYBREAKERS
Trelawney, Abigail, MOJAVE CROSSING
   see also Robiseau, Dorinda
Trelawney, Jack Ben, TREASURE MOUNTAIN
Trelawney, Nell, TREASURE MOUNTAIN
Trelawney girls, MOJAVE CROSSING; THE LONELY MEN; THE SACKETT
    BRAND
Tripp, Mary, THE DAYBREAKERS
Tristan, TO THE FAR BLUE MOUNTAINS
Turner, MOJAVE CROSSING
Tuscaroras (people), TO THE FAR BLUE MOUNTAINS; JUBAL SACKETT
Tuthill, John, SACKETT
Tyler, GALLOWAY
Tyler boys, GALLOWAY

U

Ulloa, LANDO
Ulstitlu (horned serpent), THE WARRIOR'S PATH
Ulysses, TO THE FAR BLUE MOUNTAINS
Unstwita, JUBAL SACKETT
Utes (people), JUBAL SACKETT; THE DAYBREAKERS; SACKETT; MUSTANG
    MAN; GALLOWAY; TREASURE MOUNTAIN; THE SKY-LINERS

V

Valdez, THE SKY-LINERS
Vance, Norton, THE SKY-LINERS
Vasquez, Tiburcio, MOJAVE CROSSING
Vaughn, Fred, THE SKY-LINERS
Vegetius, THE DAYBREAKERS
Vern, THE WARRIOR'S PATH
Verrazzano, Giovanni da, TO THE FAR BLUE MOUNTAINS
Victorio, THE SACKETT BRAND
Vikings (people), TO THE FAR BLUE MOUNTAINS; THE DAYBREAKERS;
    RIDE THE DARK TRAIL
Villon, Francois, JUBAL SACKETT

W

Wa-ga-su, TO THE FAR BLUE MOUNTAINS; THE WARRIOR'S PATH
Wakonda the Sky Spirit, TO THE FAR BLUE MOUNTAINS
Walford, Thomas, THE WARRIOR'S PATH
Walker, Joe, MOJAVE CROSSING
Walker, Ladder, THE SKY-LINERS
Wallen (Mrs.), THE LONELY MEN
Walton, LANDO
Warren, Ab, SACKETT
Warriors of Fire, JUBAL SACKETT
Washington, George, RIDE THE RIVER; LANDO
Watkins, Black Tom, TO THE FAR BLUE MOUNTAINS; THE WARRIOR'S
    PATH
Weaver, Paul, MOJAVE CROSSING
Webb, Ernie, THE DAYBREAKERS
Webster, Deal, THE WARRIOR'S PATH
Wellington, Con, RIDE THE DARK TRAIL
Wells, Bob, THE DAYBREAKERS
Welsh (people), TO THE FAR BLUE MOUNTAINS; THE WARRIOR'S PATH;
    JUBAL SACKETT; RIDE THE RIVER; THE DAYBREAKERS; SACKETT;
    LANDO; THE LONELY MEN; GALLOWAY; TREASURE MOUNTAIN;
    LONELY ON THE MOUNTAIN; THE SKY-LINERS
Wends (people), MUSTANG MAN
Wetzel, Lou, RIDE THE RIVER
Weymouth, SACKETT'S LAND; TO THE FAR BLUE MOUNTAINS
Wheeler, Johnny, THE LONELY MEN
Wheelwright, JUBAL SACKETT
White, Frank, THE SKY-LINERS

White, James, RIDE THE RIVER
White, Lulu, TREASURE MOUNTAIN
White Mountain Apaches (people), THE SACKETT BRAND
Wiles, Dobie, THE SKY-LINERS
Wiley, Jenny, RIDE THE RIVER
Will, GALLOWAY
William, SACKETT'S LAND; TO THE FAR BLUE MOUNTAINS; THE
    WARRIOR'S PATH
William the Conqueror, TO THE FAR BLUE MOUNTAINS; JUBAL SACKETT;
    RIDE THE DARK TRAIL
Williams, TREASURE MOUNTAIN
Williams, Old Bill, MOJAVE CROSSING, SACKETT
Willys, TO THE FAR BLUE MOUNTAINS
Wilson, Oldfast, TO THE FAR BLUE MOUNTAINS
Wilson (Pritts's man), THE DAYBREAKERS
Wilson (storekeeper), THE DAYBREAKERS
Wilton, THE DAYBREAKERS
Wingina, TO THE FAR BLUE MOUNTAINS
Winnebagos (people), LONELY ON THE MOUNTAIN
Wolf, Midah, LANDO
Wooster, Ginery, RIDE THE RIVER
Wootton, Uncle Dick, THE DAYBREAKERS
Wright, Bob, THE SKY-LINERS
Wyatt, Francis, TO THE FAR BLUE MOUNTAINS

X

Xenophon, TO THE FAR BLUE MOUNTAINS

Y

Yankees (people), MOJAVE CROSSING
Yaquis (people), LANDO; MOJAVE CROSSING
Yorkshire Swiper, RIDE THE RIVER
Yorkshiremen (people), TO THE FAR BLUE MOUNTAINS

Z

Zabrisky, Al, THE SACKETT BRAND
Zulus (people), LANDO

PLACES
IN THE
SACKETT NOVELS

A

Abajo Mountains, THE DAYBREAKERS; TREASURE MOUNTAIN

Abilene, THE DAYBREAKERS; MUSTANG MAN; LONELY ON THE MOUN-
TAIN; THE SKY-LINERS

Absaroka Mountains, TREASURE MOUNTAIN

Acaster Malbis, TO THE FAR BLUE MOUNTAINS

Adam Island, TO THE FAR BLUE MOUNTAINS

Adobe Walls, MUSTANG MAN

Africa, SACKETT'S LAND; TO THE FAR BLUE MOUNTAINS; THE WARRIOR'S
PATH; JUBAL SACKETT; LANDO; TREASURE MOUNTAIN

Alamosa, THE SKY-LINERS

Alder Gulch, SACKETT

Aleppo, JUBAL SACKETT

Alexandria, JUBAL SACKETT

Alma, RIDE THE DARK TRAIL

Alps (mountains), GALLOWAY

America, SACKETT'S LAND; TO THE FAR BLUE MOUNTAINS; THE
WARRIOR'S PATH; JUBAL SACKETT; RIDE THE RIVER; LANDO;
GALLOWAY; LONELY ON THE MOUNTAIN

Andalusia, RIDE THE DARK TRAIL

Angel Five Mountain, SACKETT

Anglesey, TO THE FAR BLUE MOUNTAINS

Animas City, TREASURE MOUNTAIN; RIDE THE DARK TRAIL

Animas River, GALLOWAY; RIDE THE DARK TRAIL

Animas Valley, TREASURE MOUNTAIN; RIDE THE DARK TRAIL

Antelope Hills, TREASURE MOUNTAIN

Antilles, TO THE FAR BLUE MOUNTAINS

Apache Ridge, THE SACKETT BRAND

Arizona, MOJAVE CROSSING; MUSTANG MAN; THE LONELY MEN; GALLO-
WAY; TREASURE MOUNTAIN; RIDE THE DARK TRAIL; THE SACKETT
BRAND

Arkansas, THE DAYBREAKERS; TREASURE MOUNTAIN; LONELY ON THE
    MOUNTAIN; RIDE THE DARK TRAIL; THE SKY-LINERS
Arkansas River, JUBAL SACKETT; MUSTANG MAN; TREASURE MOUNTAIN
Arklow Bank, TO THE FAR BLUE MOUNTAINS
Arwennack, TO THE FAR BLUE MOUNTAINS
Ashton Keynes, TO THE FAR BLUE MOUNTAINS
Asia, TO THE FAR BLUE MOUNTAINS; THE WARRIOR'S PATH; JUBAL
    SACKETT
Aspen Creek, THE SKY-LINERS
Atlanta, LANDO; THE SKY-LINERS
Atlantic Ocean, SACKETT'S LAND; TO THE FAR BLUE MOUNTAINS; JUBAL
    SACKETT; RIDE THE DARK TRAIL
Atlantis, TO THE FAR BLUE MOUNTAINS
Austin, LANDO
Azores, TO THE FAR BLUE MOUNTAINS

B

Babylon, THE WARRIOR'S PATH
Bacadeguatai, THE LONELY MEN
Bad Hills, LONELY ON THE MOUNTAIN
Badito, THE SKY-LINERS
Baghdad, TO THE FAR BLUE MOUNTAINS; JUBAL SACKETT
Bagdad (Mexico), LANDO
Baker Park, TREASURE MOUNTAIN
Baldy Mountain, GALLOWAY; TREASURE MOUNTAIN
Baltimore, THE WARRIOR'S PATH
Banded Mountain, TREASURE MOUNTAIN
Bangor, TO THE FAR BLUE MOUNTAINS
Banks, SACKETT'S LAND; TO THE FAR BLUE MOUNTAINS
Bankside, SACKETT'S LAND
Barbary Coast, SACKETT'S LAND; TO THE FAR BLUE MOUNTAINS; SACKETT
Barkerville, LONELY ON THE MOUNTAIN
Barren River, THE SKY-LINERS
Batuco, THE LONELY MEN
Bavispe River, THE LONELY MEN
Baxter Springs, THE DAYBREAKERS
Bayou Teche, TREASURE MOUNTAIN
Beacon Hill, THE WARRIOR'S PATH
Beale's Springs, MOJAVE CROSSING
Bear Creek, SACKETT; TREASURE MOUNTAIN; LONELY ON THE MOUNTAIN
Bearhide Canyon, THE SACKETT BRAND

Beaver Mountain, TREASURE MOUNTAIN
Bedford, RIDE THE RIVER
Beeville, LANDO
Bermuda, THE WARRIOR'S PATH
Bettws-y-Coed, TO THE FAR BLUE MOUNTAINS
Beverly Hills, MOJAVE CROSSING
Big Belt Mountains, TREASURE MOUNTAIN
Big Cow Creek, THE DAYBREAKERS
Big Moccasin Creek, RIDE THE RIVER
Big Sandy River, RIDE THE RIVER
Big South Fork, THE LONELY MEN; THE SACKETT BRAND
Bill of Portland, TO THE FAR BLUE MOUNTAINS
Birdlip Hill, TO THE FAR BLUE MOUNTAINS
Bitter Creek, SACKETT
Black Canyon, MOJAVE CROSSING
Black Hills, SACKETT; TREASURE MOUNTAIN
Black Lake, SACKETT
Black Mesa, THE SACKETT BRAND
Black Rock Desert, TREASURE MOUNTAIN
Black Sea, SACKETT'S LAND; JUBAL SACKETT
Blackwater, TO THE FAR BLUE MOUNTAINS
Blaine Creek, RIDE THE RIVER
Blanca Peak, TREASURE MOUNTAIN; THE SKY-LINERS
Blanket Mountain, RIDE THE RIVER
Blind Spring, MOJAVE CROSSING
Blue Mountains, *see* Abajo Mountains
Blue Ridge Mountains, TO THE FAR BLUE MOUNTAINS; THE WARRIOR'S
      PATH; LANDO; TREASURE MOUNTAIN
Boca del Rio, LANDO
Boggy Depot, MUSTANG MAN
Bombay, RIDE THE RIVER
Boone Trail, RIDE THE RIVER
Borregos Plaza, MUSTANG MAN
Boston (England), SACKETT'S LAND; TO THE FAR BLUE MOUNTAINS
Boston (Massachusetts), JUBAL SACKETT; THE LONELY MEN; GALLOWAY;
      THE SACKETT BRAND
Bourbon Street, TREASURE MOUNTAIN
Boxley Abbey, TO THE FAR BLUE MOUNTAINS
Bozeman Trail, THE DAYBREAKERS, SACKETT; LONELY ON THE MOUNTAIN
Bradshaw Road, MOJAVE CROSSING
Brazil, TO THE FAR BLUE MOUNTAINS
Brazos River, MUSTANG MAN

Brazos Santiago, *see* El Paso de los Brazos de Santiago
Brescia, JUBAL SACKETT
Bristol, SACKETT'S LAND; TO THE FAR BLUE MOUNTAINS; THE WARRIOR'S
    PATH
Bristol Mountains, MOJAVE CROSSING
Britain, SACKETT'S LAND; TO THE FAR BLUE MOUNTAINS
British Columbia, LONELY ON THE MOUNTAIN
Brittany, TO THE FAR BLUE MOUNTAINS
Broad River, TO THE FAR BLUE MOUNTAINS
Broad Street, RIDE THE RIVER
Bronco Dan Gulch, THE SKY-LINERS
Brown's Hole, SACKETT; GALLOWAY; RIDE THE DARK TRAIL
Brownsville, LANDO; TREASURE MOUNTAIN
Buckhead Canyon, THE SACKETT BRAND
Buckhead Mesa, THE SACKETT BRAND
Bull Spring Canyon, THE SACKETT BRAND
Bullfrog Ridge, THE SACKETT BRAND
Burro Creek, MUSTANG MAN

C

Cache Creek, TREASURE MOUNTAIN
Cactus Ridge, THE SACKETT BRAND
Cahuenga Pass, MOJAVE CROSSING
Cairo, THE WARRIOR'S PATH
Cajon Pass, MOJAVE CROSSING
California, THE DAYBREAKERS; SACKETT; LANDO; MOJAVE CROSSING; THE
    LONELY MEN; GALLOWAY; LONELY ON THE MOUNTAIN; RIDE THE
    DARK TRAIL
Callao, LANDO
Calle de los Negros, MOJAVE CROSSING
Callville, MOJAVE CROSSING
Cam River, SACKETT'S LAND
Camargo, LANDO
Cambridge, SACKETT'S LAND; TO THE FAR BLUE MOUNTAINS; THE
    WARRIOR'S PATH
Cambridgeshire, TO THE FAR BLUE MOUNTAINS
Camp Verde, THE SACKETT BRAND
Canada, TO THE FAR BLUE MOUNTAINS; GALLOWAY; TREASURE
    MOUNTAIN; RIDE THE DARK TRAIL
Canadian River, MUSTANG MAN; TREASURE MOUNTAIN
Caney's Fork, RIDE THE RIVER; THE SKY-LINERS

Cape Ann, THE WARRIOR'S PATH

Cape Fear, TO THE FAR BLUE MOUNTAINS

Cape Hatteras, MOJAVE CROSSING

Cape Town, RIDE THE RIVER

Cariboo River, LONELY ON THE MOUNTAIN

Carlton House, *see* Fort Carlton

Carolina, THE WARRIOR'S PATH; JUBAL SACKETT; MOJAVE CROSSING

Carolinas, LANDO; LONELY ON THE MOUNTAIN

Carizzo Creek, MUSTANG MAN; THE SACKETT BRAND

Carthage, JUBAL SACKETT

Caspian Sea, JUBAL SACKETT

Cassias Mountains, LONELY ON THE MOUNTAIN

Castlehaven, TO THE FAR BLUE MOUNTAINS

Catawba River, TO THE FAR BLUE MOUNTAINS

Cathay, SACKETT'S LAND; TO THE FAR BLUE MOUNTAINS; THE WARRIOR'S
PATH

Cattle Mountain, TREASURE MOUNTAIN

Cave-in-the Rock, RIDE THE RIVER

Caverna del Oro, THE SKY-LINERS

Chambersburg, RIDE THE RIVER

Chapultepec, LANDO

Charleston, RIDE THE RIVER; LANDO

Chatteris, SACKETT'S LAND

Cherokee Path, THE WARRIOR'S PATH

Cherry Creek, MUSTANG MAN; THE LONELY MEN; GALLOWAY; RIDE THE
DARK TRAIL; THE SACKETT BRAND

Chesapeake Bay TO THE FAR BLUE MOUNTAINS; THE WARRIOR'S PATH

Chesil Beach, TO THE FAR BLUE MOUNTAINS

Chihuahua, LANDO; THE LONELY MEN; RIDE THE DARK TRAIL; THE
SACKETT BRAND

Chilowee Mountain, THE WARRIOR'S PATH; JUBAL SACKETT

Chimala, THE LONELY MEN

China, SACKETT'S LAND; TO THE FAR BLUE MOUNTAINS; JUBAL SACKETT;
RIDE THE RIVER; GALLOWAY; LONELY ON THE MOUNTAIN

Chinapa, THE LONELY MEN

Chiricahua Mountains, TREASURE MOUNTAIN

Chittagong, THE WARRIOR'S PATH

Choccoloco River, TREASURE MOUNTAIN

Chowan River, TO THE FAR BLUE MOUNTAINS

Chunky Gal Mountain, TO THE FAR BLUE MOUNTAINS; THE WARRIOR'S
PATH; JUBAL SACKETT; LONELY ON THE MOUNTAIN

Cibecue Creek, THE SACKETT BRAND

Cienequilla Creek, MUSTANG MAN
Cienequilla del Barro Mountain, MUSTANG MAN
Cimarron, THE DAYBREAKERS; MUSTANG MAN
Cimarron River, THE DAYBREAKERS; MUSTANG MAN; THE SKY-LINERS
Cincinnati, RIDE THE RIVER
Cipango, TO THE FAR BLUE MOUNTAINS
Cirencester, TO THE FAR BLUE MOUNTAINS
Clinch Mountain, RIDE THE RIVER; MOJAVE CROSSING; MUSTANG MAN;
    GALLOWAY; TREASURE MOUNTAIN; LONELY ON THE MOUNTAIN; RIDE
    THE DARK TRAIL; THE SACKETT BRAND
Clinch River, RIDE THE RIVER
Clinch's Creek, LANDO
Clingman's Dome, RIDE THE RIVER; GALLOWAY
Clinton, LONELY ON THE MOUNTAIN
Clover Spring, THE SACKETT BRAND
Cockpit County, THE WARRIOR'S PATH
Coldwater Creek, TO THE FAR BLUE MOUNTAINS
Colorado, THE DAYBREAKERS; MUSTANG MAN; THE LONELY MEN; GAL-
    LOWAY; TREASURE MOUNTAIN; LONELY ON THE MOUNTAIN; RIDE
    THE DARK TRAIL; THE SACKETT BRAND; THE SKY-LINERS
Colorado River, MOJAVE CROSSING
Columbine Pass, SACKETT
Comanche Creek, SACKETT
Compass Creek, THE WARRIOR'S PATH
Compass Hill, TO THE FAR BLUE MOUNTAINS
Connecticut, TREASURE MOUNTAIN
Constantinople, SACKETT'S LAND; TO THE FAR BLUE MOUNTAINS
Cook's Well, MOJAVE CROSSING
Coon Creek, THE DAYBREAKERS
Coon Hollow, TREASURE MOUNTAIN
Copenhagen, RIDE THE RIVER
Cork, THE WARRIOR'S PATH
Cork Island, TO THE FAR BLUE MOUNTAINS
Cornwall, TO THE FAR BLUE MOUNTAINS
Corpus Christi, LANDO
Corrumpaw River, MUSTANG MAN
Costilla Creek, SACKETT
Cotswolds, TO THE FAR BLUE MOUNTAINS
Cottonwood, MOJAVE CROSSING
Cove Mountain, RIDE THE RIVER
Cowpens, RIDE THE RIVER
Coyote Creek, SACKETT

299

Coyote Wells, MOJAVE CROSSING

Crab Orchard, THE WARRIOR'S PATH; RIDE THE RIVER; THE SACKETT
BRAND

Crazy Mountains, TREASURE MOUNTAIN; RIDE THE DARK TRAIL

Crazy Woman Creek, SACKETT

Crete, TO THE FAR BLUE MOUNTAINS

Cricklade, TO THE FAR BLUE MOUNTAINS

Cross Creek, TO THE FAR BLUE MOUNTAINS

Cross Timbers, MUSTANG MAN

Cuba, THE WARRIOR'S PATH; JUBAL SACKETT

Cucharas River, THE SKY-LINERS

Cumberland Basin, TREASURE MOUNTAIN

Cumberland Gap, THE WARRIOR'S PATH; SACKETT; MOJAVE CROSSING;
MUSTANG MAN; THE LONELY MEN; GALLOWAY; RIDE THE DARK
TRAIL; THE SACKETT BRAND; THE SKY-LINERS

Cumberland Hills, TREASURE MOUNTAIN; RIDE THE DARK TRAIL; THE
SACKETT BRAND

Cumberland Mountain, TREASURE MOUNTAIN

Cumberland River, THE SKY-LINERS

Cumberland Valley, MOJAVE CROSSING

Cumuripa, THE LONELY MEN

D

Dakotas, THE DAYBREAKERS; LONELY ON THE MOUNTAIN; RIDE THE
DARK TRAIL

Dallas, MOJAVE CROSSING

Damariscove, THE WARRIOR'S PATH

Damascus, RIDE THE DARK TRAIL

Dan River, TO THE FAR BLUE MOUNTAINS

Dark Corner, LONELY ON THE MOUNTAIN

Davis Ridge, RIDE THE RIVER

Dead Cow Canyon, THE SACKETT BRAND

Dead Man's Tank, THE LONELY MEN

Dead Mountains, MOJAVE CROSSING

Deadwood, THE SACKETT BRAND

Deadwood Creek, GALLOWAY

Deadwood Gulch, GALLOWAY

Dease Lake, LONELY ON THE MOUNTAIN

Dease River, LONELY ON THE MOUNTAIN

Del Norte, SACKETT

Del Norte Peak, TREASURE MOUNTAIN

Demijohn Mountain, TREASURE MOUNTAIN
Denmark, TO THE FAR BLUE MOUNTAINS
Denney's Gap, GALLOWAY; THE SACKETT BRAND
Denver, MUSTANG MAN; RIDE THE DARK TRAIL; THE SKY-LINERS
Denver City, SACKETT
Devil's Dyke, SACKETT'S LAND; TO THE FAR BLUE MOUNTAINS; THE WAR-
    RIOR'S PATH
Devils Lake, LONELY ON THE MOUNTAIN
Diamond Butte, THE SACKETT BRAND
Diamond Mountains, RIDE THE DARK TRAIL
Dickey Mountains, RIDE THE RIVER
Dixie Land, TREASURE MOUNTAIN
Dock Street, RIDE THE RIVER
Dodge City, THE DAYBREAKERS; MUSTANG MAN; THE SACKETT BRAND;
    THE SKY-LINERS
Dogger, TO THE FAR BLUE MOUNTAINS
Dolores River, SACKETT; TREASURE MOUNTAIN
Double Mountain, TO THE FAR BLUE MOUNTAINS
Dublin, TO THE FAR BLUE MOUNTAINS; THE WARRIOR'S PATH
Durango, THE DAYBREAKERS; TREASURE MOUNTAIN; RIDE THE DARK
    TRAIL; THE SACKETT BRAND; THE SKY-LINERS
Durdle Door, TO THE FAR BLUE MOUNTAINS

E

Eagle Creek, LONELY ON THE MOUNTAIN
Eagle's Nest, SACKETT; TREASURE MOUNTAIN
East Boone Draw, RIDE THE DARK TRAIL
East Fork, THE SACKETT BRAND
East Verde River, THE SACKETT BRAND
Egypt, TO THE FAR BLUE MOUNTAINS
El Paso, THE LONELY MEN; TREASURE MOUNTAIN; THE SACKETT BRAND
El Paso de los Brazos de Santiago, LANDO
Eldorado Canyon, MOJAVE CROSSING
Elizabethtown, RIDE THE RIVER; THE DAYBREAKERS; SACKETT; MUSTANG
    MAN; TREASURE MOUNTAIN
Ely, SACKETT'S LAND; JUBAL SACKETT
Engineer Mountain, TREASURE MOUNTAIN
England, SACKETT'S LAND; TO THE FAR BLUE MOUNTAINS; THE
    WARRIOR'S PATH; JUBAL SACKETT; THE DAYBREAKERS; SACKETT;
    LONELY ON THE MOUNTAIN; RIDE THE DARK TRAIL

Europe, SACKETT'S LAND; TO THE FAR BLUE MOUNTAINS; THE
   WARRIOR'S PATH; JUBAL SACKETT; MUSTANG MAN; GALLOWAY;
   TREASURE MOUNTAIN; RIDE THE DARK TRAIL

F

Falmouth, TO THE FAR BLUE MOUNTAINS
Far East, THE WARRIOR'S PATH
Far Seeing Lands, JUBAL SACKETT
Fighting Creek, RIDE THE RIVER
Filey, TO THE FAR BLUE MOUNTAINS
Flanders, JUBAL SACKETT
Florence, SACKETT'S LAND; JUBAL SACKETT
Florida, SACKETT'S LAND; TO THE FAR BLUE MOUNTAINS; THE WAR-
   RIOR'S PATH; JUBAL SACKETT
Florida River, GALLOWAY
Floridy, see Florida
Foilsnashark Head, TO THE FAR BLUE MOUNTAINS
Forelands, SACKETT'S LAND
Fort Abercrombie, LONELY ON THE MOUNTAIN
Fort Arbuckle, TREASURE MOUNTAIN
Fort Bascom, MUSTANG MAN; TREASURE MOUNTAIN
Fort Carlton, LONELY ON THE MOUNTAIN
Fort Cobb, TREASURE MOUNTAIN
Fort Dodge, THE DAYBREAKERS; THE SKY-LINERS
Fort Ellice, LONELY ON THE MOUNTAIN
Fort Garland, TREASURE MOUNTAIN
Fort Garry, LONELY ON THE MOUNTAIN
Fort Gibson, TREASURE MOUNTAIN
Fort Griffin, MUSTANG MAN
Fort Hill, THE WARRIOR'S PATH
Fort Massachusetts, SACKETT
Fort Mojave, MOJAVE CROSSING
Fort Phantom Hill, MUSTANG MAN
Fort Pitt, LONELY ON THE MOUNTAIN
Fort Qu'Appelle, LONELY ON THE MOUNTAIN
Fort Stevenson, LONELY ON THE MOUNTAIN
Fort Street, MOJAVE CROSSING
Fort Union, MUSTANG MAN
Fort Whoop-Up, LONELY ON THE MOUNTAIN
Fort Worth, MUSTANG MAN; THE SKY-LINERS
Fossil Creek, THE SACKETT BRAND

Four Peaks, THE SACKETT BRAND
Fox Mountain, TREASURE MOUNTAIN
France, TO THE FAR BLUE MOUNTAINS; JUBAL SACKETT; TREASURE MOUN-
    TAIN; RIDE THE DARK TRAIL
Fraser River, LONELY ON THE MOUNTAIN
French Broad River, RIDE THE RIVER
French Quarter, TREASURE MOUNTAIN
Frog Town, LONELY ON THE MOUNTAIN

G

Gallatin Street, TREASURE MOUNTAIN
Gallatin Valley, SACKETT
Galleon Bay, THE WARRIOR'S PATH
Galley Head, TO THE FAR BLUE MOUNTAINS
Gaspe Peninsula, TO THE FAR BLUE MOUNTAINS
Gates of Hercules, RIDE THE DARK TRAIL
Gaul, THE WARRIOR'S PATH
Georgetown, LONELY ON THE MOUNTAIN
Georgia, LANDO; GALLOWAY
Ghost Trail, *see* Ute Trail
Glandore, TO THE FAR BLUE MOUNTAINS
Glandore Bay, TO THE FAR BLUE MOUNTAINS
Glassgorman, TO THE FAR BLUE MOUNTAINS
Globe, THE SACKETT BRAND
Gloucester, TO THE FAR BLUE MOUNTAINS
Golondrinos, SACKETT
Gomorrah, LANDO
Goodnight-Loving Trail, MOJAVE CROSSING
Goodnight Trail, THE SKY-LINERS
Gorontalo, THE WARRIOR'S PATH
Government Road, MOJAVE CROSSING
Grand Banks, SACKETT'S LAND; THE WARRIOR'S PATH
Granite Well, MOJAVE CROSSING
Grape Creek, THE SKY-LINERS
Grassy Cove, TO THE FAR BLUE MOUNTAINS; THE WARRIOR'S PATH;
    JUBAL SACKETT; RIDE THE RIVER
Great Plains, JUBAL SACKETT
Great Plumb Point, THE WARRIOR'S PATH
Great River (Mississippi), JUBAL SACKETT
Greater Island, TO THE FAR BLUE MOUNTAINS
Greece, TO THE FAR BLUE MOUNTAINS

Green Bottom Ripple, RIDE THE RIVER
Green River, RIDE THE DARK TRAIL
Greenhorn, THE SKY-LINERS
Greenhorn Mountains, TREASURE MOUNTAIN; THE SKY-LINERS
Grenada, THE WARRIOR'S PATH
Grenadier Mountains, SACKETT
Grouse Mountain, TREASURE MOUNTAIN
Guadalupe, LANDO
Guadalupita, SACKETT
Guinea Coasts, TO THE FAR BLUE MOUNTAINS
Gulf of Mexico, JUBAL SACKETT; SACKETT; LANDO; TREASURE MOUN-
    TAIN; LONELY ON THE MOUNTAIN
Gun Key, THE WARRIOR'S PATH
Guyundat River, RIDE THE RIVER

H

Hanging Dog Mountain, JUBAL SACKETT
Hangman's Point, TO THE FAR BLUE MOUNTAINS
Hardscrabble Mesa, THE SACKETT BRAND
Hardyville, MOJAVE CROSSING
Harmon's Station, RIDE THE RIVER
Hatteras, THE WARRIOR'S PATH
Hawk's Nest, LONELY ON THE MOUNTAIN
Haystack Mountain, TREASURE MOUNTAIN
Healthshire Hills, THE WARRIOR'S PATH
Heffernan Gulch, TREASURE MOUNTAIN
Helena, LANDO
Hell's Canyon, TREASURE MOUNTAIN
Henry Mountains, TREASURE MOUNTAIN
Hermosa Cliffs, RIDE THE DARK TRAIL
Hesperus Peak, TREASURE MOUNTAIN
Hidden Valley, MOJAVE CROSSING
High-Line Trail, see Ute Trail
Highland Rim, TREASURE MOUNTAIN; THE SACKETT BRAND
Hispaniola, THE WARRIOR'S PATH
Hiwasee River, JUBAL SACKETT
Hole-in-the-Wall, RIDE THE DARK TRAIL
Hollywood, MOJAVE CROSSING
Holston River, RIDE THE RIVER
Holy Land, TO THE FAR BLUE MOUNTAINS
Holyhead, TO THE FAR BLUE MOUNTAINS

Horse Shoe Bank, TO THE FAR BLUE MOUNTAINS
Horse Thief Valley, RIDE THE DARK TRAIL
Hudson's Bay, LONELY ON THE MOUNTAIN
Hudson's River, JUBAL SACKETT
Huerfano River, THE SKY-LINERS

I

Iceland, TO THE FAR BLUE MOUNTAINS
Idaho, THE DAYBREAKERS; SACKETT; LONELY ON THE MOUNTAIN
Illinois, RIDE THE RIVER; RIDE THE DARK TRAIL
Illinois River, JUBAL SACKETT
Independence, THE DAYBREAKERS; MUSTANG MAN; THE SKY-LINERS
India, SACKETT'S LAND; TO THE FAR BLUE MOUNTAINS; JUBAL SACKETT;
     RIDE THE RIVER; LONELY ON THE MOUNTAIN; RIDE THE DARK TRAIL
Indian Guyundat (creek), RIDE THE RIVER
Indian Ocean, TO THE FAR BLUE MOUNTAINS; RIDE THE RIVER
Indian Territory, MUSTANG MAN
Indies, TO THE FAR BLUE MOUNTAINS; THE WARRIOR'S PATH
Ireland, SACKETT'S LAND; TO THE FAR BLUE MOUNTAINS; THE WAR-
     RIOR'S PATH; JUBAL SACKETT; SACKETT
Irish Canyon, RIDE THE DARK TRAIL
Irish Sea, TO THE FAR BLUE MOUNTAINS
Isfahan, TO THE FAR BLUE MOUNTAINS
Italy, TO THE FAR BLUE MOUNTAINS; JUBAL SACKETT; THE DAYBREAKERS

J

Jackfish Lake, LONELY ON THE MOUNTAIN
Jackson Hole, SACKETT; LONELY ON THE MOUNTAIN
Jamaica, THE WARRIOR'S PATH; JUBAL SACKETT; MOJAVE CROSSING
James River, LONELY ON THE MOUNTAIN
Jamestown, TO THE FAR BLUE MOUNTAINS; THE WARRIOR'S PATH; JUBAL
     SACKETT
Java, TO THE FAR BLUE MOUNTAINS
Jefferson, LANDO
Johnson Creek, SACKETT
Jornada del Muerto, MOJAVE CROSSING
Junction Creek, TREASURE MOUNTAIN

K

Kansas, THE DAYBREAKERS; LANDO; MUSTANG MAN; GALLOWAY; LONELY
ON THE MOUNTAIN; THE SKY-LINERS
Kent Island, THE WARRIOR'S PATH
Kent Point, THE WARRIOR'S PATH
Kentucky, RIDE THE RIVER; TREASURE MOUNTAIN; LONELY ON THE MOUN-
TAIN; THE SKY-LINERS
Khurasan, TO THE FAR BLUE MOUNTAINS
Kiburi, THE LONELY MEN
King's Mountain, RIDE THE RIVER
Kinsale, TO THE FAR BLUE MOUNTAINS
Knight's Ranch, THE SACKETT BRAND
Knob Mountain, THE SACKETT BRAND
Knoxville, RIDE THE RIVER

L

La Cueva (valley), SACKETT
La Nopalera, MOJAVE CROSSING
La Paz, MOJAVE CROSSING
La Plata Canyon, TREASURE MOUNTAIN
La Plata Mountains, TREASURE MOUNTAIN
La Plata River, GALLOWAY; TREASURE MOUNTAIN; RIDE THE DARK TRAIL
La Rochelle, TO THE FAR BLUE MOUNTAINS
La Veta, THE SKY-LINERS
La Veta Pass, THE SKY-LINERS
Laguna de Brazil, LANDO
Laguna Madre, LANDO
Lake Sherwood, MOJAVE CROSSING
Lancaster, RIDE THE RIVER
Laramie, THE DAYBREAKERS
Laredo, TREASURE MOUNTAIN; RIDE THE DARK TRAIL
Las Cuevas, LANDO; THE SKY-LINERS
Las Vegas, THE DAYBREAKERS; SACKETT; MUSTANG MAN
Laurel Canyon, MOJAVE CROSSING
Leadville, SACKETT
Lepanto, SACKETT'S LAND
Levant, TO THE FAR BLUE MOUNTAINS
Levisa Fork, RIDE THE RIVER
Libya, LANDO
Lick Fork, TO THE FAR BLUE MOUNTAINS

Lightner Creek, TREASURE MOUNTAIN
Limehouse, TO THE FAR BLUE MOUNTAINS
Limestone Ridge, RIDE THE DARK TRAIL
Lincoln, THE SKY-LINERS
Lincolnshire, SACKETT'S LAND; TO THE FAR BLUE MOUNTAINS; JUBAL
    SACKETT
Little Arkansas River, THE DAYBREAKERS
Little Cow Creek, THE DAYBREAKERS
Little Crow, SACKETT; LONELY ON THE MOUNTAIN
Little Plumb Point, THE WARRIOR'S PATH
Lizard Head Peak, TREASURE MOUNTAIN
Llano Estacado, MUSTANG MAN
    see also Staked Plains
Loma Parda, MUSTANG MAN
London, SACKETT'S LAND; TO THE FAR BLUE MOUNTAINS; THE
    WARRIOR'S PATH; JUBAL SACKETT; RIDE THE RIVER; MOJAVE
    CROSSING; GALLOWAY; RIDE THE DARK TRAIL
London Bridge, SACKETT'S LAND
Lone Rock Hill, THE SKY-LINERS
Long Creek, TO THE FAR BLUE MOUNTAIN
Los Angeles, MOJAVE CROSSING; LONELY ON THE MOUNTAIN
Los Redos Creek, MUSTANG MAN
Loudon, RIDE THE RIVER
Louisa, RIDE THE RIVER
Louisiana, GALLOWAY; TREASURE MOUNTAIN
Louisville, THE SKY-LINERS
Low Countries, SACKETT'S LAND; THE WARRIOR'S PATH
Lulworth Cove, TO THE FAR BLUE MOUNTAINS

M

Madagascar, TO THE FAR BLUE MOUNTAINS
Madden Peak, GALLOWAY
Magnetic Gulch, TREASURE MOUNTAIN
Maiden Lane, SACKETT'S LAND
Main Street, MOJAVE CROSSING
Maine, THE LONELY MEN
Mal Pais, THE DAYBREAKERS
Malabar Coast, SACKETT'S LAND; THE WARRIOR'S PATH
Malachite, THE SKY-LINERS
Mancos River, GALLOWAY
Marble Mountain, THE SKY-LINERS

Marl Spring, MOJAVE CROSSING
Martinique, THE WARRIOR'S PATH
Marv, TO THE FAR BLUE MOUNTAINS
Maryland, THE WARRIOR'S PATH; RIDE THE RIVER
Massachusetts Bay Colony, THE WARRIOR'S PATH; JUBAL SACKETT
Matamoras, LANDO
Matape, THE LONELY MEN
Mayenne, SACKETT'S LAND
Mazatal Mountains, THE SACKETT BRAND
McCauleyville, LONELY ON THE MOUNTAIN
McClean Rock, MOJAVE CROSSING
McClellan Creek, TREASURE MOUNTAIN
McConnell's Town, RIDE THE RIVER
Mecca, JUBAL SACKETT
Medano Creek, THE SKY-LINERS
Mediterranean Sea, SACKETT'S LAND; RIDE THE DARK TRAIL
Menai, TO THE FAR BLUE MOUNTAINS
Merionethshire, TO THE FAR BLUE MOUNTAINS
Merrimack River, THE WARRIOR'S PATH
Mesa Verde, GALLOWAY; RIDE THE DARK TRAIL
Meshed, TO THE FAR BLUE MOUNTAINS
Mexico, SACKETT'S LAND; TO THE FAR BLUE MOUNTAINS; THE
      WARRIOR'S PATH; JUBAL SACKETT; THE DAYBREAKERS; LANDO;
      MUSTANG MAN; THE LONELY MEN; RIDE THE DARK TRAIL; THE
      SACKETT BRAND
Mexico City, MUSTANG MAN
Middle Creek, TREASURE MOUNTAIN
Middle Prong, RIDE THE RIVER
Middletown, RIDE THE RIVER
Midnight Mesa, THE SACKETT BRAND
Miles City, THE SACKETT BRAND
Mimbres Mountains, GALLOWAY
Mimbres River, RIDE THE DARK TRAIL
Minnesota, SACKETT; LONELY ON THE MOUNTAIN
Mississippi River, JUBAL SACKETT; RIDE THE RIVER; SACKETT; LANDO;
      MUSTANG MAN; TREASURE MOUNTAIN; LONELY ON THE MOUNTAIN;
      THE SKY-LINERS
Missouri, RIDE THE RIVER; THE DAYBREAKERS; MOJAVE CROSSING;
      MUSTANG MAN; GALLOWAY; TREASURE MOUNTAIN; THE SACKETT
      BRAND; THE SKY-LINERS
Missouri River, RIDE THE RIVER; THE DAYBREAKERS; LONELY ON THE
      MOUNTAIN; RIDE THE DARK TRAIL

Mobeetie, THE SACKETT BRAND
Mobile, LANDO; THE SKY-LINERS
Mogollon Mountains, TREASURE MOUNTAIN
Mogollon Rim, THE LONELY MEN; THE SACKETT BRAND; THE SKY-LINERS
Mogollon River, TREASURE MOUNTAIN; RIDE THE DARK TRAIL
Mojave Desert, MOJAVE CROSSING
Moluccas, TO THE FAR BLUE MOUNTAINS
Mona, *see* Anglesey
Montana, THE DAYBREAKERS; SACKETT; GALLOWAY; LONELY ON THE
    MOUNTAIN; RIDE THE DARK TRAIL; THE SACKETT BRAND; THE
    SKY-LINERS
Monterey, GALLOWAY
Montreal, LONELY ON THE MOUNTAIN
Moose Mountains, LONELY ON THE MOUNTAIN
Mora, THE DAYBREAKERS; SACKETT; LANDO; MOJAVE CROSSING; MUS-
    TANG MAN; THE LONELY MEN; TREASURE MOUNTAIN; THE SACKETT
    BRAND
Mora Creek, THE SACKETT BRAND
Mora River, SACKETT
Moreno Creek, SACKETT
Mosca Pass, THE SKY-LINERS
Moselle, THE WARRIOR'S PATH
Mount Vernon, RIDE THE RIVER
Mountain Branch, THE DAYBREAKERS
Mouse River, LONELY ON THE MOUNTAIN
    see also Souris River
Mud Creek, THE DAYBREAKERS
Muleshoe, THE SKY-LINERS
Musketaquid River, THE WARRIOR'S PATH
Muskrat Branch, THE WARRIOR'S PATH
Muskrat Creek, TO THE FAR BLUE MOUNTAINS
Musselshell River, THE DAYBREAKERS

N

Nacori, THE LONELY MEN
Nantahala Mountains, THE WARRIOR'S PATH; JUBAL SACKETT
Nantahala River, TO THE FAR BLUE MOUNTAINS; THE WARRIOR'S PATH
Naples, SACKETT'S LAND
Nashville, RIDE THE RIVER; THE SKY-LINERS
Natchez, TREASURE MOUNTAIN
Natchez Trace, RIDE THE RIVER; SACKETT; LANDO; MOJAVE CROSSING

O

Oak Spring, THE SACKETT BRAND
Oakville, LANDO; TREASURE MOUNTAIN
Odihan, TO THE FAR BLUE MOUNTAINS
Ohio, SACKETT; LONELY ON THE MOUNTAIN; THE SACKETT BRAND
Ohio River, JUBAL SACKETT; RIDE THE RIVER; LONELY ON THE MOUN-
    TAIN; THE SKY-LINERS
Okitoa, THE LONELY MEN
Old Dad Mountains, MOJAVE CROSSING
Old Head, TO THE FAR BLUE MOUNTAINS
Old Taos Pass, SACKETT
Ontario, LONELY ON THE MOUNTAIN
Oregon, THE LONELY MEN; RIDE THE DARK TRAIL
Ottertail River, LONELY ON THE MOUNTAIN
Ouse River, SACKETT'S LAND
Outer Banks, TO THE FAR BLUE MOUNTAINS
Outlaw Trail, RIDE THE DARK TRAIL
Overland Trail, RIDE THE DARK TRAIL
Owl Creek, THE DAYBREAKERS; MOJAVE CROSSING
Oxford, TO THE FAR BLUE MOUNTAINS
Ozark Mountains, THE DAYBREAKERS

P

Pacific Ocean, THE WARRIOR'S PATH; MOJAVE CROSSING; LONELY ON THE
    MOUNTAIN
Padre Island, LANDO
Pagosa Springs, GALLOWAY; TREASURE MOUNTAIN
Painted Desert, TREASURE MOUNTAIN
Paintsville, RIDE THE RIVER
Pajaritos Mountains, THE LONELY MEN
Pallisadoes, THE WARRIOR'S PATH
Palo Duro Canyon, MUSTANG MAN
Pamber Forest, TO THE FAR BLUE MOUNTAINS
Pamirs, TO THE FAR BLUE MOUNTAINS
Panama, MOJAVE CROSSING
Panhandle, MUSTANG MAN; TREASURE MOUNTAIN; RIDE THE DARK TRAIL;
    THE SACKETT BRAND
Paris, TO THE FAR BLUE MOUNTAINS; MOJAVE CROSSING; RIDE THE DARK
    TRAIL
Park Creek, TREASURE MOUNTAIN

Powell River, RIDE THE RIVER
Prescott, MOJAVE CROSSING; RIDE THE DARK TRAIL
Prince Rupert's Land, LONELY ON THE MOUNTAIN
Providence Mountains, MOJAVE CROSSING
Prussia, RIDE THE DARK TRAIL
Pueblo, THE SKY-LINERS
Punta de Aguas Creek, MUSTANG MAN
Purgatoire River, THE DAYBREAKERS
Pyrenees (mountains), GALLOWAY

Q

Qu'Appelle River, LONELY ON THE MOUNTAIN
Quartz Creek, TREASURE MOUNTAIN

R

Rabbit Ear Creek, MUSTANG MAN; TREASURE MOUNTAIN
Rabbit Ears Mountain, MUSTANG MAN
Raleigh's land, TO THE FAR BLUE MOUNTAINS
Rancho Malibu, MOJAVE CROSSING
Rancho Rodeo de las Aguas, MOJAVE CROSSING
Rangoon, THE WARRIOR'S PATH
Rapidan, THE WARRIOR'S PATH
Rappahannock, THE WARRIOR'S PATH
Raton, THE DAYBREAKERS
Ravenna, SACKETT'S LAND
Reach, SACKETT'S LAND; TO THE FAR BLUE MOUNTAINS
Red River, TREASURE MOUNTAIN
Red River of the North, LONELY ON THE MOUNTAIN
Red Sea, TO THE FAR BLUE MOUNTAINS; THE WARRIOR'S PATH
Remedios, THE LONELY MEN
Ribbon Mesa, TREASURE MOUNTAIN
Richmond, LANDO; LONELY ON THE MOUNTAIN
Rio Cobre, THE WARRIOR'S PATH
Rio Grande, SACKETT; LANDO; MUSTANG MAN; RIDE THE DARK TRAIL
Rio Grande City, LANDO
Rio Grande del Norte, TREASURE MOUNTAIN
Rio Grande Pyramid, TREASURE MOUNTAIN
Rita Blanca Creek, MUSTANG MAN
Roan Mountain, LONELY ON THE MOUNTAIN
Roanoke, TO THE FAR BLUE MOUNTAINS

Robbers' Roost, MUSTANG MAN; RIDE THE DARK TRAIL
Rock Creek, SACKETT
Rock Springs, MOJAVE CROSSING
Rocky Mountains, THE DAYBREAKERS; SACKETT; TREASURE MOUNTAIN;
    RIDE THE DARK TRAIL; THE SKY-LINERS
Rocky River, TO THE FAR BLUE MOUNTAINS
Rocky Run, LONELY ON THE MOUNTAIN
Rome, RIDE THE DARK TRAIL
Romero, MUSTANG MAN
Rose-Marie, THE DAYBREAKERS
Ruby Gulch, TREASURE MOUNTAIN
Ruidoso, THE DAYBREAKERS
Russell, THE SKY-LINERS
Russell Fork, RIDE THE RIVER
Russia, THE SACKETT BRAND
Rye Creek, THE SACKETT BRAND

S

Saint-Quentin, SACKETT'S LAND
Salish Mountains, TREASURE MOUNTAIN
Salt Lick Canyon, THE SACKETT BRAND
Salt Ponds, THE WARRIOR'S PATH
Salt River, THE SACKETT BRAND
Samarkand, JUBAL SACKETT
San Antonio, LANDO; MUSTANG MAN; THE SACKETT BRAND
San Augustine, LANDO
San Bernardino, MOJAVE CROSSING
San Carlo, THE LONELY MEN
San Diego, MOJAVE CROSSING
San Francisco, MOJAVE CROSSING; LONELY ON THE MOUNTAIN; RIDE THE
    DARK TRAIL; THE SACKETT BRAND
San Gorgonio River, MOJAVE CROSSING
San Juan Basin, GALLOWAY
San Juan Mountains, SACKETT; MUSTANG MAN; GALLOWAY; TREASURE
    MOUNTAIN; RIDE THE DARK TRAIL
San Juan River, TREASURE MOUNTAIN
San Luis, SACKETT; TREASURE MOUNTAIN
San Pedro Street, MOJAVE CROSSING
San Rafael Swell, RIDE THE DARK TRAIL
San Vincente Spring, MOJAVE CROSSING
Sand Creek, THE SKY-LINERS

Sandy River, TREASURE MOUNTAIN
Sangre de Cristo Mountains, JUBAL SACKETT; THE DAYBREAKERS;
    SACKETT; MUSTANG MAN; TREASURE MOUNTAIN; THE SKY-LINERS
Santa Fe, JUBAL SACKETT; THE DAYBREAKERS; SACKETT; MUSTANG MAN;
    TREASURE MOUNTAIN; LONELY ON THE MOUNTAIN; THE SACKETT
    BRAND; THE SKY-LINERS
Santa Fe Trail, THE DAYBREAKERS; MUSTANG MAN; THE SKY-LINERS
Santa Gertrudis, LANDO
Santa Margarita Mountains, THE LONELY MEN
Santa Monica, MOJAVE CROSSING
Santa Monica Range, MOJAVE CROSSING
Santa Rosalia, THE LONELY MEN
Santa Teresa, LANDO
Santee River, TO THE FAR BLUE MOUNTAINS
Santiago de la Vega, THE WARRIOR'S PATH
Saratoga, SACKETT; THE LONELY MEN
Sawatch Mountains, TREASURE MOUNTAIN
Sawmill Canyon, GALLOWAY
Scagg's Creek, THE SKY-LINERS
Scilly, TO THE FAR BLUE MOUNTAINS
Scotland, JUBAL SACKETT; SACKETT; RIDE THE DARK TRAIL
Secret Pass, MOJAVE CROSSING
Secret Spring, MOJAVE CROSSING
Sedalia, THE SKY-LINERS
Seine River, JUBAL SACKETT
Senokipe, THE LONELY MEN
Sequatchie River, JUBAL SACKETT; LONELY ON THE MOUNTAIN
Serbin, MUSTANG MAN
Settlements (Philadelphia), RIDE THE RIVER; LANDO
Severan, TO THE FAR BLUE MOUNTAINS
Shadow Cave, JUBAL SACKETT
Shalako, GALLOWAY; TREASURE MOUNTAIN; RIDE THE DARK TRAIL
Shanghai, THE WARRIOR'S PATH
Sharkstooth Peak, TREASURE MOUNTAIN
Shawmut, THE WARRIOR'S PATH
Shawnee Trail, LANDO
Sheep Hole Mountains, MOJAVE CROSSING
Sheyenne River, LONELY ON THE MOUNTAIN
Shiloh, MOJAVE CROSSING; THE LONELY MEN
Shining Mountains (Rocky Mountains), JUBAL SACKETT; RIDE THE RIVER
Shooting Creek, TO THE FAR BLUE MOUNTAINS; THE WARRIOR'S PATH;
    JUBAL SACKETT; RIDE THE RIVER

Shropshire, TO THE FAR BLUE MOUNTAINS
Sidelong Hill, RIDE THE RIVER
Sidon, JUBAL SACKETT
Sierra Grande (peak), MUSTANG MAN
Sierra Madre (mountains), THE LONELY MEN
Siler's Bald, RIDE THE RIVER
Silver City, THE DAYBREAKERS
Silver Creek, TREASURE MOUNTAIN
Silver Falls, TREASURE MOUNTAIN
Silverton, SACKETT
Sinepuxtent, THE WARRIOR'S PATH
Sinking Creek, THE SKY-LINERS
Sinks, the, RIDE THE RIVER
Siwash, RIDE THE DARK TRAIL
Sleeping Ute Mountain, TREASURE MOUNTAIN
Smithland, THE SKY-LINERS
Smoky Mountains, LANDO; MOJAVE CROSSING; TREASURE MOUNTAIN;
    THE SACKETT BRAND
Snake Range, TREASURE MOUNTAIN
Snowstorm Peak, TREASURE MOUNTAIN
Socorro, THE DAYBREAKERS
Sodom, LANDO
Soledad, THE LONELY MEN
Solomonville, THE SACKETT BRAND
Sonora, LANDO; THE LONELY MEN; RIDE THE DARK TRAIL
Sonora River, THE LONELY MEN
Sonora town, MOJAVE CROSSING
Souris River, LONELY ON THE MOUNTAIN
    see also Mouse River
South Africa, LANDO
South America, TREASURE MOUNTAIN
South Dakota, LONELY ON THE MOUNTAIN
South Pass, SACKETT; RIDE THE DARK TRAIL
South Pass City, THE DAYBREAKERS; SACKETT; RIDE THE DARK TRAIL
South Saskatchewan River, LONELY ON THE MOUNTAIN
Southwark, SACKETT'S LAND; TO THE FAR BLUE MOUNTAINS
Soyopa, THE LONELY MEN
Spain, TO THE FAR BLUE MOUNTAINS; THE WARRIOR'S PATH; JUBAL
    SACKETT; RIDE THE DARK TRAIL
Spanish Indies, TO THE FAR BLUE MOUNTAINS
Spanish Islands, TO THE FAR BLUE MOUNTAINS
Spanish Main, TO THE FAR BLUE MOUNTAINS; THE WARRIOR'S PATH

Spanish Peaks, THE SKY-LINERS
Spanish Trail, SACKETT; MOJAVE CROSSING; TREASURE MOUNTAIN
Spice Islands, SACKETT'S LAND
Spring Street, MOJAVE CROSSING
St. Cloud, LONELY ON THE MOUNTAIN
St. John's, TO THE FAR BLUE MOUNTAINS
St. Louis, TREASURE MOUNTAIN; THE SKY-LINERS
St. Paul, LONELY ON THE MOUNTAIN
St. Paul's Walk, SACKETT'S LAND; TO THE FAR BLUE MOUNTAINS; THE
     WARRIOR'S PATH
Staked Plains, MUSTANG MAN; TREASURE MOUNTAIN; THE SKY-LINERS
     see also Llano Estacado
Stamford, SACKETT'S LAND
Starvation Creek, GALLOWAY
Stein's Peak, THE LONELY MEN
Stikine River, LONELY ON THE MOUNTAIN
Stone Mountain, RIDE THE RIVER
Storm King Mountain, TREASURE MOUNTAIN
Storm King Peak, SACKETT
Straits of Gibraltar, TO THE FAR BLUE MOUNTAINS
Suffolk, SACKETT'S LAND
Sulphur River, LONELY ON THE MOUNTAIN
Sulphur Springs Valley, THE LONELY MEN
Sumatra, TO THE FAR BLUE MOUNTAINS
Susquehanna River, RIDE THE RIVER
Sweden, TO THE FAR BLUE MOUNTAINS
Swift Run Gap, THE WARRIOR'S PATH
Swineshead, TO THE FAR BLUE MOUNTAINS

T

Taklamakan, TO THE FAR BLUE MOUNTAINS
Taos, MUSTANG MAN
Tara, TO THE FAR BLUE MOUNTAINS
Tarshish, RIDE THE DARK TRAIL
Tartary, TO THE FAR BLUE MOUNTAINS
Tartessus, RIDE THE DARK TRAIL
Tascosa, SACKETT; THE SACKETT BRAND; THE SKY-LINERS
Tashkent, JUBAL SACKETT
Tazewell, THE SKY-LINERS
Tellico, LONELY ON THE MOUNTAIN
Tennessee River, JUBAL SACKETT; RIDE THE RIVER

Tug Fork, RIDE THE RIVER
Tule Creek, MUSTANG MAN
Turkey Flat, THE DAYBREAKERS
Turtle Mountains, LONELY ON THE MOUNTAIN
Tusquitee Creek, THE WARRIOR'S PATH
Tusquitees, THE WARRIOR'S PATH
Twenty-Nine Palms, MOJAVE CROSSING
Twin Buttes, TREASURE MOUNTAIN
Two Buttes, THE SKY-LINERS
Two Buttes Creek, THE DAYBREAKERS
Tyburn, TO THE FAR BLUE MOUNTAINS
Tyre, JUBAL SACKETT

U

Uinta Mountains, TREASURE MOUNTAIN
Uncomphagre (plateau), SACKETT
Union Pass, MOJAVE CROSSING
United States, THE DAYBREAKERS; MUSTANG MAN
Upper Cove, TO THE FAR BLUE MOUNTAINS
Utah, RIDE THE DARK TRAIL
Ute Peak, GALLOWAY
Ute Trail, TREASURE MOUNTAIN
Uvalde, SACKETT

V

Vallecitos, TREASURE MOUNTAIN
Vallecitos (basin), SACKETT
Valley Forge, RIDE THE RIVER
Venice, SACKETT'S LAND
Verde River, THE SACKETT BRAND
Vermilion Creek, RIDE THE DARK TRAIL
Vermont, THE LONELY MEN
Vicksburg, SACKETT
Victoria, LONELY ON THE MOUNTAIN
Virginia, TO THE FAR BLUE MOUNTAINS; THE WARRIOR'S PATH; JUBAL
    SACKETT; SACKETT; LANDO; MUSTANG MAN; GALLOWAY
Virginia City, THE DAYBREAKERS; SACKETT; MOJAVE CROSSING

W

Wales, TO THE FAR BLUE MOUNTAINS; JUBAL SACKETT; SACKETT; RIDE
THE DARK TRAIL; THE SKY-LINERS

Walks, the, THE WARRIOR'S PATH

Wallen Creek, RIDE THE RIVER

Walsenburg, THE SKY-LINERS

Warrior's Path, SACKETT'S LAND; THE WARRIOR'S PATH; JUBAL SACKETT

Wash, the, SACKETT'S LAND; TO THE FAR BLUE MOUNTAINS; THE WAR-
RIOR'S PATH; JUBAL SACKETT

Washington, D.C., THE LONELY MEN; THE SACKETT BRAND

Washington Gardens, MOJAVE CROSSING

Washita River, TREASURE MOUNTAIN

Water Holes, THE DAYBREAKERS

Water Street, RIDE THE RIVER

Wateree River, TO THE FAR BLUE MOUNTAINS

Waterloo, LANDO

Webber's Falls, TREASURE MOUNTAIN

Weisbeck, TO THE FAR BLUE MOUNTAINS

West Boone Draw, RIDE THE DARK TRAIL

West Bottom Creek, THE SACKETT BRAND

West Indies, TO THE FAR BLUE MOUNTAINS; THE WARRIOR'S PATH

West Keal, TO THE FAR BLUE MOUNTAINS

West Point, THE DAYBREAKERS

West Virginia, RIDE THE RIVER; THE LONELY MEN; RIDE THE DARK
TRAIL

Wheeling, RIDE THE RIVER

White Dome, TREASURE MOUNTAIN

White Sands, MOJAVE CROSSING

Whittlesey, TO THE FAR BLUE MOUNTAINS

Wicklow Head, TO THE FAR BLUE MOUNTAINS

Wicklow Point, TO THE FAR BLUE MOUNTAINS

Wild Rice Creek, LONELY ON THE MOUNTAIN

Wild Rye, THE SACKETT BRAND

Wilderness Road, LANDO

Wilderness Trail, MOJAVE CROSSING

Willestream, TO THE FAR BLUE MOUNTAINS

Williamsburg, TO THE FAR BLUE MOUNTAINS; THE WARRIOR'S PATH

Willoughby, JUBAL SACKETT

Willow Spring, MOJAVE CROSSING

Wilson's Cove, LONELY ON THE MOUNTAIN

Winchester, TO THE FAR BLUE MOUNTAINS

Windy Pass, TREASURE MOUNTAIN
Winnesimmet, THE WARRIOR'S PATH
Winnipeg, LONELY ON THE MOUNTAIN
Wisconsin, LONELY ON THE MOUNTAIN
Wolf Creek, TREASURE ON THE MOUNTAIN
Wolf Creek Pass, SACKETT; TREASURE MOUNTAIN
Wolf Rock, TO THE FAR BLUE MOUNTAINS
Wood Ditton, SACKETT'S LAND
Wrangell, LONELY ON THE MOUNTAIN
Wyoming, SACKETT; THE LONELY MEN; LONELY ON THE MOUNTAIN;
 RIDE THE DARK TRAIL; THE SKY-LINERS

XYZ

Yadkin River, TO THE FAR BLUE MOUNTAINS
Yankton, LONELY ON THE MOUNTAIN
Yellow House Canyon, MUSTANG MAN

RANCHES AND BRANDS
IN THE
SACKETT NOVELS

RANCHES

Buzzard Roost Ranch, THE SKY-LINERS
MT (ranch), RIDE THE DARK TRAIL
San Francisco Ranch, MOJAVE CROSSING
Tumblin' R Ranch, THE DAYBREAKERS
Two-Bar Ranch, THE DAYBREAKERS

BRANDS

Clover Three (brand), GALLOWAY
Eight-Ladder-Eight (brand), RIDE THE DARK TRAIL
Flower (brand), GALLOWAY
Fork Over (brand), SACKETT
Half-Box H (brand), THE SKY-LINERS
JBF Connected (brand), THE SKY-LINERS
Lazy A (brand), THE SACKETT BRAND
Lazy Y (brand), LONELY ON THE MOUNTAIN
NH Connected (brand), MUSTANG MAN
Pig-Pen (brand), THE SKY-LINERS
Pitchfork Bar (brand), SACKETT
Rafter Open A (brand), GALLOWAY
Rocking D (brand), GALLOWAY
Six-Four-Six (brand), RIDE THE DARK TRAIL
Slash B (brand), THE SKY-LINERS
Spider-Web (brand), THE SKY-LINERS
Three Eights (brand), TREASURE MOUNTAIN

RIFLES AND PISTOLS
IN THE
SACKETT NOVELS

RIFLES

Ballard (rifle), LANDO
Henry (rifle), THE DAYBREAKERS
Henry (rifle), LANDO
Henry (rifle), THE SKY-LINERS
Sharps (rifle), THE DAYBREAKERS
Sharps (rifle), MUSTANG MAN
Sharps (rifle), TREASURE MOUNTAIN
Sharps (rifle), RIDE THE DARK TRAIL
Spencer (rifle), THE DAYBREAKERS
Spencer (rifle), THE LONELY MEN
Spencer (rifle), TREASURE MOUNTAIN
Spencer (rifle), RIDE THE DARK TRAIL
Spencer (rifle), THE SKY-LINERS
Winchester (rifle), THE DAYBREAKERS
Winchester (rifle), SACKETT
Winchester (rifle), LANDO
Winchester (rifle), MOJAVE CROSSING
Winchester (rifle), MUSTANG MAN
Winchester (rifle), THE LONELY MEN
Winchester (rifle), GALLOWAY
Winchester (rifle), TREASURE MOUNTAIN
Winchester (rifle), LONELY ON THE MOUNTAIN
Winchester (rifle), RIDE THE DARK TRAIL
Winchester (rifle), THE SACKETT BRAND
Winchester (rifle), THE SKY-LINERS

PISTOLS

Colt (pistol), THE DAYBREAKERS
Colt (pistol), MOJAVE CROSSING
Colt (pistol), THE LONELY MEN
Colt (pistol), GALLOWAY
Colt (pistol), THE SACKETT BRAND
Colt (pistol), THE SKY-LINERS
Colt (pistol), *see also* Dragoon Colt; Navy Colt
Dance & Park (pistol), GALLOWAY
Doune (pistol), RIDE THE RIVER
Dragoon Colt (pistol), RIDE THE DARK TRAIL
Navy Colt (pistol), THE DAYBREAKERS
Navy Colt (pistol), MOJAVE CROSSING
Remington .36 (pistol), MOJAVE CROSSING
Remington Navy (pistol), THE LONELY MEN
Smith & Wesson .44 (pistol), TREASURE MOUNTAIN
Smith & Wesson Russian (pistol), TREASURE MOUNTAIN
Smith-Percival (pistol), MOJAVE CROSSING
Walch Navy (pistol), LANDO

SALOONS, TAVERNS, RESTAURANTS, INNS, AND HOTELS IN THE SACKETT NOVELS

SALOONS

101 Ranch (saloon), TREASURE MOUNTAIN
Absinthe House (saloon), TREASURE MOUNTAIN
Amsterdam (saloon), TREASURE MOUNTAIN
Baca's (saloon), MUSTANG MAN
Baltimore (saloon), TREASURE MOUNTAIN
Blue Anchor (saloon), TREASURE MOUNTAIN
Bon Ton (saloon), RIDE THE DARK TRAIL
Buffalo Bill House (saloon), TREASURE MOUNTAIN
Buffum's (saloon), MOJAVE CROSSING
Canton House (saloon), TREASURE MOUNTAIN
Congress Hall Saloon, THE LONELY MEN
Dutchman's (saloon), RIDE THE RIVER
End of Track (saloon), RIDE THE DARK TRAIL
Five Dollar House (saloon), TREASURE MOUNTAIN
Frenchman's (saloon), TREASURE MOUNTAIN
Gold Miner's Daughter, The (saloon), GALLOWAY
La Fonda (saloon), THE DAYBREAKERS
Lady Gay (saloon), THE SKY-LINERS
Long Branch (saloon), THE SKY-LINERS
Mahogany Hall (saloon), TREASURE MOUNTAIN
Mother Burke's Den (saloon), TREASURE MOUNTAIN
Murphy's Dance House (saloon), TREASURE MOUNTAIN
Quartz Rock Saloon, THE LONELY MEN
Rose-Marie Saloon, THE DAYBREAKERS
Schwenk and Will's (saloon), TREASURE MOUNTAIN
Uncle Ben Dowell's (saloon), THE SACKETT BRAND

TAVERNS

Bristol (tavern), THE WARRIOR'S PATH
Noble's Tavern, RIDE THE RIVER
Sevenoaks (tavern), SACKETT'S LAND

RESTAURANTS

Delmonico's (restaurant), MOJAVE CROSSING
Delmonico's (restaurant), GALLOWAY
Drover's Cottage (restaurant), THE DAYBREAKERS
Drover's Cottage (restaurant), LONELY ON THE MOUNTAIN
Shoo-Fly Restaurant, THE LONELY MEN

INNS

George Inn, SACKETT'S LAND
Grapes, The (inn), TO THE FAR BLUE MOUNTAINS
Greenhorn Inn, THE SKY-LINERS
Inns of Court, THE WARRIOR'S PATH
Prospect of Whitby (inn), TO THE FAR BLUE MOUNTAINS
Tabard (inn), SACKETT'S LAND
White Hart (inn), SACKETT'S LAND

HOTELS

Baker Block (hotel), MOJAVE CROSSING
Bella Union Hotel, MOJAVE CROSSING
Bella Union Hotel, *see also* Saint Charles Hotel
Bratton's (hotel), THE DAYBREAKERS
Pico House (hotel), MOJAVE CROSSING
Saint Charles Hotel, TREASURE MOUNTAIN
Santa Monica Hotel, MOJAVE CROSSING
St. James Hotel, THE DAYBREAKERS
United States Hotel, RIDE THE RIVER

BOOKS
IN THE
SACKETT NOVELS

Advancement of Learning, THE WARRIOR'S PATH
Arabian Nights, JUBAL SACKETT
Bleak House, THE DAYBREAKERS
Commerce of the Prairies, THE DAYBREAKERS
Compleat Gentleman, The, THE WARRIOR'S PATH
Country Justice, THE WARRIOR'S PATH
Deerslayer, The, THE DAYBREAKERS
Essays, THE WARRIOR'S PATH
Ivanhoe, THE SKY-LINERS
Katha Sarit Sagara, TO THE FAR BLUE MOUNTAINS
Lochinvar, RIDE THE RIVER
Marmion, RIDE THE RIVER
Method of Physics, THE WARRIOR'S PATH
Muquaddimah, TO THE FAR BLUE MOUNTAINS
Pilgrim's Progress, GALLOWAY

Bible, THE DAYBREAKERS
Bible, SACKETT
Bible, MOJAVE CROSSING
Bible, GALLOWAY
Bible, RIDE THE DARK TRAIL

SHIPS
IN THE
SACKETT NOVELS

Abigail, TO THE FAR BLUE MOUNTAINS
Abigail, THE WARRIOR'S PATH
Eagle, TO THE FAR BLUE MOUNTAINS
Eagle, THE WARRIOR'S PATH
Hayda, TO THE FAR BLUE MOUNTAINS
Jolly Jack, SACKETT'S LAND
Jolly Jack, TO THE FAR BLUE MOUNTAINS
Lion, TO THE FAR BLUE MOUNTAINS
Mayflower, THE WARRIOR'S PATH
Mayflower, JUBAL SACKETT
Philadelphia, SACKETT
Scamp, The, TO THE FAR BLUE MOUNTAINS
Sprite, TO THE FAR BLUE MOUNTAINS
Tiger, SACKETT'S LAND
Vestal, THE WARRIOR'S PATH

SONGS
IN THE
SACKETT NOVELS

"Barbry Allen," RIDE THE RIVER
"Barbry Allen," THE DAYBREAKERS
"Barbry Allen," SACKETT
"Barbry Allen," TREASURE MOUNTAIN
"Black, Black, Black," THE DAYBREAKERS
"Black, Black, Black," SACKETT
"Black, Black, Black," TREASURE MOUNTAIN
"Black Jack Davy," RIDE THE RIVER
"Brennan on the Moor," SACKETT
"Brennan on the Moor," TREASURE MOUNTAIN
"Brennan on the Moor," LONELY ON THE MOUNTAIN
"Darlin' Corey," TREASURE MOUNTAIN
"Golden Vanity, The," SACKETT
"Green Coffee Grows on High Oak Trees," RIDE THE DARK TRAIL
"Greensleeves," RIDE THE RIVER
"Hello, Susan Brown," RIDE THE DARK TRAIL
"Hunters of Kentucky, The," THE SACKETT BRAND
"John Hardy," THE LONELY MEN
"Lord Lovell," RIDE THE RIVER
"Lord Randall," THE DAYBREAKERS
"My Darling Nellie Gray," THE DAYBREAKERS
"Oh, Bury Me Not on the Lone Prairee," THE LONELY MEN
"On Jordan's Stormy Banks," THE LONELY MEN
"Rickett's Hornpipe," RIDE THE RIVER
"Rock of Ages," THE LONELY MEN
"Rock of Ages," THE SKY-LINERS
"Skip to My Lou," TREASURE MOUNTAIN
"Sweet Betsy," THE DAYBREAKERS
"Tenting Tonight on the Old Camp-Ground," TREASURE MOUNTAIN
"Zebra Dun," THE LONELY MEN

NARRATORS
OF THE
SACKETT NOVELS

SACKETT'S LAND	Barnabas Sackett
TO THE FAR BLUE MOUNTAINS	Barnabas Sackett
THE WARRIOR'S PATH	Kin-Ring Sackett
JUBAL SACKETT	Jubal Sackett
RIDE THE RIVER	Echo Sackett
THE DAYBREAKERS	Tyrel Sackett
SACKETT	William Tell Sackett
LANDO	Orlando Sackett
MOJAVE CROSSING	William Tell Sackett
MUSTANG MAN	Nolan Sackett
THE LONELY MEN	William Tell Sackett
GALLOWAY	Flagan Sackett
TREASURE MOUNTAIN	William Tell Sackett
LONELY ON THE MOUNTAIN	William Tell Sackett
RIDE THE DARK TRAIL	Logan Sackett
THE SACKETT BRAND	William Tell Sackett
THE SKY-LINERS	Flagan Sackett

CHRONOLOGY
OF THE
SACKETT NOVELS

SACKETT'S LAND	c. 1600
TO THE FAR BLUE MOUNTAINS	c. 1600–1620
THE WARRIOR'S PATH	c. 1620s
JUBAL SACKETT	c. 1620s
RIDE THE RIVER	c. 1840s–1850s (before Civil War)
THE DAYBREAKERS	c. 1870–1872
SACKETT	c. 1874–1875
LANDO	c. 1873–1875
MOJAVE CROSSING	c. 1875–1879
MUSTANG MAN	c. 1875–1879
THE LONELY MEN	c. 1875–1879
GALLOWAY	c. 1875–1879
TREASURE MOUNTAIN	c. 1875–1879
LONELY ON THE MOUNTAIN	c. 1875–1879
RIDE THE DARK TRAIL	c. 1875–1879
THE SACKETT BRAND	c. 1875–1879
THE SKY-LINERS	c. 1875–1879

INDEX
TO ENTRIES IN
THE SACKETT
COMPANION

ABOUT LOUIS L'AMOUR

"I think of myself in the oral tradition—as a troubador, a village taleteller, the man in the shadows of the campfire. That's the way I'd like to be remembered—as a storyteller. A good storyteller."

It is doubtful that any author could be as at home in the world recreated in his novels as Louis Dearborn L'Amour. Not only could he physically fill the boots of the rugged characters he wrote about, but he literally "walked the land my characters walk." His personal experiences as well as his lifelong devotion to historical research combined to give Mr. L'Amour the unique knowledge and understanding of people, events, and the challenge of the American frontier that became the hallmarks of his popularity.

Of French-Irish descent, Mr. L'Amour could trace his own family in North America back to the early 1600s and follow their steady progression westward, "always on the frontier." As a boy growing up in Jamestown, North Dakota, he absorbed all he could about his family's frontier heritage, including the story of his great-grandfather who was scalped by Sioux warriors.

Spurred by an eager curiosity and desire to broaden his horizons, Mr. L'Amour left home at the age of fifteen and enjoyed a wide variety of jobs including seaman, lumberjack, elephant handler, skinner of dead cattle, assessment miner, and officer on tank destroyers during World War II. During his "yondering" days he also circled the world on a freighter, sailed a dhow on the Red Sea, was shipwrecked in the West Indies and stranded in the Mojave Desert. He won fifty-one of fifty-nine fights as a professional boxer and worked as a journalist and lecturer. He was a voracious reader and collector of rare books. Mr. L'Amour's personal library of some 10,000 volumes covers a broad range of scholarly disciplines including many personal papers, maps, and diaries of the pioneers.

Mr. L'Amour "wanted to write almost from the time I could talk." After developing a widespread following for his many adventure stories written for the fiction magazines, Mr. L'Amour published his first full-length novel, HONDO, in the United States in 1953. Every one of his more than 100 books is in print; there are nearly 200 million copies of his books in print worldwide, making him one of the bestselling authors in modern literary history. His books have been translated into twenty languages, and more than forty-five of his novels and stories have been made into feature films and television movies.

His hardcover bestsellers include THE LONESOME GODS, THE WALKING DRUM (his twelfth century historical novel), JUBAL SACKETT, LAST OF THE BREED, and THE HAUNTED MESA.

The recipient of many great honors and awards, in 1983 Mr. L'Amour became the first novelist ever to be awarded the National Gold Medal by the United States Congress in honor of his life's work. In 1984 he was also awarded the Medal of Freedom by President Ronald Reagan.

Louis L'Amour died on June 10, 1988. His wife Kathy, and their two children, Beau and Angelique, carry the L'Amour tradition forward.